Agency-Based
Program
Evaluation

We would like to dedicate this book to evaluation practitioners, to the many social work and human service evaluation scholars, to the agencies engaged in evaluation, and to the consumers who inform and hopefully benefit from evaluation efforts.

Agency-Based
Program
Evaluation

Lessons From Practice

Stephen A. Kapp

University of Kansas

Gary R. Anderson

Michigan State University

Los Angeles | London | New Delhi
Singapore | Washington DC

For information:

SAGE Publications, Inc.
2455 Teller Road
Thousand Oaks,
   California 91320
E-mail: order@sagepub.com

SAGE Publications India Pvt. Ltd.
B 1/I 1 Mohan Cooperative
   Industrial Area
Mathura Road, New Delhi 110 044
India

SAGE Publications Ltd.
1 Oliver's Yard
55 City Road
London EC1Y 1SP
United Kingdom

SAGE Publications Asia-Pacific
   Pte. Ltd.
33 Pekin Street #02-01
Far East Square
Singapore 048763

Printed in the United States of America

Library of Congress Cataloging-in-Publication Data

Kapp, Stephen A.
Agency-based program evaluation: lessons from practice /
Stephen A. Kapp, Gary R. Anderson.
    p. cm.
Includes bibliographical references and index.
ISBN 978-1-4129-3984-3 (pbk.)
   1. Human services—Evaluation. I. Anderson, Gary R., 1952– II. Title.

HV41.K277 2010
361.0068 4—dc22   2009028255

This book is printed on acid-free paper.

09   10   11   12   13   10   9   8   7   6   5   4   3   2   1

Acquisitions Editor:	Kassie Graves
Associate Editor:	Leah Mori
Editorial Assistant:	Veronica K. Novak
Production Editor:	Astrid Virding
Copy Editor:	Jovey L. Stewart
Typesetter:	C&M Digitals (P) Ltd.
Proofreader:	Scott Oney
Indexer:	Diggs Publication Services
Cover Designer:	Gail Buschman
Cover Artist:	Nyvya Washburn
Cartoonist:	Kristen Gish
Marketing Manager:	Stephanie Adams

Contents

Foreword

The concept of *agency-based social work* was introduced by Weissman, Epstein, and Savage-Abramovitz (1985) and intended to convey the fact that however it is discussed theoretically, social work practice typically occurs in an organizational context. That context significantly shapes, facilitates, constrains, sustains, and renews social workers' capacity to serve individuals, groups, families, and communities. Our eponymous book on this subject was subtitled "Neglected Aspects of Clinical Practice."

Likewise, both the concept of *agency-based program evaluation* and this valuable and value-informed book by Kapp and Anderson observes that effective evaluation of social work programs requires an understanding of organizational dynamics and the stakeholders that are implicated in these. Inevitably then, program evaluation is a political process. Because many existing evaluation texts (and there are many) give scant attention to these organizational dynamics, Kapp and Anderson's book could have been subtitled: "Neglected Aspects of Program Evaluation Practice."

Instead, these broadly experienced evaluation researchers and educators emphasize the positive lessons learned from years spent working and consulting in the evaluation trenches. Rather than writing yet another predominantly technical book, however, they have written a book that is both moral and humane, without being moralistic. Hence their book gives as much attention to the ethical dimensions and interpersonal aspects of evaluation as it does to evaluation techniques, methodology, and design.

Additionally, Kapp and Anderson suggest that the practice of agency-based evaluation not only parallels other forms of social work practice—casework, group work, community organization, and administration—but requires the skills of each. In so saying, the authors join Patton (1997) in asserting that evaluation implementation and utilization is ultimately about people. And whether these people are conceptualized as "stakeholders," "clients," "consumers," "service providers," "practitioners," or "administrators," successful evaluation requires their *engagement*.

So does successful authoring. In writing this thoroughly engaging and practitioner-friendly book, the authors correctly assume that as practitioners and as evaluators our ultimate purpose as social workers is helping, and that true helping requires systematic reflection about the results of our efforts. However, in conveying this central message, Kapp and Anderson do not resort to research jargon or to the moralistic hectoring common to other social work research and evaluation texts. Nor do they echo the shrill threats of Evidence-Based Practice (EBP) proponents who preach social work's destruction if we do not limit ourselves to interventions that are "scientifically proven" to be effective.

Thus, throughout their book, both explicitly and implicitly, the reader is gently reminded of its "initial premise," that being that

> the use of evaluation findings has great potential for helping the consumers of service programs. This belief is at the heart of this work. While it is frustrating and tenuous, the risks of investing in these activities are worth the potential payoff of improving the lives of service recipients. (p. 194)

Unlike the many evaluation texts that emphasize research methods (and I've written a few), this book does have "heart." Atypically, evaluation designs, sampling, and other research techniques are discussed toward the end rather than up front. To hard-nosed academic researchers, this may seem counterintuitive and pedagogically unsound. But while Kapp and Anderson are well-grounded in evaluation techniques, such as focus groups, information technology, logic modeling, Ongoing Monitoring, and so forth, they recognize that their readers are likely to be "research-reluctants" (Epstein, 1987) and that the case for agency-based evaluation is better made through the accumulation of rich anecdotal material based on years of rich evaluation experience.

Still, at the end of every chapter, Kapp and Anderson make a point to "check the vital signs" of their readers to see to it that they have "understood the previous information and are ready to move on to some new content" (p. 9).

To me this metaphor conjured up an image of a wise, technically up-to-date, but humane, "g.p." who teaches medical students by example, who makes complex decisions look easy, and who takes into account the dynamic interaction between the patient, his environment, and all that medical technology has to offer. And also one who communicates with his students through easily understandable and useful diagrams, using occasional self-effacing humor to break the tension. Kapp and Anderson are not physicians, but they are wise and subtle practitioners of their craft.

Another reflection of their practice wisdom is their *methodological pluralism.* Unlike EBP "fundamentalists" who worship at the foot of the currently fashionable "hierarchy of evidence" (Adams, Matto, & LeCroy, 2009; Epstein, 2001) and who extol the superiority of randomized controlled, quantitative research experiments at the expense of other legitimate forms of inquiry, Kapp and Anderson give major attention to descriptive and quasi-experimental designs as well as to qualitative forms of evaluation (McNeill, 2006).

In addition, they enthusiastically discuss the evaluative uses of *available data,* an informational resource that other evaluation research texts reject out of hand. Yet available information often is (and certainly should be) the starting point in all "real life" agency-based evaluations. Though I have dedicated much of my previous decade's work to exploring the evaluative potential of "mining" available data (Epstein, 2009), Kapp and Anderson correctly treat it as just one of several both useful and admittedly imperfect evaluation strategies.

Similarly, consumer satisfaction instruments and strategies are considered for what they contribute as well as for their limitations. Often satisfaction data are summarily rejected by evaluation methodologists as being "too soft" to have any research utility. But when *original* data collection is considered in agency-based evaluation, client satisfaction is often (and should be) the clinical practitioner's first thought.

Ultimately, *Agency-Based Program Evaluation: Lessons From Practice* is an easy, evenhanded, and informative read about a complex and politically charged set of professional activities. With this complexity in mind, the authors consider the importance of cultural competency in the conduct of evaluation as well as issues that arise when agency administrators must decide whether to employ internal or external, university-based evaluators.

The book ends with a chapter on how to promote dissemination and utilization, recognizing that meaningful "endings" are an essential component of meaningful human relationships as well as of evaluation. Too many program evaluations are quickly read and unreflectively filed or perhaps never read, let alone utilized. Subtitled "Spreading the News," Kapp and Anderson's final chapter on utilization acknowledges that evaluation reports are only worth the effort if they reinforce what is programmatically worth keeping and help change what isn't. This Foreword is intended to spread the news that this book is well worth buying, reading, keeping, and ultimately using.

Irwin Epstein, PhD
H. Rehr Professor of Applied Social Work Research
Hunter College School of Social Work
New York, NY

REFERENCES

Adams, K. B., Matto, H. C., & LeCroy, C. W. (2009). Limitations of evidence-based practice for social work education: Unpacking the complexity. *Journal of Social Work Education, 45,* 165–186.

Epstein, I. (1987). Pedagogy of the perturbed: Teaching research to the reluctants. *Journal of Teaching in Social Work, 1,* 71–89.

Epstein, I. (2001). Using available information in practice-based research: Mining for silver while dreaming of gold. *Social Work in Health Care, 33,* 15–32.

Epstein, I. (2009). *Clinical data-mining: Integrating practice and research.* New York: Oxford University Press.

McNeill, T. (2006). Evidence-based practice in an age of relativism: Toward a model for practice. *Social Work, 51,* 147–156.

Patton, M. Q. (1997). *Utilization-focused evaluation* (3rd ed.). Thousand Oaks, CA: Sage.

Weissman, H., Epstein, I., & Savage-Abramovitz, A. (Eds.). (1985). *Agency-based social work: Neglected aspects of clinical practice.* Philadelphia: Temple University Press.

Acknowledgments

Steve Kapp: My wife, Carolyn, and daughter, Hannah, made colossal investments in this book with endless patience and support throughout this seemingly endless project.

The idea for this book was hatched by my co-author Gary, after a colloquium at my alma mater about my evaluation work. Since then we have both sent children off to college and developed a solid friendship around this work and our other commonalities. It has been a treat to work with him.

The crew at Sage has done a great job putting up with our antics while exploiting our ideas. Kassie Graves has integrated tolerance, persistence, and wit as she has gingerly shepherded us through this arduous process. Jovey Stewart's artful copy-editing and Astrid Virding's graceful management of production made the most of our often fractured prose.

My extended family rallied my reserves through their feigned interest and enthusiasm in exactly all the right places. I want to thank, H. L. Manding, Esquire; C. D. Baker; the Ro's: J and She; the LLene Sisters: Beau, Jollene, Dwa, and Donna; and finally, Judge Winks and her partner, Randy. My canine companion, Max sat at my feet for nearly every word of text. His devout medical team, lead by Dr. Bill, kept him alive for the duration of the project.

April Rand offered valuable editorial and research support, as did Ariel Ludwig. Cheri L'Ecuyer did formatting when and how I asked for it. Kristen Gish emerged as a promising textbook cartoonist. She should only be held responsible for artwork as the demented ideas forwarded by the cartoons belong to this author. Nyvya Washburn did a great job with the cover art.

This book is grounded in our years of experience in and with agency settings. I need to recognize a broad range of agency-based evaluation practitioners that have been critical to my skill development. Irwin Epstein and the late

Tony Grasso gave me my first evaluation job in an agency setting and a lot of my capabilities can be traced back to those years. My skills were continually developed through my experience with the Office of Mental Health Policy at Social and Rehabilitation Services in Kansas. Finally, my ideas about evaluation have continued to develop through my affiliation with my colleagues at the University of Kansas School of Social Welfare, especially Chris Petr, Charlie Rapp, Mark Holter, and Ed Scanlon.

Gary Anderson: I would also like to acknowledge and thank my wife, Valerie, and my daughters—Lauren and Elizabeth—for their patience and support. Their encouragement in this project, and many others, is deeply appreciated. As Steve noted, his presentation on agency-based research inspired our thoughts about the importance of the broader context in conducting program evaluations and agency-based research. I have learned a lot from Steve and the development of our friendship has been one of the most valued outcomes of this project. I agree with Steve that the professional staff at Sage has been a pleasure to work. I appreciate their knowledge and skill, patience and wisdom. Their help and talent were invaluable.

In writing this book, I have become more aware of my debt and gratitude to a number of colleagues who have been teachers and partners in social work education and in working with agencies. These include: Sarah Greenblatt, formerly from Hunter College and now at Casey Family Services; Deb Adamy from Hunter College; Andrea Savage and Irwin Epstein and other colleagues from Hunter College School of Social Work; Mary Davidson, former Dean at Rutgers University; my colleagues at Michigan State University School of Social Work, particularly Rena Harold, Paul Freddolino, and JoAnn McFall; Margie Rodriguez LeSage and Suzanne Cross, also at MSU School of Social Work; Peg Whalen, at the Alliance for Children and Families; and to Joan Pennell, from North Carolina State University Department of Social Work. I also want to express my appreciation to numerous agency and department administrators and social workers who over the years have worked with me and patiently taught and worked alongside me on evaluation projects. The lessons noted in this book have been oftentimes imperfectly learned and practiced and I am grateful for the collaborative and generous spirit displayed by many colleagues in agency practice.

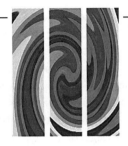

Introduction

The Purpose of This Book

Program evaluation is essential to demonstrate effective practice, advance an organization's mission, and powerfully respond to one's internal and external stakeholders. This ability to articulate the value of one's interventions and programs and satisfy constituents becomes heightened when facing times of economic stress, difficult funding decisions, and an increased demand for services. The ethical principles and challenges and political and cultural considerations that provide the context for the evaluation process can significantly shape the ability to implement an evaluation and promote value. In addition, the reality of an agency's day-to-day functioning can complicate the elements of an evaluation plan and its steps and strategies. The purpose of this book is to articulate the elements of program evaluation, to deepen our understanding of the contextual issues that surround and shape an evaluation, and to anticipate and make sound decisions in balancing techniques and strategies and the realities of the agency environment.

GUIDING PRINCIPLES

This book is guided by three principles: (1) the importance of understanding agency-based practice and the crucial role of real-world facilitating factors and obstacles; (2) the conceptualization of program evaluation as a macro-practice skill that requires a set of values, behaviors, and skills that correspond to other aspects of professional work; and (3) program evaluation as a vital part of effective agency practice, which can have a positive impact on the lives of those individuals, families, and communities receiving services.

1. *Practice-focused perspective.* This book is designed to be used by professionals in an agency setting, academics who engage in and teach program evaluation, and future professionals in graduate schools of social work or related human service professions. Consequently, the tone of the book is frequently and deliberately conversational and straightforward. Our intent is to reinforce the evaluation process; it should not be shrouded in mystery or academic language but should be relatively clear and comprehendible to most audiences. Clear communication in terms that are not foreign or intimidating to persons working in agencies is essential to advance a commitment to and the practice of program evaluation.

Correspondingly, we have selected the topics for this book to provide a foundation for understanding the complexity and challenges associated with program evaluation. It is our hope that the core evaluative elements are presented in a manner that provides a foundation for approaching and understanding evaluation. In tandem, we will be presenting the complexity of decision making. This complexity is magnified by the identification of classic ethical considerations, ethical dilemmas, cultural competency and sensitivity as values and components, and the social and political context of an evaluation process.

2. *Macro-practice orientation.* Although program evaluation can be presented and viewed as a discrete set of skills and strategies, our approach identifies evaluation as a professional practice skill associated with macro-perspectives, that is, examining larger programs and systems. Focusing on evaluation as a macro-practice skill. Given this orientation, this book will not include how to evaluate one's individual clinical practice or the effectiveness of therapeutic interventions as applied to individual clients, families, or treatment groups. As macro-practice, the emphasis is on large systems and the dynamics, effectiveness, and interaction of those systems. Program evaluation informs management decisions, is guided by and influences agency leadership, supports or amends or contributes to the elimination of programs, and has implications for organizational practice and policy.

As program evaluation is a form of professional practice, it is crucial for evaluators to consider and display the elements associated with that practice. These elements include the ability to form relationships and to operate within the context of those relationships. This may challenge some views of evaluation that describe the evaluator as more distant and separate from the participants of a study and the organizations that seek or are subject to an evaluation.

Similar to a traditional social work problem-solving process, there are elements of an assessment and the need to employ ecological and systemic thinking in understanding an evaluation process. A well-planned process that frequently involves collaboration and requires cultural sensitivity will lead to a set of strategies and actions with varying degrees of effectiveness. The process itself requires self-awareness and self-reflection. The ability to evaluate one's evaluation and its impact also is important. This book will describe program evaluation as a form of professional practice with specific knowledge and skills embedded and intertwined with other elements of professional practice.

3. *A valuable tool for service improvement.* Program evaluation is often separated from critical actions like service delivery in the agency world, much like it is taught as a distinct entity in social work and other social science curricula. Evaluation is cast in a view as superfluous paperwork that gets addressed after the real work is completed. This book promotes program evaluation as a vital aspect of practice; as a fundamental strategy for engaging agency staff at all levels, along with consumers and other constituents, around the improvement of services. Multiple voices can be engaged rationally and productively to describe their understanding of the intended function and actual performance of real-life services. Credible information about the intended plan for services, the degree to which services are being delivered in accordance with that plan, and the eventual impact of those services can fuel essential advocacy efforts directed at improving the lives of those who choose and need services.

RATIONALE FOR CHAPTERS

This book lays a foundation for a deliberative and strategic approach to program evaluation elements and their effectiveness. However, a number of factors need to be considered as an evaluation is being formulated prior to the implementation of the plan. Consequently, a number of topics are front-loaded before the mechanics of the evaluation are introduced:

Chapter 1. This chapter presents the rationale for conducting program evaluations and the importance of these evaluations. Graduate students and agency practitioners oftentimes focus on learning intervention skills and delivering quality services; this focus needs to expand to include evaluation. Although instrumental to program quality, appreciating the role of program evaluation may be an acquired taste. We hope that readers will be more firmly convinced of the value of an evaluation process, able to articulate the rationale for program evaluation and advocate for evaluating programs, and for some, discover a commitment to building and participating in a learning community.

Chapter 2. The purpose of the second chapter is to present the steps for conducting a program evaluation. While aiming to describe a logical and linear progression of decisions and actions, this chapter will also acknowledge and begin to describe the complexity and creative aspects of the evaluation process. It will provide an outline for the evaluative process that will parallel the organization of the book. Key terms will also be identified and defined. We expect that a reader will gain or reaffirm the steps needed to conduct an evaluation and accompanying decision points, while gaining an appreciation for the complexity of the evaluation process.

Chapter 3. This is the first of two chapters on ethical issues. This chapter will identify and describe ethical concerns that are classic to many areas of research methods. Building on fundamental ethical principles that affirm the importance of minimizing harm, advancing one's best interests, respecting autonomy, and promoting justice, this chapter will identify ethical principles that are essential for the conduct of evaluation and research. These principles are aligned with the NASW Code of Ethics. A reader should be able to identify the central ethical issues inherent in an evaluation and research study and assess the usefulness of a number of practical methods for addressing and implementing these principles.

Chapter 4. This chapter continues the consideration of ethical challenges. Oftentimes the most confusing and troubling elements of an evaluation process are the result of or are intertwined with ethical questions and concerns. This chapter will identify and examine ethical and moral dilemmas that are encountered in agency practice and settings. A reader will be able to recognize these dilemmas and list principles that can assist in making ethical choices.

Chapter 5. Similar to ethical considerations, this chapter looks at how political and social issues can support, complicate, or impede an agency-based evaluation process. This includes a careful look at who is conducting the evaluation. There are multiple dimensions to these considerations, beginning with the recognition that an evaluation takes place in the context of a social system with multiple subsystems and structures and system dynamics. Whether an evaluation is conducted by internal agents or external agents may introduce additional complications and opportunities, but both will face a common set of challenges. The evaluator may quickly learn that she or he is in the midst of a complicated set of relationships, roles, expectations, and pressures. Even more complicated, an evaluator may be oblivious to the social and political factors that may ultimately shape the validity and value of the evaluator's efforts. Alerting readers to these potential dynamics is the goal of this chapter.

Chapter 6. This chapter will look at a range of examples and issues that address cultural competency and evaluation. The conceptualization of research methods and program evaluation activities as mostly neutral, objective, and scientific processes may minimize one's attentiveness to the cultural context. However, this cultural context will shape the elements of the evaluation, the participants in the evaluation, and the activities and views of the evaluator. Appreciating and attending to the culture of the participants increases the likelihood of an accurate and useful evaluation. Attentiveness to culture also increases the trust and participation of participants. Readers will be able to identify a number of steps designed to assure a more culturally competent evaluation.

Chapter 7. Evaluation questions are always surrounded by the context of a living, breathing program. Each program usually carries a series of assumptions about its history and functioning that impact the evaluation. This chapter delineates a concrete process using program logic models to flesh out multiple perspectives on a program's functioning, develop a united view, and generate specific questions (program information needs) in the context of the agreed-upon program model. Varieties of models are included along with some illustrations of how to use the models to critique and promote the program.

Chapter 8. There are some stereotypical notions that all evaluation projects include the development of a survey that will provide vital information when it is administered. Actually, many agencies have data repositories, some known and some not, that can be very useful in meeting program needs. This chapter describes a process for finding those data sources and organizing them to address the program's needs for information. We provide a number of examples that illustrate the value of these available sources. We also identify some caveats along with strategies for enlisting agency staff to assess and bolster the credibility of the information.

Chapter 9. One of the most complicated and critical aspects of all evaluation is getting users to integrate the information into their decisions and practices aiming to improve services. This unique chapter addresses this challenge directly. In it we outline a process to assess an agency's past history and enumerate a list of concrete strategies along with an argument as to why social workers and other human service professionals are well-equipped to provide these types of support.

Chapter 10. This chapter will present group designs and methods that will inform the strategic choices that determine the evaluation. The key considerations in crafting and selecting such designs are related to securing agency commitment and addressing a range of threats to internal validity. In the end, the goals of credibility and confidence in the results of the study and the effectiveness of the program need to guide the design. These goals are balanced with the resources and stressors affecting the organization.

Chapter 11. Oftentimes evaluations tackle service challenges that present program information needs and evaluation questions that are not conducive to a structured questionnaire or numbers that can be extracted from an existing database. Addressing these questions may draw on qualitative methodologies with strong histories in a variety of social science disciplines. This chapter describes a variety of these techniques and offers some relevant examples. The use of these techniques in an evaluation is complicated, as most agency-based evaluation questions need answers in a rapid fashion that may cause the evaluator to customize the use of the technique. At the same time, these techniques are useful because they accommodate the exploratory nature of the ambiguous inquiry that may be required. In addition, these methods also provide a viable forum for the inclusion of service recipients' ideas and opinions in an unencumbered fashion.

Chapter 12. As stated in Chapter 11, it is difficult to complete a comprehensive evaluation without including the voices of service consumers. They have a unique view of the service experience. Furthermore, including their opinions fits with social work principles related to the dignity of the client and a commitment to quality service. This chapter references some historical and empirical support for consumer satisfaction. Methodological and historical factors are considered, along with several ideas about effective strategies for choosing and implementing a consumer satisfaction survey. Finally, we include a variety of consumer satisfaction instruments as examples.

Chapter 13. The last step in the evaluation process is to get the word out about the wonderful things that were learned and how agencies can use that information to make their services better and more beneficial for those receiving the services. Although this usually occurs in a written report, this chapter discusses a variety of techniques that address how to frame and disseminate the evaluation information for various user groups, as well as some activities that can support the utilization process.

TARGET AUDIENCE

This book is primarily designed to assist in the preparation of those professionals who will be the future conductors and leaders of program evaluations, the future participants in program evaluations, and the consumers of information gained from program evaluations—that is, graduate students in social work and other helping professions. We offer this assistance by identifying the basic elements of program evaluation, focusing on the special challenges associated with program evaluation in the real world and providing discussion questions, activities, and resources to deepen and expand one's application and knowledge of this content. The book's chapters will provide some measure of traditional program evaluation content, and each will include sources of additional information. This book particularly emphasizes elements of the evaluative process—such as ethics, culture, and politics—that are sometimes overlooked or discussed in briefer terms but in our experience can contribute significantly to the success and impact of the evaluation.

A second audience for this book is agency-based practitioners, program managers, and agency leaders. In response to the demands and needs for information from external funding sources, or as an integral part of an agency's mission to develop a learning community and model learning organization, program evaluation is a crucial aspect of an agency's operation. Internal agency-designated evaluators, staff members participating in an evaluation or committed to understanding the impact and success of their programs, and agency leaders responsible for allocating funds and achieving positive outcomes can benefit from this focus on program evaluation in an agency context.

A third audience for this book is university and academic-based teachers and evaluators. It is our responsibility to support professional values associated with evaluation and promoting programs that are just and helpful. Preparing future participants and leaders in evaluation requires a systemic approach to program evaluation in addition to the techniques, technologies, and methodologies associated with research and evaluation. The book is presented in 13 chapters to correspond with the length of an academic semester and a course with a specialization in program evaluation.

In addition, with the requirement for outside evaluators and the opportunities that present themselves due to academic expertise in program evaluation, universities are a primary source of program evaluators. In some professions, such as social work, there is the expectation for, or, at least, the recognition of engagement in the community and the value of outreach and professional service. This engaged scholarship, which includes creating and disseminating knowledge, propels a number of academic leaders, oftentimes with research teams that include students, into the community and program evaluation activities. University researchers have a special opportunity to provide responsive, ethical, and effective program evaluation that promotes best practices, strengthens agency practice, and develops an appreciation for and commitment to evaluation and research.

HOW TO USE THIS BOOK

Although this book can be read from cover to cover in the prescribed order—particularly for a graduate program evaluation class over the course of a semester—each chapter is designed to stand on its own and provide a focused presentation for an interested reader.

Common organizational features in each chapter include the following:

1. Each chapter will begin with an affirmation of the rationale for the content of the chapter.

2. Each chapter will contain numerous examples to illustrate the concepts and processes described in the chapter. These examples will be derived from our real-life experiences (with details slightly altered to protect the identity of organizational partners), from the experience of colleagues, or from professional literature.

3. As relevant, chapters will contain figures and sample forms to illustrate concepts or actions described in the chapter.

4. As relevant, we will review information in each chapter through a narrative recapitulation or a series of checklists that review and highlight the content presented. Reviewing content parallels the process of in-class checking with students to present the information in segments, to encourage the understanding of these sections, and to increase the likelihood that there is some measure of understanding before introducing new content. We rely on this technique in teaching and training and activities. In the text, these summaries

are highlighted with a stethoscope as if to say we want to make sure all of your vital signs are vibrant; meaning, you have understood the previous information and are ready to move on to some new content.

5. Each chapter will conclude with additional information to advance one's understanding of the topic and deepen and broaden the information that a student or practitioner might want to consider:

    a. *Big Ideas:* While intending to present a range of information and communicating the complexity of factors that may influence the design and implementation of a program evaluation, this end note is intended to identify and highlight the most salient points in the chapter.

    b. *Discussion Questions:* To reinforce learning, to encourage critical thinking, and in recognition of the fact that there may not be "right" answers, we pose a number of questions at the end of each chapter. These questions can be considered individually. We encourage using these as group discussion questions as we believe the evaluation process benefits from sharing and examining multiple perspectives, dialogue, and group reflection.

    c. *Activities:* Each chapter will provide topics for further consideration and deliberation, actions to illustrate or apply information from the chapter, and possible areas for debate.

With regard to the debate topics, within each area of study, oftentimes there are multiple courses of action, with no clear right or wrong approach, and oftentimes advantages and disadvantages to each choice. Sifting through these questions, options, and alternatives is an essential skill. Ideally, this debate would take place among the members of an evaluation team or between the team and an advisory board. Here, we will often present potential debate topics, because the ability to see and argue multiple perspectives is, in our opinion, a desirable trait. We challenge the readers with topics to consider, actions to try, and ideas to critique.

    d. *Resources:* The topics introduced in each chapter could conceivably comprise their own entire book. We recognize that some areas for consideration could be explored in greater detail, and that there are additional practical guides and instructions that the reader could find valuable (for example, there are more than 10 ways to present a logic model!). Each chapter will identify a number of annotated resources for further study.

e. *References:* The professional literature that informs each chapter will be identified at the end of the book. There are many excellent books on program evaluation, and a number of those authors have informed and guided the content in this book. In addition, a significant portion of the content reflects our own experience and observations. These experiences and observations have not been subjected to a rigorous evaluation. Their value and validity will be, in part, determined by the reader's critique and evaluation of the information. This quality of critical thinking is essential for program evaluation!

This book should be sufficiently broad and detailed to serve as a primary text on program evaluation. It can be supplemented by collections of complete program evaluations in the professional literature, program reports, or other resources developed by experienced program evaluators and research faculty members. This book can also be used as a supplement to a standard text on the mechanics of program evaluation. As noted earlier, certain chapters may supplement or enrich other resources in teaching program evaluation.

Knowing how to conduct a program evaluation and placing that outline in the context of multiple systemic considerations is a vital process for organizational improvement and the advancement of best practices in human and social services. There are multiple obstacles and challenges in conducting this vital work. Hopefully the value of the process, the knowledge of the process, and awareness of these complicating factors will increase the probability of a successful evaluation experience that advances knowledge and improves professional practice.

CHAPTER 1

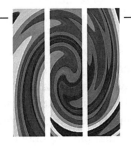

Making the Case for Program Evaluation

Program evaluation has unlimited potential for improving services. It can help to clarify and develop the kinds of services that recipients need. It also can help to identify and/or adjust services that are not being delivered to more effectively serve the appropriate people. Crucial information can be discovered about the benefit of services through questions like these: Are program participants getting anything out of the programs? Are recipients doing better after receiving the services? Is everyone better off? If not, who is better off and who is not? What aspects of the program are associated with those who seem to be doing well? How can the program be managed to ensure that everyone gets the service that seems to have the greatest impact?

While this list of questions seems very relevant to social work practice, social worker practitioners and research/evaluators seem to operate on different planets. Practitioners are usually committed to delivering the best possible service that directs attention to their immediate interactions with the client, for example, such as a counseling session or the completion of a referral. This orientation does not leave excess time or energy for evaluation. Additionally, research and evaluation activity is often separated from practice. Many agencies have distinct departments and/or staff functions that perform these duties. Research or quality assurances arms in organizations usually are separate from direct-service wings. The schism is further reinforced in most social work curricula where there is a clear distinction between practice courses and evaluation/research courses.

The primary focus of social work intervention is to improve the lives of individuals, families, and their communities by working with them to assist them with helpful services and resources. Consistent with organizational and educational reinforcements, when thinking about this mission to improve the lives of clients, it is unlikely that program evaluation is one of the first topics that comes to your mind. While we understand that, we would like to argue that an effective evaluation can be a very powerful tool for improving the quality of services and increasing the positive impact on service recipients.

ETHICAL OBLIGATIONS

As social workers, we have an ethical responsibility to exploit all resources in our repertoire in the interest of improving the lives of the clients we are serving. While our Code of Ethics guides us in the treatment of clients and the clarification of moral dilemmas that may arise in social work practice, there is also attention focused on the importance of providing services that are effective and helpful to clients (NASW, 1999).

Additionally, our Code of Ethics emphasizes a social worker's mandate to focus on social justice in the interest of interrupting the oppression of high-risk groups dispensed by prominent social institutions (NASW, 1999). If you are truly committed to at-risk individuals, families, and/or their communities, then program evaluation is a great ally. You can discover if services are actually being delivered to targeted groups or find out if services are being delivered as intended or if services are having the desired impact. Evaluation can also help to identify the services that are actually needed. When you consider the array of tools a social worker has at his or her disposal, program evaluation techniques have great potential for assisting in this fundamental mission to improve lives.

Checking Vitals

The Code of Ethics focuses on the importance of providing services that are effective and helpful to clients (NASW, 1999).

The Code of Ethics emphasizes a social worker's mandate to focus on social justice in the interest of interrupting the oppression of high-risk groups dispensed by prominent social institutions (NASW, 1999).

A recent trend in social work service is the choice of services models based on evidence-based practice. Social workers with this orientation would choose service treatment modalities that have been proven to work with the specific target population of interest. Choosing a model with an empirical history of effectiveness is an excellent practice; however, it does not ensure that the service will benefit the service recipients. In addition, evidence-based practitioners need to evaluate specific services to ensure that the model's effectiveness generalizes to that setting (Yeager & Roberts, 2003).

Social workers in managerial and supervisory capacities often practice from a consumer-centered management framework. The use of evaluative information to assess consumer needs, the effectiveness of the implementation of services, and the eventual impact of services is central to a consumer-centered approach to administrative practice (Poertner & Rapp, 2007).

Very similar arguments about the needs for service and its respective effectiveness are critical in the process of securing funds. Evaluation findings can be invaluable in the process of seeking new funding or continuing existing funds for services. When seeking grant monies, public or state contracts, or foundation dollars, it is likely that some type of evaluation will be required to enhance the likelihood of securing the award.

Checking Vitals

Evidence-based practitioners need to evaluate specific services to ensure that the model's effectiveness generalizes to that setting (Yeager & Roberts, 2003).

The use of evaluative information to assess consumer needs, the effectiveness of the implementation of services, and the eventual impact of services is central to a consumer-centered approach to administrative practice (Poertner & Rapp, 2007).

When seeking grant monies, public or state contracts, or foundation dollars, it is likely that some type of evaluation will be required to enhance the likelihood of securing the award.

PUTTING IT INTO CONTEXT

In addition to the practical and ethical arguments, evaluation is useful in service delivery efforts that are exceedingly complex. Clients bring complex sets of needs to the service setting, with economic and social challenges often at the center of those needs. Client families often come from racial or ethnic groups who have faced a lengthy history of injustice and discrimination. Additionally, individuals and families may have received services from established systems that do not have a track record of helping their clients. Despite these challenges, individuals and their families seem to find personal strengths that allow them to endure and survive.

In most cases, social work services are housed in extremely complex organizations. Ongoing discussion of organizational politics does not necessarily cast a favorable light on the individuals who participate in processes that impede the use of evaluation data (Rubin & Babbie, 2005). Our experience indicates that various players within these organizations engage in these processes as a part of their jobs, and the accompanying complexities come with the territory. When you look at these services systems you will find that different individuals design, implement, fund, and often evaluate the same services from different vantage points in the organization. For example, while direct service staff actually deliver the service, supervisors, managers, and administrators hire, fire, and manage these staff. Depending on the size of the organization, other staff functions may manage the payroll and benefits of these staff, deal with computers and technology, and also raise funds for the services. Finally, executive directors and upper management personnel usually oversee the operation at the top level of the organization.

All of these parties rely on external constituencies for many critical things. Funding and contractual arrangements may come from public or private entities. Favorable laws that support the mission of the organization require the agency to lobby legislators (local, state, and federal) and their supporters. The point of this discussion is not to review your organizational theory, but to keep in mind that doing evaluation and using data to improve services often gets lost in the shuffle. The staff at various levels of the organization are forced to deal with pressing matters, and unfortunately, in most cases, evaluative work is not viewed as the most pressing matter.

The low priority of evaluation within social service organizations is also complemented by the aforementioned historical schism that exists in the social work world between research and practice. Research is often viewed as something outside of practice. This is often reinforced in schools of social work where research and evaluation courses are taught in isolation from direct practice. In our conversations with students about research and taking additional research courses, even those who do well in the research course see it as a separate and less critical part of their professional development. This is further supported in organizations where ongoing evaluation is often excluded from the "real work" of the agency.

SO WHY BOTHER?

Despite the challenges, the potential payoffs for program evaluation efforts are significant. We have said it before and we will say it again: Program evaluation data can be used toward the betterment of social work practice in a number of ways. When agency staff at all levels participates in evaluation, it enhances the quality of the evaluation, the evaluation process, and the prognosis for securing credible and useful information. Additionally, social workers who participate in the evaluation process pick up skills that can improve their skills as practitioners. Patton (1997) describes the skills that participants in the evaluation process acquire that make them better practitioners as "process use" (p. 88). Participants are better able to concisely and concretely conceive and define an intervention and employ information to determine if it works. These skills put practitioners in a better position to develop interventions that are more likely to be effective, even before any evaluation has taken place.

Beyond the advancement of conceptual skills, evaluation can help to more effectively identify the services needs of client populations. Before any service can be successful, the specific needs to be addressed must be clear, and evaluative research can be instrumental in clarifying individual, family, and community needs. Evaluative efforts can make the intended outcomes of services more clear and meaningful (see Chapter 7). Surprisingly, practitioners who work in the same program can often have vastly different views on the intended outcomes of a program. Evaluation can help practitioners to flesh out and unify their unique perspectives, putting everyone on the same page of program intentions, which inevitably enhances the program's potential for impact.

Checking Vitals

Participation of all levels of staff in evaluation enhances the quality of evaluation, the evaluation process, and the prognosis for securing credible and useful information.

Social workers who participate in the evaluation process pick up skills that can improve their skills as practitioners:

Participants are better able to concisely and concretely conceive and define an intervention and employ information to determine if it works.

These skills put practitioners in a better position to develop interventions that are more likely to be effective, even before any evaluation has taken place.

Evaluation can help to more effectively identify the services needs of client populations.

Evaluation can help practitioners to flesh out and unify their unique perspectives, putting everyone on the same page of program intentions, which inevitably enhances the program's potential for impact.

One of the increasing demands for program evaluation is the development and completion of evaluation plans for program funders to demonstrate the program's impact. Most major funding sources require a program evaluation as part of the program proposal. However, the evaluations are often treated as a box to check in the interests of meeting funder reporting requirements. It is our hope that the ideas and concepts presented in this book will encourage practitioners to view these evaluation opportunities as viable methods for improving services.

The insights gained from evaluation can be used to make a myriad of different types of changes in the interest of better services. For example, one process evaluation about family therapy discovered that family therapists were spending time doing things that did not facilitate contact with families, such as supervising work and lunch activities. As a result, the supervisors reassigned these tasks and gave the family workers more time to meet with families. In another case, the staff from a children's group home found out the successes from the program were not succeeding in the community 3 months after release. To compensate, the program manager adjusted significant program resources to expand the aftercare services for their clients in community placement.

A somewhat unique use of program evaluation is the promotion of programs. Social workers engage in a litany of amazing practices within program models that are often very impressive. They engage with individuals and families who have often been effectively excluded from services previously. They help consumers to identify and accomplish specific goals under dire circumstances. They implement complex treatment plans in the community by working around barriers and taking advantage of existing resources. However, social workers are really not committed to telling the world about the great things they accomplish (Kapp, 2000), most likely because they are too busy doing the job to tell folks about it. Additionally, social workers often perceive marketing and advertising as self-aggrandizing. While that may be true, it is also true that social workers need to let their various constituents know about the wonderful things they do, as other professions are often being considered as cheaper or more convenient alternatives. Furthermore, program advocacy can often result in additional resources for the individuals, families, and communities receiving services. Models constructed in the process of evaluation and evaluative data are excellent tools for telling our many stakeholders about the great things being accomplished by individuals, families, and communities with the support of social workers.

Checking Vitals

Most major funding sources require a program evaluation as part of the program proposal.

Social workers need to let their various constituents know about the wonderful things they do, as other professions are often being considered as cheaper or more convenient alternatives.

Program advocacy can often result in additional resources for the individuals, families, and communities receiving services.

WHY ISN'T EVERYONE DOING IT?

If evaluation is so fantastic, why is this book opening with such a shameless promotion about the wonders of evaluation? If it is so wonderful, should it not be integrated into all aspects of agency practice? Right? As mentioned earlier, most social workers have minimal training in research and evaluation skills. The lack of significant background is nicely complemented by the view that evaluation does not fit into most notions of social work practices. Even when evaluation is completed, the lacking skill sets, conceptual frames, and interest levels that preclude evaluation work do not help. The track record of getting evaluation findings integrated into practice decisions is not good. Busy practitioners do not naturally find ways to assimilate evaluation data into the routine decision frameworks. Much of this book is directed at that challenge.

Poertner and Rapp (2007) argue that using evaluation is an excellent way to organize and focus all of the disparate factors that go into service on the effectiveness of those services. The potential benefits of evaluation outweigh the complexities associated with implementing an evaluation. For example, a clinical social worker might report to a supervisor, "You know, this family could really benefit from family therapy, but with what they have been through, it is just too hard. I am not going to even attempt to work with them!" There are many likely responses, ranging from telling the social worker to work with the family or lose his or her job, to engaging in a more supportive process that might help the social worker to more constructively deal with some of the barriers. But it is unlikely that the supervisor would say, "No problem, I don't blame you!" Evaluation has similar potential for improving the lives of those being served by social workers and likewise, it is unacceptable to avoid because of its inherent complexity.

Despite these challenges, evaluation is still conducted, maybe not in all organizations, but in many cases. This may occur at the behest of a funding source, or an organization may have a commitment to evaluation despite the complexities identified. If evaluative activity is going to be initiated, the evaluators or those acting in that capacity need to plan to invest the time and resources into the project in a manner that addresses the organizational and political dynamics of the organization. In cases where the evaluation is conducted oblivious of the organization, we feel it is unlikely that positive changes in the interest of clients will occur.

The purpose of this book is to prepare those who are doing evaluation to complete the work in a meaningful fashion that will promote positive changes for clients. We also hope to make people aware of various land mines and to offer suggestions for transforming those impediments into assets for completing an evaluation that will be helpful, useful, and lead to better services.

Checking Vitals

The potential benefits of evaluation outweigh the complexities associated with implementing an evaluation.

If evaluative activity is going to be initiated, the evaluators or those acting in that capacity need to plan to invest the time and resources into the project to address the organizational and political dynamics of the organization.

From a minor clarification of a program expectation . . . to promoting a plan to a funding source . . . to making a significant change in program operation based on evaluative data—services can be improved in innumerable ways using program evaluation. The point of this book is that evaluations are overcome by a variety of barriers and impediments when social workers try to take the research concepts learned in their research courses and apply them in the dynamic confines of agency social work practice. Unfortunately, research courses often focus more on methodological issues and never get around to the feisty matters that crop up when an evaluation is being implemented in an agency. Our plan is to apprise readers of what they will face in this enterprise and to give them ideas, skills, and techniques to address and optimize those same factors in the completion of an evaluation that facilitates the improvement of services.

This book promotes the idea that conducting program evaluation in an agency is a type of practice; there are specific pieces to the practice; and those pieces are clearly defined. In this book, we will define these specific aspects of program evaluation practice and ground our explanation in our experience as evaluators. While social workers and social work students are exposed to research methods, very little discussion addresses the application of these methods within an agency context.

Patton (1997) speaks intelligently about the craft of evaluation, focusing on the use of the information. He insightfully describes the most critical part of evaluation as "People, People, People" (p. 39). Our emphasis on practice speaks directly to finding ways to engage "people" in the evaluation process who would otherwise abstain from or impede the process. While agency practitioners are busy going about their particular aspect of service delivery, they prefer to stay out of evaluation practice or obstruct its implementation. This activity is often perceived as interfering with the business of service delivery. The practice of program evaluation presents numerous opportunities for engaging practitioners in the evaluative process, hoping that, at the least, they will not interfere with the process, but most likely participate in the use of the evaluation data.

Checking Vitals

Conducting program evaluation in an agency is a type of practice; there are specific pieces to the practice; and those pieces are clearly defined.

 KEY PIECES OF PROGRAM EVALUATION PRACTICE

Program evaluation practice involves the following:

1. Engage stakeholder in the evaluation process.
   a. Find the individuals with the information needs.
   b. Find the individuals needed to support the process.
   c. Find the individuals necessary to help with conducting the evaluation.
   d. Engage them in the evaluation process.
      i. Secure an initial investment.
      ii. Maintain their engagement throughout the process.

2. Assess and address agency political factors.
   a. Conduct an assessment of the agency's readiness to participate in an evaluation.
   b. Use the learning from the political assessment to implement and complete the evaluation.

3. Choose an evaluation design.
   a. Describe the program in a participative fashion.
   b. Identify information needs in the context of the program.
   c. Examine data sources to fulfill the information needs.

    d. Determine research methods based on information needs.

    e. Develop strategies to maintain the integrity of the evaluation process during implementation.

4. Data collection.

    a. Develop plans to collect information that require original data collection.

    b. Develop plans to acquire and organize data from available sources.

    c. Develop plans to support the data collection action throughout the process.

5. Reporting and using data.

    a. Develop methods for presenting data to different groups of users in a timely manner.

    b. Work with users to determine their plans for using the data.

    c. Practice using data with them.

    d. Support them in the use of the data.

6. Addressing culturally competent program evaluation.

    a. Identify insensitivities that are often reinforced in evaluation methods.

    b. Develop techniques for addressing those insensitivities.

The practice of program evaluation addresses these dimensions of the process. If you were to compare this list of activities to other evaluation texts, the treatment of methodology might look similar, but the emphasis on engaging agency staff in the process is the raison d'être of this book. Not only do we think that the process of engaging key organizational and service actors is critical to evaluation, we feel that social workers are the ideal candidates for taking on this role. The same clinical or interpersonal skills that social workers have acquired to assess and intervene with clients will suit them well in the practice of program evaluation. The remainder of the book will develop this notion of program evaluation practice by describing these concepts in more detail and sharing multiple examples of the application.

REVIEW AND REFLECT

Big Ideas

- Program evaluation is a critical part of practice that is consistent with our Code of Ethics, emphasizing effective services and advocating on behalf of oppressed groups.

- Program evaluation is regularly required to secure funding for services addressing the needs of underserved populations.

- Practitioners interested in evaluation can have a significant impact on the use of evaluation to improve services by involving agency personnel in the process.
  - Defining the program.
  - Identifying information needs and methods.
  - Developing plans for eventual use of the information.

Discussion Questions

- List and discuss some of the typical attitudes toward program evaluation. You may have experienced these attitudes or simply heard of them.

- Pick two of the attitudes identified in the previous question; then discuss the way they may impact program evaluation in an agency.

- How is the Code of Ethics tenet about effective services related to program evaluation?

- What is the relationship between social justice and program evaluation?

- What are some benefits of involving agency staff in the program evaluation process?

Activities

- The authors of this book make a huge deal about the value of program evaluation for improving services. Do you buy their argument? Why or why not? If you assume this argument is true why would you think program evaluation is not a more critical part of every service?

- Make a list of three barriers to using program evaluation to improve services. Comment on the validity of the barrier, whether it is really a barrier, and then suggest some ways to address it.

- The authors make a somewhat unique argument about program evaluation as an essential element of a social justice approach to advocating on behalf of underserved people. Critique this argument. Present a position in favor of this position and one against. Then, defend the position that is most consistent with your point of view.

Resources

- *Evaluation terminology*. Retrieved from http://www.irvine.org/assets/pdf/ evaluation/evaluation_terminology.pdf

- Hatry, H. (2007). *2006 performance measurement: Getting results* (2nd ed.). Baltimore, MD: Urban Institute Press. Retrieved from http://www.urban.org/ books/pm/chapter1.cfm

- Morley, E., & Lampkin, L. M. (2004, July). *Using outcome information: Making data pay off*. Retrieved from Urban Institute: http://www.urban.org/ publications/311040.html

- Urban Institute. (2002, June). *How and why nonprofits use outcome information*. Retrieved from http://www.urban.org/url.cfm?ID=310464

CHAPTER 2

Steps in Program Evaluation

I am sure you will find that survival analysis will be the
ideal technique for evaluating any of your programs.

T his chapter will forward an overall framework for designing and conducting an evaluation. We will describe a series of steps that are usually included in every evaluation project and frame those steps according to
our ideas about an agency-based approach. This scheme will serve a number
of purposes:

Provide a context and a framework for the upcoming discussion of evaluation activity in the book.

Define a model that will serve as a foundation for applying various facets of program evaluation forwarded in the book.

Begin to articulate the authors' basic notions about the process of evaluation.

SPELLING OUT THE EVALUATION PROCESS

The process for conducting an evaluation can be elusive and requires a basic structure. For purposes of clarity, most evaluation and research texts describe an overall research process that is similar to the one outlined in Figure 2.1. A clear structure is articulated that not only describes the overall process but also enumerates a sequence of steps. The steps provide a beginning and an ending to what could otherwise be an ambiguous process.

Obviously, before the evaluation project can progress, the evaluation question needs to be spelled out. Steps 1, 2, and 3 describe the onset of that process:

Step 1: *Identify* the evaluation question is the part of the process where the general focus of the project is stated in the form of a research question. Examples of an evaluation question could range from "Is the family preservation program effective?" to "Should we continue the family preservation program?"

Step 2: *Conceptualize* the question puts greater detail around the question. This step clarifies the key concepts in the evaluation question. For example, if you were to ask five people to define a concept like poverty, most likely you would get five different definitions. The point of this step is to consider different approaches, develop the one that best fits your interests, and make the chosen conceptual framework clear. The question, "Is the family preservation program effective?" could take many different forms. The question could ask: Are families better off than if they did not receive the service? Or the evaluation could focus on the delivery of the service, specifically: Was it implemented as intended according to a specific model of family preservation? Another option would be to examine the impact the program had on the recipient families. This step fleshes out more detail around the evaluation question. Clearly, each evaluation question can be developed in a variety of ways.

Step 3: *Operationalize* the question adds further detail to the question. The conceptual work spelled out in Step 2 provides a conceptual orientation for the evaluation question. This step defines specific concepts of the evaluation question.

Figure 2.1	Steps in an Evaluation

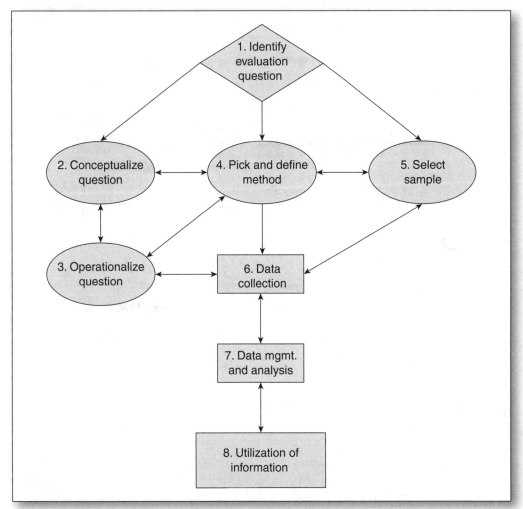

If in Step 2 the question, "Are families better off than if they did not receive the service?" was chosen, then efforts would be devoted to developing clear definitions. Does the term "family" refer to the parents and the child, or does it refer to all members of the family? What does "better off" mean? Is the focus on whether the child is home, or is it about the child's overall well-being? This step defines each of the key concepts. These initial steps set up the choice of the actual design by putting some detail around the intended question.

defines terms used in conceptualization stage

Checking Vitals

The fundamental steps of the evaluation process are as follows:

Step 1: *Identify* the evaluation question:

> The general focus of the project is stated in the form of a research question.

> Example: Is the family preservation program effective?

Step 2: *Conceptualize* the question:

> The key concepts in the evaluation question are clarified.

> The point of this step is to consider different approaches, develop the one that best fits your interests, and make the chosen conceptual framework clear.

> Example: The question could ask, "Are families better off than if they did not receive the service?"

Step 3: *Operationalize* the question:

> Specific concepts of the evaluation question are defined.

> Example: Does the term "family" refer to the parents and the child, or is it all members of the family?

RATING THE LEVEL OF STRUCTURE VERSUS FLUIDITY

The eight steps shown in Figure 2.1 as well as the initial steps defined above appear straightforward and clear. At first glance, the model also seems linear and consistent; however, if you look closely at the model you will see a number of lines with arrowheads on both ends. These bi-directional arrows depict the evaluation process as a fluid and dynamic process where the steps may be highly interdependent. The project may start with a specific question, but that question may be influenced or changed by the subsequent steps.

The fluidity of the evaluation process is heightened by the agency environment. Evaluation practitioners need to be attentive to this active context. The vignette described in the boxed example (below) illustrates that an evaluation question can be influenced by the subsequent steps in the evaluation process. Often program evaluation texts (Rossi, Lipsey, & Freeman, 2004) distinguish between a *process* evaluation (p. 56)—designed to improve the program—versus a *summative* evaluation (p. 36) that is focused on assessing the effectiveness of the program. Even if such distinctions are made at the onset of a project, it is the authors' experience that oftentimes the purpose of an evaluation may change during the process, as the context of an agency evaluation is a vibrant setting where information needs change. Agency dynamics, such as political factors and organizational traditions, often alter the design and implementation of evaluation. This is one of the unique points of view offered in this book; that is, the agency world where program evaluation resides is an ever-changing venue where services are usually primary and change is inevitable.

Example

The manager and funder of a tutoring program for urban youth made a commitment to evaluate the degree to which high-risk youth were receiving the service. The evaluator met with them and one of the lead tutors to discuss a strategy for determining the sample of youth to contact to discern this information, but the question changed. The tutor informed the group that the youth who predominantly used the service were highly motivated youth with sophisticated questions about more advanced projects and extra-credit assignments. After further discussion, the question evolved into a pilot test of a strategy to promote the program to high-risk youth to increase their involvement.

A second tenet of this book is that the purpose of a program evaluation is the generation of quality information for the improvement of services. For example, in Figure 2.1, the oversized box around Step 8, Utilization of Information, is symbolic. The book addresses many important factors in evaluation—like an ethical approach to practice and the utilization of different methods to collect credible information, which might be more likely to include service users in the development and collection of the evaluation—but all of this is focused around the primary purpose of generating information that can be used to improve the service delivery process. The steps of the evaluation process need to be framed with an appreciation of two fundamental notions: (1) The use of information for service improvement is primary, and (2) the context for evaluation is an agency where evaluation must compete with many enterprises for attention. To address these beliefs, the prescribed evaluation process attends to these notions in a number of different fashions.

Checking Vitals

The purpose of an evaluation may change during the process, as the context of an agency evaluation is a vibrant setting where information needs change.

Agency dynamics, such as political factors and organizational traditions, often alter the design and implementation of an evaluation.

Fundamental notions:

The use of information for service improvement is primary.

The context for evaluation is an agency where evaluation must compete with many enterprises for attention.

THE AGENCY CONTEXT

The evaluation process occurs in an agency setting which is dynamic and constantly focused on the delivery of services. Given this consideration, the approach presented in this book proposes a variety of accommodations. For example, before a meaningful discussion of the evaluation question occurs, it is vital to develop a solid grasp of the program. Chapter 7, Program Definition: Using Program Logic Models to Develop a Common Vision, provides a strategy for taking evaluation one step back from the evaluation question and focusing on the specification of the program model. Before any discussion of an evaluation can be complete, energy needs to be devoted to developing a clear, concise, and collective vision of the program.

The chapter describes a process for getting input about the program model and synthesizing the information into a supported model. The program model discussion elicits varying points of view and encourages assimilation of differing ideas into a collective model depicting the program. In this context, where the program model is central, evaluation questions are often viewed as program information needs. Specific program information needs emerge from program model discussions. Key constituents, staff, clients, funders, and so forth, identify program components where information is needed. Additionally, the participative nature of this process encourages the investment of key parties (stakeholders) in the definition of the program and the delineation of information needs for the program. As a result, not only are both the model and the development of the evaluation questions more comprehensive; critical players have a stronger identification with them as well.

Checking Vitals

Before any discussion of an evaluation can be complete, energy needs to be devoted to developing a clear, concise, and collective vision of the program.

Program model discussion:

Elicits varying points of view and encourages assimilation of differing ideas into a collective model depicting the program.

Evaluation questions are often viewed as program information needs.

The participative nature of this process encourages the investment of key parties (stakeholders) in the definition of the program and the delineation of information needs for the program.

The discussion (outlined in Figure 2.1) then proceeds to Step 4: *Pick and Define* the method. The choice of the method is first identified in Chapter 7, Program Definition: Using Program Logic Models to Develop a Common Vision. The discussion is driven by the context developed around the program model and its associated information needs. Again, this chapter describes a process for discussing the program's information needs and methods for collecting the best data to inform those needs. As you will find in Chapter 7, key actor involvement builds commitment to the specific information needs and leads to a more thorough consideration of these needs given the breadth and depth of the key actors' collective knowledge. It should also be noted that the process outlined for choosing information needs, as opposed to defining a single evaluation question, may lead to a variety of pieces of information coming from multiple sources as opposed to a single evaluation method.

Chapter 7 also describes an inclusive process for actively involving stakeholders in the process of defining the program model, information needs, and method options. Chapter 9, Evaluation Design: Options for Supporting the Use of Information, adds a critical dimension to the discussion of information needs and potential designs. The inclusive process is expanded to include a deliberate discussion of the intended use of the information. The discussion allows the identified parties to consider the most important information needs and how the information will be used. Consideration is given to the format that best suits the user as well as the organizational context for the possible usage. If the intended users are individual program managers, then the form of the data and method may look different than it would if the intention were to convince external funders to expand resources. Briefly, program managers most likely would want information that matches their specific programs, whereas funders may prefer information that would complement their standard evaluation and reporting conventions. This discussion examines various ideas about use of the information in a time frame that can influence specification of the design. Additionally, the chapter describes strategies to make sure that the collective ownership of the evaluation developed in the definition of the program and the choice of the method continues while the data is being collected and during the use of the information. Discussion of the usage in the early stage of the evaluation process allows the users to tailor the type of information to be collected to suit their needs. We feel strongly this contributes to ownership of the evaluation during the implementation and its eventual use.

Chapter 9 also examines the organizational context for using the data. The chapter outlines some basic methods for assessing the organization's readiness for using the data and possible strategies to support the users in specific political contexts. More discussion about the presentation of information for users is presented in Chapter 13, Dissemination: Spreading the News.

Checking Vitals

When an evaluation question is raised in the context of a specific program, it usually translates to a variety of program information needs from multiple sources.

Stakeholders (key actors associated with a program) need to discuss the potential use of the information in the very beginning of the process as this discussion can influence the collection and future use of the data.

Likewise, the ways for disseminating the information require attention in the beginning as this can influence design and usage.

Figure 2.2 describes a process for evaluation that is more consistent with the text presented in this book. Steps 1 through 3 (as shown in Figure 2.1 as Identifying, Conceptualizing, and Operationalizing the evaluation question) are now focused around program information needs. These steps, along with Picking and Defining the method (which includes sampling, data collection, and analysis issues) now reside on the right side of Figure 2.2. The right side of Figure 2.2 captures the more customary steps. The left side of Figure 2.2

Figure 2.2   Agency-Based Steps in Evaluation

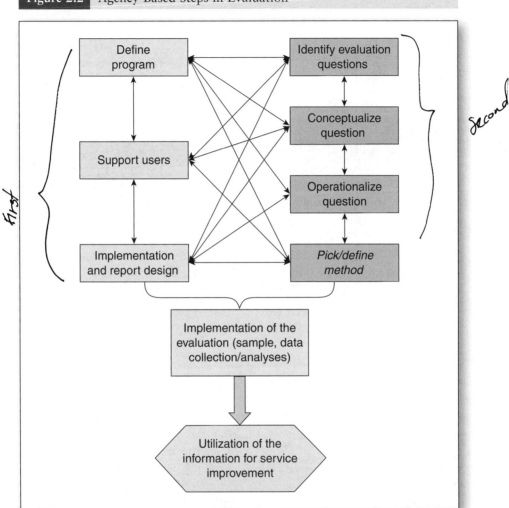

augments the aforementioned steps with inclusive processes for program definition, supporting the users, and dissemination. This broader perspective—attending to the specifics of the program, the organizational context, and the eventual use of the information—usually creates an evaluation that is more attentive to the agency context and the information needs. In addition, this approach typically elicits valuable support during the implementation of the evaluation. Most important, this sensitivity to the agency context has great potential for increasing the eventual use of the evaluation information for service improvement. Obviously, these steps do not guarantee the celebratory utilization of the information for bettering the lives of children, families, and their communities. However, it has been our experience that the chances of evaluation findings making their way into program decision processes without similar efforts is less likely.

Checking Vitals

 When an evaluation question is raised in the context of a specific program it usually translates to a variety of program information needs from multiple sources.

Stakeholders (key actors associated with a program) need to discuss the potential use of the information in the very beginning of the process as this discussion can influence the collection and future use of the data.

Likewise, the ways for disseminating the information require attention in the beginning as this can influence design and usage.

APPLYING CREDIBLE EVALUATION
METHODS IN AN AGENCY SETTING

Thus far, this chapter has focused on a process for including the perspectives of key actors in the evaluation and the accommodation of the agency context. While that is critical, it is also vital to discuss the application of plausible and honorable evaluation methods. Not surprisingly, the aforementioned agency factors influence the choice and implementation of various methodologies. We would like to share some of the lessons that have been learned about the design and implementation of a variety of different evaluation methods. You will find a range of different and well-known options described with a focus on agency-based implementation. For example, Chapter 8, Program Description: Evaluation Designs Using Available Information, describes evaluation designs that exploit existing agency information sources. This chapter discusses various information sources along with strategies for linking the data with key program information needs. Some examples are given of the more common uses of the alternative data sources.

Chapter 10, Evaluation Design: Group Designs and Methods, addresses more traditional evaluation methods requiring comparison groups and a prescribed methodology. This set of methods raises a series of unique methodological and ethical challenges in an agency context. The specialized requirements of this orientation are discussed, and some techniques for their implementation are illustrated. Sometimes program evaluation questions are not well-suited to quantitative methods of evaluation. Chapter 11, Evaluation Design: Qualitative Designs and Applications, identifies a variety of qualitative techniques and highlights some workable examples for agency evaluation.

Evaluation in social work often utilizes methods that are consistent with ethical considerations that suit the field. Chapter 12, Consumer Satisfaction, explicates the practice of including feedback from recipients into the evaluation process. This approach raises some unique considerations covered in this chapter, along with many examples.

Last, but not least, the book covers some unique principles that govern our approach to program evaluation. Many of these ideals come from ethical considerations forwarded in social work. Social work is not only the background of the authors; we also find these standards very applicable to evaluation practice. Chapter 3, Ethics and Program Evaluation: Applying a Code of Ethics to Field-Based Research, discusses a set of values that can be used to guide evaluation in agency settings where multiple agendas tend to operate. Chapter 4, Ethical Challenges for Evaluators in an Agency Setting: Making Good Choices, describes some guidelines for the respectful treatment of the individual agency staff and service consumers that are included in evaluation practice. Chapter 6, Cultural Competency and Program Evaluation, presents a specialized view of the treatment of service recipients in an evaluation context that is less likely to perpetuate the types of oppression they may have faced in service settings and society in general.

Checking Vitals

Implementing various evaluation methods in agency settings can be tricky. We discuss some ways of addressing these complications in the methods chapters in the book.

Agency-based evaluation presents a set of ethical concerns around the treatment of agency staff and service recipients that we also confront.

This chapter presents a way of conducting evaluation that keeps the agency context and the potential use of the data for service betterment at the forefront. As a result, we cover a fairly unique set of topics in detail that may not be highlighted in other texts. Additionally, this book covers useful methodological and ethical approaches that are typical in agency evaluation.

REVIEW AND REFLECT

Big Ideas

- The linear approach to evaluation methods often presented is problematic in an agency setting.

- The design and implementation of an evaluation needs to always attend to two basic concepts: (1) The agency setting is where the evaluation will occur; and (2) the use of evaluation data for improvement is most often the eventual goal.

- Given this context, the design and implementation must be centered on the program context and the process needs to be highly participative.

Discussion Questions

- What are some difficulties of the evaluation model initially presented in Figure 2.1?

- Why is a firm grasp of the program such a key aspect of the design and implementation of the evaluation?

- What is the authors' concern with the notions of a summative and process evaluation?

- What are some of the key differences between the first model of evaluation offered and the second model of evaluation?

- How are the differences presented in the second model related to agency-based evaluation?

Activities

• Do you agree with the authors' description of the problems associated with the first model of evaluation?

• In Figure 2.2, pick one of the boxes located on the left and discuss how you think it would contribute to accomplishing the goal related to the boxes on the right; then list some of the drawbacks that you see between the same boxes.

• In Figure 2.2, the authors' propose that attention paid to the boxes on the left will enhance the eventual use of the data. Discuss what part of this argument appeals to you and what part does not.

Resources

• Hatry, H. P., & Lampkin, L. (2003, May 9). *Key steps in outcome management*. Retrieved from Urban Institute: http://www.urban.org/publications/ 310776.html

• W. K. Kellogg Foundation. (n.d.). *Evaluation questions*. Retrieved from http://wkkf.org/Default.aspx?tabid=90&CID=281&ItemID=2810011&NID= 2820011&LanguageID=0

• W. K. Kellogg Foundation. (n.d.). *The evaluation plan*. Retrieved from http://wkkf.org/Default.aspx?tabid=90&CID=281&ItemID=2810015&NID= 2820015&LanguageID=0

CHAPTER 3

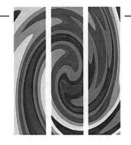

Ethics and Program Evaluation

Applying a Code of Ethics to Field-Based Research

"After reviewing these comprehensive data sources it is clear this program is very effective!"

The process of conducting research and the evaluation of programs and the outcomes associated with these activities have the potential to be helpful or harmful to individuals, groups, organizations, and the broader society. When professional activities have the capacity to help or hurt, there is a crucial role for ethical thinking and ethical decision making (Royse, 1992). The practice of program evaluation, by its very nature, is often concerned with the positive or negative outcomes of certain organizational actions or programs and the consequences for the organization and the persons served by the agency (Rubin & Babbie, 2005).

The discovery of the positive benefits of a program, its neutral effects, or its negative consequences has implications for ethical practice. An effective social service program, for example, may lead to a strong commitment to continue the program, expand the program, or replicate the program. However, a social service program with inconclusive or neutral results may mean that additional information needs to be gathered to assess its costs and benefits and weigh the investment of energy, funding, and time. An ineffective program, on the other hand, or one with negative consequences, should result in an imperative to stop the program, to reinvest the resources supporting the ineffective program, or at least to change the program. There may even be the obligation to repair any harm that has been done by the program. In addition to outcomes, the process of conducting the evaluation and the process of delivering an intervention or program may create areas of scrutiny with regard to the effects on participants and the consequences for stakeholders. With limited resources, multiple needs, and the potential for helpful and harmful processes and outcomes, it is essential to consider ethical practice, principles, and processes in program evaluation.

The process of identifying problems and programs to study, designing and implementing those studies, and reporting and responding to these studies creates numerous opportunities for conflicts and dilemmas. Not limited to being rude or impolite, disrespectful, ignorant, or foolish, some of these complications rise to the level of moral and ethical considerations and standards. In fact, some of the most vexing aspects of a program evaluation might involve the ethical challenges and issues that are laced throughout the project or study. The failure to consider these potential issues in constructing and implementing an evaluation plan will leave a researcher vulnerable to being blindsided by accusations and ethical binds and multiple troubles that might sabotage or undermine one's work.

This chapter will provide a foundation for examining ethics and program evaluation. It will describe principles that are central to professional practice. The ethical conduct of evaluation and research is explicitly addressed in the Code of Ethics of the National Association of Social Workers (NASW). The Social Work Code of Ethics also provides a rubric for identifying and analyzing a range of ethical considerations in relation to clients, organizations, and the profession. Understanding and adherence to this professional code is expected for evaluators and researchers just as for clinicians, community organizers, and organizational leaders. Chapter 4 will identify and expand on additional ethical dilemmas central to the conduct of a program evaluation.

Checking Vitals

When professional activities have this capacity to help or hurt, there is a crucial role for ethical thinking and ethical decision making.

The discovery of the positive benefits of a program, its neutral effects, or its negative consequences has implications for ethical practice.

With limited resources, multiple needs, and the potential for helpful and harmful processes and outcomes, it is essential to consider ethical practice, principles, and processes in program evaluation.

The failure to consider potential issues in constructing and implementing an evaluation plan will leave a researcher vulnerable to being blindsided by ethical binds and multiple troubles that might sabotage or undermine one's work.

CODES OF ETHICS

Organizations that initiate or participate in the evaluation of their programs and researchers who conduct such studies are frequently members of professional organizations. As professionals, in general, they are committed to ethical practice, as professionalism assumes the ability to examine one's own behavior and align one's practice with ethical standards. In addition, as professionals, the conduct of those leading the evaluation of a program are guided and governed by professional codes of ethics: "To interact professionally is to take an ethical stance. When these ethical positions are pointed out, we realize that taking professional action automatically involves operating within our codes of ethics" (Bloom, Fischer, & Orme, 2003, p. 12). Adherence to such codes raises a number of questions and may provide some guiding principles for professionals engaged in evaluation work (NASW, 1999; Royse, 1992; Rubin & Babbie, 2005).

Ethical Responsibilities to Clients

The primary responsibility of professionals is to conduct their work in such a manner as to promote the well-being of clients. Fundamentally, why engage in program evaluation? There is an ethical imperative to provide interventions/programs/services that promote the well-being of clients; thus, determining if and to what extent such help is taking place is an ethical imperative for a program or professional.

This central responsibility to clients raises a number of practical and theoretical questions for program leadership and evaluators:

1. Who is the client? Is the primary responsibility to the persons who receive the services? In an evaluation, are the agency personnel involved in the program also defined as clients of the evaluation?

2. Are there any limits to this responsibility to clients? When is a responsibility to larger society sufficient enough to trump one's responsibility to clients or to the agency? Should clients be advised that there may be situations in which the researcher has a duty to report or draw attention to a set of circumstances that are troublesome? If so, when is this discussed with clients or with the agency?

3. With respect to informed consent, to what extent should the evaluator inform subjects as to the nature of the evaluation? When should this information be shared? How often and in how much detail? Whose responsibility is it to inform participants? Are there exceptions to informed consent or its full implementation?

4. With regard to data collection, how is data collected, reviewed, and stored? Should participants be audiotaped or videotaped? If so, then when and to what extent? Are there circumstances under which it would be harmful or impermissible to in some way record a client? Whose purposes does such data collection serve?

5. What competencies are required to conduct or lead a program evaluation? What qualities should an organization look for in an evaluator? Assuming that competency correlates with one's ability to act responsibly toward clients, how does one acquire or recognize these competencies? Is it possible to gain assurances that an evaluation team has the necessary ability and competency to conduct a responsible study?

6. To what extent does an evaluator need to know and understand the culture of the agency? Is there an obligation to approach work with an agency from the same perspective as work with clients, recognizing the strengths of the culture? If understanding culture is essential to competent and responsible work, how does one acquire this knowledge and understanding?

7. What if one's responsibility to clients is in conflict with one's own interests? What are some areas that may pose a conflict of interest? How can one avoid these areas of conflict? What if these areas of conflict are not apparent in the early stages and arise suddenly in the process of the evaluation? How does one overcome lack of awareness and learn to recognize areas of potential conflict?

8. Is there a duty to inform clients and other stakeholders of a real or potential conflict of interest? If so, how do you do this and when? Are there times when one should not take an assignment due to a conflict of interest? If so, then why and when? Are there times when one should terminate a relationship—why and when? Can a conflict of interest be effectively managed?

9. How do you recognize a dual relationship? What if the dual relationship, in fact, is what secured the contract or opportunity to conduct the evaluation? What are the clear and appropriate boundaries between an evaluator and an organization and its clients? What if the evaluator is working with two or more agencies that have a relationship to each other and to the evaluator, with conflicting interests?

Checking Vitals

There is an ethical imperative to provide interventions/programs/ services that promote the well-being of clients; thus, determining if and to what extent such help is taking place is an ethical imperative for a program or professional.

Privacy and Confidentiality

Respect for the privacy and the confidentiality of subjects is an important aspect of overall responsibility for clients (Reamer, 2001). This commitment to confidentiality is a central tenet of professional behavior. Without some assurance of confidentiality, it may not be possible to gain information from persons who participate in one's study. It may be possible to get persons to participate, but without the sense that their privacy was protected, the honesty and overall validity of information gained may be suspect. One of the primary responsibilities of an administrator is to protect the information about and the privacy of one's employees and the persons served by the agency (O'Sullivan & Rassel, 1989). Respect for confidentiality is important as a professional duty, as a practical consideration to gain accurate information, and to conduct a study in accord with agency regulations.

This central principle of privacy that is translated into professional practice as a commitment to confidentiality leads to a number of ethical issues for evaluators and administrators:

1. Does an agency have the right to privacy? What if you discover information that is troublesome or private information that is not related to the focus of your study?

2. What constitutes valid consent to disclose confidential information?

3. Are there compelling professional reasons that would lead you to disclose information? If so, for what reasons and to whom would you disclose it?

4. How do you protect the identities of research/evaluation subjects, particularly when one is evaluating a small program or agency or a distinctive program? How is privacy protected when the study takes place in small or rural communities?

5. Should you sign a confidentiality agreement and what does that entail?

6. How should you respond to the media?

7. How do you protect written and electronic records and other sensitive information?

8. Is there an agency Institutional Review Board process to review the evaluation's provisions to protect privacy and assure confidentiality of participants and information?

9. How do you handle presentations and publications beyond and after an evaluation report to the agency?

Certain topics will raise heightened concerns about confidentiality: (1) when information is solicited from vulnerable subjects; (2) when information is sought on stigmatized topics, such as drug use or sexual behavior; or (3) when data collection techniques expose subjects to considerable scrutiny, for example, in participant observation in which multiple areas of one's behavior or life space may be available for discovery and scrutiny.

Example

The study on organizational climate and culture involved interviews with a range of employees. The questions addressed the workers' relationships with their supervisors and other agency managers. Fearful of losing their jobs or experiencing some form of retaliation, the workers had little to say to the interviewer. Concurrent focus groups were also constrained as a middle manager sat in on each focus group. Conducting the interviews off-site, individually, with assurances of privacy, resulted in gaining more detailed information. One worker related how she sat alone in her office and cried on several occasions, after experiencing harsh criticism and lack of support from coworkers and supervisors. A range of positive and negative experiences were reported in the interviews. In the focus groups, the staff member did not realize that a middle manager was sitting in on the first focus group. When that person also attended a second focus group, the person's identity was clearly established. The staff member respectfully spoke with the middle manager after the second group and asked if he would refrain from attending future focus groups. He agreed, appearing unaware that his presence may have shaped the workers' responses. Subsequent focus groups were livelier and more vocal.

How should an agency that is involved in program evaluation support confidentiality as an ethical principle?

1. An agency has a limited right to confidentiality—an organization can reasonably expect that its inner processes and procedures that are beyond the scope of the evaluation will not be exposed to public broadcast or scrutiny due to deliberate dissemination by the evaluator.

2. The potential for accidental discovery of troublesome or private information should be anticipated by the evaluator and the agency, and conditions for disclosure and reporting such discoveries should be addressed up front. This involves some risk because if an evaluator belabors the possible points of discovery, an agency that is already skittish about an evaluation, has a relatively closed culture to begin with, or is in a politically vulnerable position may be disinclined to initiate or participate in program evaluation. Conversely, a clear discussion and clear plan may be reassuring to agency administrators.

3. An agency administrator and the program evaluator should together, up front, identify any conditions that would potentially require some degree of setting aside confidentiality and privacy requirements.

Example

The researcher had a preliminary conversation with the child welfare program manager about the study and its strategy for data collection. To identify the decision-making elements in relation to child maltreatment, the evaluator would be relying primarily on reading case records and interviews with a number of key informants, including frontline workers. The program manager was fully supportive of the study and stated, "As you read the case records and talk to our case managers, if you find examples of poor casework and practices that appear to be problematic, please inform me." The researcher replied, "The information that I gain from records and information is, for the most part, confidential. If I discover something that is unethical and harmful, I will let you know but for the most part I expect that the information I gain will either have to remain confidential or not be directly attributable to any worker." The manager continued, "OK, but I want to know if workers are not doing their jobs well and children or families are suffering." She replied, "I appreciate your commitment to good practice. If there are alarming incidents involving serious harm I will bring them to your attention, but I want workers to be honest with me so that overall performance can be informed and potentially improved by this study. Primarily, the information that I learn will be reported back as group information, rather than individual performance." The program manager was sufficiently assured that dangerous behavior would be brought to his attention, and the researcher was assured that she would protect worker identities and information. Both needed these assurances to proceed with the study.

Example

When interviewing the mother about the nature of the intervention and relationship with her caseworker, the mother reported that the worker stated that the mother's life must be dull now that she had given up her substance abuse habit. The mother was distressed about her conversations with the worker as she was struggling with abstinence. In an interview with a second client served by the same caseworker, the woman reported to the interviewer that the caseworker encouraged her to party and have fun, including drinking alcohol.

The woman had been struggling with parenting problems that were linked to her drinking behavior. She thought her caseworker was a fun and lively person, and she enjoyed her conversations with her worker. The interviewer had to consider the accuracy of the information reported by both clients. She also had to consider whether or not to bring the worker's behavior to the attention of anyone associated with the project or agency.

4. For the sake of clarity, draft a confidentiality agreement that spells out the range and limitations on disclosure and dissemination of evaluation processes and outcomes, and other agency business. For example, the evaluator could sign a statement that said he or she would not release or divulge information that could be considered confidential—such as identifying information (names, addresses, or any other information that would disclose the identity of a person). Collecting social security numbers should be avoided—if a numerical code is needed to identify a response for matching purposes, a numerical code should be invented rather than using social security numbers or other potentially identifying or private information. In a confidentiality agreement, in addition to the promise to keep information private and restrict gaining identifying information, the project should be identified, a date should be noted, and an expiration date and signatures should be witnessed.

5. The evaluator and any evaluation team members need to be careful about discussing the study. Conversations about the evaluation should not take place in public places inside or outside the research site.

6. If the evaluator is affiliated with a university, the study should follow the guidelines of the university's institutional review board (IRB) with regard to confidentiality and should follow agency guidelines about conducting research and respecting confidentiality. If the evaluator is not affiliated with a university, it may still be possible to contract with a nearby university IRB to review one's evaluation plan and develop an agency IRB review process. Although time-consuming and adding a step to one's process, this review may be particularly helpful in gaining perspective and sanction if there is no agency-based review process.

7. Research records should be stored in a secure, locked cabinet and in a private, locked office. Records should be disposed of carefully. Shredding documents is recommended.

8. Some information can be gathered through mechanisms that assure respondent anonymity. Protect privacy by not asking for identifying information and through establishing reporting methods that do not require any form of self-disclosure or exposure.

9. University-based evaluators will often want the option to publish their findings. Negotiate this before the evaluation begins with questions like these: Can it be published? Does the evaluator agree to have the agency read the article before publication? Is agency approval necessary for publication? Can the agency request or insist upon revisions? How will the agency be acknowledged? Will there be coauthors, and will an agency person(s) be included as an author? Where will the report be published? To what extent will the publication/report use pseudonyms or disguise the agency identity and location? If the findings are positive, the agency may want to encourage publication!

Following are some guidelines to govern the sharing of information:

• Evaluators who want to share the information learned in the evaluation process should obtain a release of information from the agency or organization being studied and from relevant stakeholders, such as funders.

• Evaluators should establish ownership of the data prior to the collection of data, as ownership defines the authority to share information.

• Evaluators should identify how, when, and where the data is to be presented as soon as possible. Academic researchers will want to publish and present the data. When a program is doing well, an agency will generally see sharing the information as a good thing; in fact, the organization may press the researcher to present the data/report. However, findings are rarely purely wonderful, or negative, and the researcher has the obligation to present the information in an honest, thoughtful form, even if the agency or evaluation team members prefer broadly worded positive descriptors. To the extent possible, discuss and plan for how information will be presented ahead of time.

Checking Vitals

Respect for confidentiality is important as a professional duty, as a practical consideration to gain accurate information, and to conduct a study in accord with agency regulations.

One of the primary responsibilities of an administrator is to protect the information about and the privacy of one's employees and the persons served by the agency (O'Sullivan & Rassel, 1989).

Certain topics will raise heightened concerns about confidentiality:

Information is solicited from a vulnerable subject.

Information is sought on stigmatized topics, such as drug use or sexual behavior.

Data collection techniques expose subjects to considerable scrutiny.

Role Clarity

Ethical responsibilities to clients for evaluators include respecting boundaries and maintaining a professional relationship. For example, a participant may seek consultation or counseling from an evaluation team member. Whether or not the evaluator or team member is competent and licensed to provide therapeutic services, this is not the evaluator's role, so a referral should be made to an appropriate counselor. Although rarely addressed, it should be noted that in parallel with professional behavior with clients, a research team member should not have sexual relations with research subjects and evaluation participants.

Ethical Responsibilities to Colleagues

In designing and implementing a program evaluation, evaluators have a responsibility to both colleagues and clients. This responsibility is evidenced through how evaluators conduct themselves as professionals and with regard to certain complicated relationships with other professionals. Central to ethical professional conduct is respect for others. This respect includes truthfulness about one's abilities, background, and credentials as well as avoiding unwarranted negative criticism in the evaluation process.

Some potentially complicated professional relationships can surface when an evaluator learns about the strengths and weaknesses of program staff members. What should an evaluator do if one discovers that a professional is impaired? What if an evaluator discovers that an employee is incompetent? What if one learns about or observes unethical behavior? Evaluators have a responsibility to warn a program administrator about harmful or potentially harmful behavior and a seriously impaired state of an employee. This should be balanced with a commitment to accuracy, carefulness, respect for privacy, and an assessment about the severity and frequency of compromising behaviors. To the extent possible, the evaluator's response to these troubling conditions should be noted up front in the negotiations and design of the evaluation, rather than after a disturbing discovery.

Sometimes, however, this has not been addressed in the early stages; a researcher needs to make sure he or she has accurate information, that it is a potentially harmful situation, and then precisely and privately report the matter to an appropriate administrator. Even if addressed up front, discovering and deciding to report and then dealing with any ramifications is an uncomfortable and stressful experience for the evaluator.

Example

The research assistant was reading case records and discovered that the worker had not made any home visits to meet with the child in foster care for over half a year.

Example

A member of the evaluation team was scheduled to conduct an interview with one of the supervisors. The supervisor missed the appointment and missed the subsequent two appointments. Finally, the interviewer met the supervisor. The supervisor had bloodshot eyes, seemed unfocused, spoke with slurred speech, and smelled like alcohol.

Checking Vitals

Ethical responsibilities to clients for evaluators include respecting boundaries and maintaining a professional relationship.

Central to ethical professional conduct is respect for others; this includes truthfulness about one's abilities, background, and credentials as well as avoiding unwarranted negative criticism in the evaluation process.

Evaluators have a responsibility to warn a program administrator about harmful or potentially harmful behavior and a seriously impaired state of an employee.

To the extent possible, the evaluator's response to potential troubling conditions should be noted up front in the negotiations and design of the evaluation, rather than after a disturbing discovery.

Ethical Responsibilities in Practice Settings

A number of challenging situations can present themselves in conducting an evaluation, particularly when that evaluation process extends over a number of months or years. These situations include clarity about boundaries and the evaluator's level of involvement with the practice and policies of the agency. Some questions are the following:

1. To what extent, if any, should evaluators provide training for agency professionals or provide educational resources or consultation to the workers or others involved in the evaluation?

2. To what extent, if any, should evaluators work to improve an agency's policies, procedures, and practices?

3. What if there is discrimination at the agency? Or unfair personnel practices?

4. What if there is a labor dispute at the agency? What if there is a pending strike? What if you are asked for information to support one side or the other in an agency conflict?

5. What if policies or practices appear to violate a code of ethics? What if these practices are merely troubling, or rude, or ineffective? How can one tell if there is an ethical violation?

Evaluators need to have a clear sense of their role. The initial clarity that may be shared by the evaluator and the organization will most likely be tested at some point in time during the course of the evaluation. With an active, community-based evaluation process that extends over a period of time, a relationship builds with the agency administrators, workers, and other study stakeholders.

This relationship provides some opportunities and advantages and some potential complications for the evaluation. The evaluator may feel tempted to engage in a conversation with the worker to balance the relationship and provide some reciprocity in information sharing. It might be natural to feel sympathetic to the worker, and the evaluator might sense the worker's need for feedback or reassurance. However, this is not the evaluator's role. The evaluation team members will need to kindly reiterate the scope of their relationship with the persons they work with on the project. The researcher should resist exploring the worker's feelings beyond the interview protocol. Even suggesting that the worker speak to his supervisor may be too much a directive and subject to interpretation. Providing feedback, in a careful, planful, thoughtful manner to project and agency leaders, needs to be weighed based on the seriousness of the concerns or questions expressed by workers. The nature of the study and the agreed-upon process will also guide an evaluator's reporting back to the project team and administration. For example, if there is an agreed-upon process of providing regular and extensive feedback on the process elements of the study, then providing feedback in regard to workers' questions or requests for assistance may be appropriate if done in a manner that respects the worker's privacy.

Example

An evaluation team member was asking a family service worker a number of questions about how the worker made decisions with regard to his cases. The questions were from a project questionnaire to assure that the same questions were asked about each case and of each worker. After asking a question about problem identification, the worker asked the team member if she agreed with the worker's observations. The team member gently stated that she did not have an opinion and that she was there to learn about the worker's views. As the interview came to a close, the worker asked the team member for some assurances. "Did I do the right things in that case? Am I a good caseworker?" the worker asked. "What should I do if I face this case situation again in the future? Is there anything I can read that will help me respond to these concerns?" The team member replied, "I appreciate your responding to these questions associated with the project. I am sorry, but I am not in a position to comment on your work, and it is not my place to provide advice." The team member reported the results of the interview but did not add the worker's comments to her report or recordings nor did she bring them to the attention of anyone outside of the evaluation team.

It makes sense to acknowledge that a relationship develops between the researcher and his or her human subjects. The nature of this relationship should have some of the qualities of a positive relationship. For example, evaluators should be generally warm and cordial and strive to be genuine. However, this is not a therapeutic relationship, a managerial relationship, or a collegial relationship. If the researcher is perceived to be arrogant, aloof, and cold, it may be difficult to engage project stakeholders in the evaluation process. However, the focus needs to be on the goals and processes of the evaluation, not the evaluation team member's likability. The goal is to strive for engagement with human subjects while maintaining clear boundaries and parameters.

Example

The researcher had been visiting the agency for several days at a time over a 12-month period. During these visits, she had been conducting individual interviews and meeting with the agency team that was implementing the program that was being evaluated. During one visit, several months into the study, the evaluator was invited to join the rest of the staff in celebrating one of their coworkers' birthdays. The celebration was being held in the agency conference room. The evaluator went to the party and the staff cheered as she entered the room. She was quickly offered a piece of cake, asked to sign a birthday card, and expected to sing along with the staff. She ate the cake, signed the card, and sang "Happy Birthday." Staying for a relatively short period of time, as she exited, one of the workers told her that another coworker had a baby shower coming up and asked if the researcher wanted to contribute to the office gift.

Example

The evaluation was drawing to a close. There were just a few more interviews and case records to examine. After a long day of sitting alone in a basement room reading case records, two staff members dropped by and invited the evaluator to join them for a drink at a local pub.

Evaluators do not want to alienate the people involved in the study. There is the need to foster cooperation in participating in interviews, locating case records, and other data collection activities. However, role clarity is needed. Evaluators do not want to get entangled in organizational politics. It is not the evaluator's place to directly improve the agency through consultation and a significant advocacy role. The study findings may provide information that informs agency practice and supports others' advocacy activities, but that is different than evaluator intervention. Managing relationships and boundary issues is easier if the evaluator is a member of a team and can use team member colleagues in a supervisory manner to explore and affirm appropriate and ethical responses to others in a practice setting.

Checking Vitals

The evaluator needs to have a clear sense of her or his role.
Providing feedback in a careful, planful, thoughtful manner to project and agency leaders, needs to be weighed based on the seriousness of the concerns or questions expressed by workers.

The nature of the study and the agreed-upon process will guide an evaluator's reporting back to the project team and administration.

The goal is to strive for engagement with human subjects while maintaining clear boundaries and parameters.
It is not the evaluator's place to directly improve the agency through consultation and a significant advocacy role.
Managing relationships and boundary issues is easier if the evaluator is a member of a team and can use colleagues in a supervisory manner to explore and affirm appropriate and ethical responses to others in a practice setting.

Ethical Responsibilities as Professionals

In addition to one's responsibilities to clients and to colleagues, there are general duties for an evaluator. These duties are linked to the evaluator's responsibility to the agency and to the public. One of the core considerations is whether or not the persons conducting the program evaluation value the interests of the project and the purposes of the evaluation over their own self-interest and personal advancement (Reamer, 2001). This prioritization of a public good and service over self-promotion can be assessed by examining the evaluator's competence, business practices, and attributions. For example:

1. Does the person(s) conducting the program evaluation accurately present her or his qualifications so that funding groups, agencies, and peers can assess the person's competence to conduct the study? How does one assess competency?

2. Does the evaluator accurately present the costs associated with the evaluation, and are funds spent appropriately?

3. Is there evidence during the evaluation process that the evaluator or any members of the evaluation team are impaired?

Example

The agency workers reported to the conference room first thing in the morning for their scheduled focus group. The focus group facilitator was not in the conference room and did not show up at the agency until later in the morning. This happened several mornings. When the facilitator walked into a late morning focus group later that week, he seemed unprepared and a bit confused about the format for the group. Some of the workers reported that he looked disheveled.

---

4. Does the evaluator attempt to gain other business while doing business with the agency?

Example

One of the recommendations of the evaluation was that workers in the agency needed to be trained in areas of best practices in the field of mental health. While crafting the report, the evaluator shared with agency leaders that he had a training curriculum addressing best practices in mental health and that his curriculum and training regime were a good match for the needs of the agency as identified through the evaluation.

---

5. Does the evaluator give credit to the persons who have contributed to the evaluation process?

Example

The agency's in-house coordinator for quality assurance worked extensively with the evaluation team. She provided a thorough briefing about the agency and its programs, facilitated data collection, helped interpret and understand the data, and contributed to the drafting of the report and read and commented on its early versions. However, the final report was presented as the sole product of the university-based evaluation team.

Even as a funding entity or organization would be asking these questions about an evaluator, the person conducting the evaluation would be asking complementary questions:

1. Can the methodological and other challenges be completely known and identified at the beginning of a project? What happens when evaluators find themselves in an unfamiliar situation or facing challenges for which they are not prepared or qualified in the middle of the evaluation? Is there a standard of competence that is good enough? Do evaluation skills generalize to all or most situations? How does one competently evaluate pioneering innovations?

2. Evaluation skills and business skills are two different sets of abilities. What if you are a good evaluator but inexperienced at or incapable of projecting expenses? Perhaps the greatest danger is that the evaluation team will be underpaid and undercompensated rather than becoming financially enriched by a project?

3. How does one define impairment? What if personal tragedies or family emergencies take place during an evaluation?

4. While one should not be self-promoting or pushing one's own business, is it wrong to inform others of one's evaluation business or to inform an agency of additional services that might be offered by the evaluation team?

5. How do you determine who should be given credit for an evaluation, for an evaluation report, or for other products from the evaluation? To what extent is that credit proportional to effort or contribution?

With regard to business practices, the extent of funding may have a number of ramifications for the conduct of the project. The commitment to advance knowledge, improve practice, and support positive outcomes for clients may motivate an evaluator to be involved in a project with insufficient financial support. Whether a business decision—as a loss leader—or as an expression of one's higher values, a person might provide a service without financial compensation. However, providing an evaluation that is significantly underfunded can have a number of troubling ramifications. Insufficient funding may be an expression of lack of investment and lack of serious interest in the outcome. There may be serious intent, but without sufficient resources the work might not get done in a timely manner or as thoroughly as desired by the funding agency. Being held to timelines, methodological rigor, and reporting requirements without adequate funding can engender resentment on the part of the evaluation team and conflict with the evaluation's sponsor. What if the research team is underpaid while the agency proceeds to contract with expensive consultants for other tasks? Are the research team members highly committed professionals or chumps? It is possible to decline an invitation to conduct an underresourced evaluation, to accurately project one's expenses and expect that the project budget will approximate those costs, or to craft a plan that matches the project's resources (if a minimal standard of quality can be assured).

Evaluators have the ethical responsibility to conduct themselves in a manner that is directed by the best interests of the project. The honest and trustworthy behavior and motivation of the evaluation team gives the agency and external audiences confidence in the findings of the study. This integrity is essential to contribute to knowledge and to improve policy and practice.

Checking Vitals

The core consideration is whether or not the persons conducting the program evaluation value the interests of the project and the purposes of the evaluation over their own self-interest and personal advancement.

This prioritization of a public good and service over self-promotion can be assessed by examining the evaluator's competence, business practices, and attributions.

(Continued)

(Continued)

The commitment to advance knowledge, improve practice, and support positive outcomes for clients may motivate an evaluator to be involved in a project with insufficient financial support.

Providing an evaluation that is significantly underfunded can have a number of troubling ramifications.

Insufficient funding may be an expression of lack of investment and lack of serious interest in the outcome.

Work might not get done in a timely manner or as thoroughly as desired by the funding agency.

Being held to timelines, methodological rigor, and reporting requirements without adequate funding can engender conflict and resentment on the part of the evaluation team.

Ethical Responsibilities to the Profession

The behavior of the person conducting an evaluation reflects on that person, his or her professionalism, and his or her profession. This individual could be identified as a program evaluation professional or a professional social worker or psychologist, or associated with an academic position and university. Ethical responsibilities to one's profession include a commitment to promote high standards of practice and to advance ethical practice as described in this chapter.

Ethical Responsibilities to Society

Codes of ethics address a professional's responsibility to the broader society. In the case of program evaluation, it advances a public good to conduct an evaluation of interventions and agency practices. Providing the information that gives the public confidence in specific approaches or interventions is helpful. An agency's commitment to examine its practices and to seek to assure that it at least does not harm people and, in fact, promotes health and well-being is the right thing for an agency and for society. To assure that funds, particularly when resources are scarce, are directed to effective purposes and well invested is a responsibility to broader society and makes ethical sense. Confidence in an agency and its services is supported by effective evaluation practices, and this promotes the well-being of society. To fail to conduct an evaluation may be unethical (Grinnell, 1997, pp. 8–9).

In review, attentiveness to professional codes of ethics and ethical principles highlights a broad range of issue for the evaluator and the subjects of the evaluation. However, no code of ethics can completely address all factors that an evaluation will encounter. Conditions may present situations beyond the scope of present-day codes of ethics, for example, in relation to the emerging uses of technology. In addition to new and unfamiliar situations, researchers may find that some aspects of ethical codes are unclear or appear contradictory. The ability to make an ethical judgment may require more than knowledge of codes of ethical conduct. For ethical clarity, it is important to keep the focus of helping on the client rather than promoting one's self-interest (Bloom et al., 2003). As it may be difficult to determine a client's or one's own interests, it is essential that ethical decision making take place through dialogue and result from collaboration, discussion, debate, and supervision. Finally, throughout the centuries, philosophers have promoted variations on a Golden Rule principle to guide moral thinking: "Do unto others as you would have them do unto you." So, if you were a participant in a study, what would you want to know? If you are a program director, how would you want evaluators to conduct themselves? If the evaluation of your program found a number of faults, how would you want these to be reported? Professional practice, including program evaluation, is full of ethical challenges and issues requiring thoughtful attention.

Checking Vitals

Ethical responsibilities to one's profession include a commitment to promote high standards of practice and to advance ethical practice.

An agency's commitment to examine its practices and to seek to assure that it at least does not harm people and, in fact, promotes health and well-being is the right thing for an agency and for society. No code of ethics can completely address all factors that an evaluation will encounter.

The ability to make an ethical judgment may require more than knowledge of codes of ethical conduct.

It is essential that ethical decision making take place through dialogue and result from collaboration, discussion, debate, and supervision.

REVIEW AND REFLECT

Big Ideas

• The conduct of a program evaluation requires attentiveness to moral issues and ethical guidelines because the process and outcome of an evaluation can harm or help a range of stakeholders.

• In determining the ethical guidelines that should inform and shape an evaluative process, there are relevant principles identified in professional codes of ethics.

• There are ethical responsibilities to multiple entities in an evaluation, including the recipients of services, the participants in the evaluation, and the agency that offers the program, and to other professionals and society.

Discussion Questions

• What are the strengths and what are the limitations of professional codes of ethics?

• Why is confidentiality frequently viewed as one of the most prominent ethical principles that require one's professional attention? Under what circumstances should a program evaluator set aside confidentiality and share identifying information?

• If an ethical dilemma arises that is not addressed in a professional code of ethics, what should a researcher do to determine the right course of action?

Activities

• Write a confidentiality agreement that would assure an agency or relevant organization that information would be handled with care and respect.

• Check with your university's IRB board concerning the assurances and processes that a researcher must follow to protect human subjects. Examine the required forms and fill out the portions that address issues of confidentiality and privacy.

• Check with local social service organizations to discover if they have a formal process that is required to gain permission to conduct research or conduct an evaluation in the agency. Examine the required forms, particularly those sections addressing confidentiality. Compare them to the university's IRB forms and assurances.

Resources

• American Evaluation Association. (2004). *Guiding principles for evaluators* [Fact sheet; Revisions reflected herein ratified by AEA membership, July 2004]. Retrieved from http://www.eval.org/Publications/GuidingPrinciplesPrintable.asp

• National Association of Social Workers. (2008). *Code of ethics*. Retrieved from http://www.socialworkers.org/pubs/code/code.asp

CHAPTER 4

Ethical Challenges for Evaluators in an Agency Setting

Making Good Choices

I'm sure when you fill out this form saying that Ms. Davidson is pushy
and never listens to you, it will have no impact on your eligibility.
Yeah, I wouldn't worry about that.

Aligning one's actions with a professional code of ethics addresses a range
of ethical considerations and duties in program evaluation. Paying particular attention to the protection of human subjects is central to one's planning for and conducting an evaluation study. This attentiveness to protecting

human subjects from harm leads to strong consideration for those actions that promote informed consent. Additional ethical issues can be identified and examined in connection to the stages of an evaluation process, ranging from the early stages of planning the evaluation through the final steps after implementation. This chapter will further explore the central issues of protection, privacy, and informed consent and discuss ethical considerations throughout the life span of the evaluation.

PROTECTION OF HUMAN SUBJECTS

Gaining knowledge about people, their life circumstances, and the interventions that may improve their safety and well-being requires human subjects as the focus of study. Many research activities call upon the direct cooperation and permission of other persons to conduct the study, particularly in regard to data collection at varying stages of a research and evaluation process. For example, researchers may need the persons engaged in the program being evaluated to fill out a survey truthfully before, during, and after an intervention. A need may also exist for people to participate in an interview and answer a range of questions with a sense of confidence and openness that results in honest and trustworthy information. A small group may be asked to share their experiences, thoughts, or feelings in a focus group. As most evaluation research involves human subjects, these are primary areas of concern and interest for the evaluator and the evaluation team.

In studies that do not require face-to-face or direct data collection from human participants, there still exists the indirect exposure of personal information and potentially private content. Reading a case record provides considerable information about a person's history as well as documentation about a range of areas of functioning. For example, a child welfare record may contain a psychiatric or psychological assessment, in addition to health care information and the worker's assessment notes. Secondary data and agency reports may provide data that is not as strongly linked to an individual identity but may still reveal information about an individual or group of individuals that includes personal or private information. Gaining knowledge about people and the programs in which they are enrolled or receive some form of service exposes them to some measure of disclosure and potential harm.

This potential risk may not be identified or may be minimized by either the agency or the researcher. A variety of dynamics can contribute to undervaluing or overlooking the potential risks associated with research and program evaluation:

1. The administrator or researcher simply may not think there are any risks to participants or, if any risks exist, they are trivial and best labeled an inconvenience.

2. The administrator might trust the researcher or the researcher's sponsoring organization, believing the researcher would not hurt anyone or engage in dangerous behavior.

3. The administrator or researcher may be motivated by positive and pure motives such that it is inconceivable to them that their actions would be harmful.

4. Those leading the study may be ignorant of certain risks, particularly if the researchers are not familiar with the culture and practices of the agency.

5. Based on their analysis of the risk, the administration may believe that any risks are overridden by the positive results that could be gained.

6. The evaluator may believe that certain steps designed to protect human subjects would compromise the conduct of the study and dilute the findings of the study.

The assessment and planning in relation to protecting human subjects may be time-consuming. Political or other organizational factors may be pushing for a speedy and streamlined process that can quickly produce results. However, this protective analysis and planning should not be minimized.

Unfortunately, the history of conducting research provides some troubling examples of the failure to consider the protection of human subjects. One of the early examples of the negative effects of research was the harmful and unethical research conducted by Nazi scientists during World War II. The examples of torture and pain inflicted by scientists was exposed during the Nuremberg trials in 1945 and resulted in the 1946 Nuremberg Code's protections for human subjects (Reamer, 2001). A primary American example of conducting research and the ethical issues related to the potential harm to participants is the Tuskegee Syphilis Study conducted by the U.S. Public Health Service (O'Sullivan & Rassel, 1989). In this infamous study, African American men were exposed to syphilis and left untreated so that researchers could observe the illness. Participants in this study were not provided information about the true conduct of the study or the risks involved. This study was conducted over a 40-year period (1932–1973). Yale psychologist Stanley Milgram also conducted a research study in the summer of 1961 that deceived participants as well. The volunteer participants were recruited for an experiment in which the volunteer was instructed to administer progressively more painful electric shocks to a pupil (a research team member). The willingness of volunteers to obey instructions and administer pain to another person, in this case the team member posing as the person to be shocked, was the object of the study (Grinnell, 1997, pp. 36–37). Another example of using deception to gain data was the observational study of the Tearoom Trade. This study, conducted by sociology doctoral student Laud Humphreys from 1965 through 1968, involved the disguised researcher observing and interviewing persons engaged in sexual behavior in public restrooms (Humphreys, 1970). The awareness and knowledge of these historical examples may affect the current willingness of persons to participate in research studies.

Based on these historical and egregious experiences, there are a number of guiding principles that should point to an evaluation plan that could be supported by an agency administrator seeking to understand a program and an evaluator designing and/or implementing the evaluation plan:

1. *Assume harm and risk.* Any time an agency evaluates a program or seeks to gain an understanding of its programs and those served by it, there should always be the assumption of some measure of risk.

2. *Identify and address risks.* In each study, there should be an explicit component that identifies and documents risks and the processes and procedures that will be implemented to address and minimize or remove these risks.

3. *Cultivate mutual responsibility* in risk assessment and planning. The assessment of risk and the response to such risk is the mutual responsibility of the agency as well as the researcher. Both parties should identify and address risk, minimize the potential for harm, and plan for protecting human subjects. In the university, an institutional review board (IRB) facilitates this examination. In an agency, a formal method for reviewing and assessing risk might not exist; therefore, a process should be established and implemented for such purposes. Even if the researcher is an independent contractor, the responsibility to identify risks and identify procedures to protect human subjects still exists.

4. *Incorporate scrutiny.* There should be a mutual acknowledgment that "good people" can still harm others, and that unintentional harm is still harm. The persons responsible for the study need to maintain an acceptable level of self-evaluation and criticalness. In addition, stakeholders should subject this evaluation plan to outside scrutiny to challenge the potential

rationalizations, justifications, or "blind spots" that may be in evidence for those invested in the study.

5. *Understand the setting.* The outside evaluators need to gain an orientation to the agency and its people and practices so that an evaluation plan can be crafted that is informed by the agency context and culture. For example, evaluators need to be aware of the vulnerabilities of study participants. The researchers should also proceed with caution and periodic re-examination as they learn more about the people and the organization and become more competent in their ability to assess the impact and consequences of their actions.

6. *Avoid deception.* The use of deceptive tactics and the deliberate withholding of information to ensure innocent and honest responses should be challenged repeatedly. An evaluator choosing to use such tactics should be required to present significant justifications for such deception and lack of disclosure, and this strategic choice should be subject to scrutiny by competent, external critics. The study designers should construct a plan that does not rely upon or use deceptive tactics but rather seeks alternative methods that fully protect human subjects.

Practically speaking, adherence to codes of ethics and ethical standards of practice and research protects an organization from negative scrutiny and criticism, even loss. Morally, protecting the rights of those who participate in research and evaluation is an ethical imperative based on respect for individual autonomy, privacy, and the duty to treat people with fairness and with social justice. Central to ensuring this respectful treatment of others is the principle and practice of informed consent.

Checking Vitals

Gaining knowledge about people and the programs in which they are enrolled or receive some form of service exposes them to some measure of disclosure and potential harm.

It is important to assess the risks associated with the evaluation process to ensure the protection of human subjects.

Protecting the rights of those who participate in research and evaluation is an ethical imperative based on respect for individual autonomy, privacy, and the duty to treat people with fairness and with social justice.

INFORMED CONSENT

It is a basic tenet of respect for human beings that people have the right to be given information relevant to their well-being and be fully informed about an action or procedure that involves them in some way. A person has the right to be informed about the purpose of an evaluation project along with the right to be informed of the methods that will be used in the evaluation (e.g., interviews or surveys). One cannot assume that participants can accurately or fully identify and comprehend the potential dangers and risks they might encounter or experience through their involvement in the evaluation. Persons who participate in an evaluation project need to be informed of the risks and the benefits associated with their participation in the project. These persons should be informed by the evaluation team about how the information provided will be reported and used. The informed consent process includes providing information about confidentiality. These features constitute the basis for assessing the informed nature of the project. This attentiveness to informed consent is the responsibility of the evaluator.

Elements of a Consent Form:

1. Identify the person being asked for consent.

2. Identify the evaluators and their affiliations.

3. State the purpose of the study.

4. Describe how the evaluation will be conducted and the participant's role in the study.

5. Identify and describe the potential risks related to participation in the study.

6. Identify and describe the potential benefits related to participation in the study.

7. State the length of time of the study and the amount of time required for the person's participation.

8. Provide a place for the person's signature if agreeing to participate.

9. Provide a place for the evaluator's signature and information on how to contact the evaluator.

10. Date the consent form.

In addition to being fully informed, the person must be in a position to voluntarily agree and consent to participate in the project. It is possible to be fully informed but feel coerced or constrained to participate. Respect for human beings requires that a person be fully informed, so the person can voluntarily choose to participate or not participate based on accurate and complete information.

This fundamental right for participants can be addressed by the evaluator and the organization involved in the evaluation through the following avenues:

1. Recognize that clients and workers may feel intimidated by a project initiated by management or an external funding source and conducted by a university-based scientist. This may be heightened for vulnerable populations. This will require some assurances, oftentimes in writing, to support the voluntary nature of one's consent to participate.

2. Assure potential participants that they can choose to participate or not participate and that they will not lose or gain benefits based on their decision. Potential participants may worry that failing to agree to participate might cause an agency benefit or service to be withheld. Gaining a benefit, a significant monetary reward, or a prominent gift may also feel compelling for a potential participant. Positive or negative pressures are counter to a standard of voluntary participation (NASW, 1999).

3. Identify risks and benefits and state assurances in writing. Provide a copy of the document that provides information and gains one's agreement for the client and for the project manager.

4. Assess the ability to give consent as some people may be unable to give a valid consent for participation due to their age, a disability, or some other circumstance that may compromise their ability to understand and appreciate the information provided by the evaluator. In some cases, such as with minor children, consent may be given by legal guardians.

5. Revisit the information provided and update it as appropriate. Typically, gaining informed consent is a single-point-in-time action, but it makes sense to review the information and reassess consent if circumstances change in the study or to assure ongoing consent and voluntary participation.

An organization that is initiating or participating in an evaluation should ask the evaluator to describe the process that will be used to address informed consent. The organization may have its own forms or process that should be used to assure informed consent. Consent forms can have a number of features that unintentionally sabotage the form's purpose. For example, the language could be overly loaded with jargon or technical descriptions that are incomprehensible to nonscientists. The form may be vague or overly long and wearisome to read and digest. The language needs to be clear, comprehendible to a non-technical reader, and complete. In addition to gaining written agreement, the document should be verbally reviewed, and the participant should be encouraged to ask questions or raise concerns. This process also needs to be sensitive to the language and culture of participants.

Checking Vitals

A person has the right to be informed about the purpose of an evaluation project and has the right to be informed of the methods that will be used in the evaluation.

Persons participating in an evaluation project need to be informed of the risks and the benefits associated with their participation in the project.

Respect for human beings requires that a person be fully informed, so the person can voluntarily choose to participate or not participate based on accurate and complete information.

An organization that is initiating or participating in an evaluation should ask the evaluator to describe the process that will be used to address informed consent.

In some circumstances, particularly when gaining information from employees, when there is less vulnerability, there may be implied consent. The person's participation in an interview, a focus group, or filling out a survey constitutes agreement to participate. There may also be cases in which the participant does not have total freedom to choose—for example, if a program is being evaluated by an external reviewer for a government, legal, or funding agent, employee participation may be a requirement of employment. Regardless of the level of voluntary participation, even with implied consent or participation as a condition of employment, participants should be fully informed about the purposes, methods, benefits, risks, and reporting associated with the project.

If the evaluation uses information that is already in the public domain, such as statistics reported to a governmental body, informed consent does not apply. If the evaluation uses agency documents, a number of safeguards need to be put in place to assure confidentiality, but most often informed consent does not apply. Although applicable in a range of situations in which data is being collected directly from an administrator, employee/worker, or client, particular concern for informed consent is heightened with the vulnerability of the population under study. There are also heightened concerns and risks when the information gathered relates to stigmatized or criminal behavior. The informed consent process may require legal consultation or review.

Checking Vitals

Regardless of the level of voluntary participation, even with implied consent or participation as a condition of employment, participants should be fully informed about the purposes, methods, benefits, risks, and reporting associated with the project.

If the evaluation uses information that is already in the public domain, or agency documents, with certain safeguards, informed consent does not apply.

An evaluator should seek to maximize respect for autonomy and confidentiality.

DESIGNING THE EVALUATION

One of the early decisions in an evaluation study is selecting and planning a design, a set of approaches to collecting information, analyzing that information, coming to conclusions, and reporting those findings. The type of design that is used in the evaluation may reduce or heighten concerns about privacy, informed consent, or harm to participants. For example, a number of funding agencies may encourage the use of experimental designs in conducting program evaluations. The use of experimental methods, particularly the denial of services to some persons, raises a number of ethical and practical issues (Royse, 1992). Denying a vulnerable group of clients an intervention or service solely for the purpose of creating a control group is generally not acceptable to an IRB, and such a strategy will often raise concerns among agency-based personnel. One might argue that it is unethical to provide an untested intervention or service, but such arguments rarely are persuasive with community agencies. Using evidence-based practices may reduce the need for extensive further evaluation, but there is still a need to examine the application of the practice to a particular population, program, or place. Building evidence-based practices is at the core of this design dilemma. How does one balance the need to demonstrate the effectiveness of an intervention or program with the reluctance and resistance that comes from concerns about denying or delaying treatment or program participation? This resistance can be particularly acute if a case manager or program manager perceives that the persons they are responsible for are denied the promising intervention. There can be a shared commitment to evaluation and providing effective services, however this leads to and supports the search for alternate means to accomplish this desired end.

There may be less problematic ways to ascertain program effectiveness than denying services. Alternate strategies include locating a naturally occurring control group for the study, such as (1) conducting a comparative study by using a comparable or matched group in a geographical location where the service is not available; (2) comparing the experimental subjects to recipients of a similar service at another agency with a similar mission; (3) using a group of persons who choose not to participate in the study to compose a natural comparison group; (4) using a long waiting list as a group of clients who have not yet received the intervention; or (5) using a strategy of providing the service through different venues (e.g., group treatment versus individual treatment versus an online treatment option) that provides treatment but also sets up points of comparison (Royse, 1992). It may also be possible to continue one's regular services with some clients and introduce the innovation to others.

In some settings, the use of a control group is not only precluded by ethical concerns but may simply be impractical. Reasons for impracticality may include the fact that the number of persons being served is so small that it is not possible to create a group awaiting services. Particularly in building a new pilot program, constructing a control group may be at cross-purposes with the program's goals of building a strong and sustainable base of persons receiving the new services. Evaluating different programs or ways of delivering an intervention without denying services may require considerable creativity, compromises, or adaptations that will affect one's confidence in the study's conclusions, but ethical and political considerations may require an approach that does not harm clients by withholding needed help (see Chapter 10 on Group Designs and Methods).

Checking Vitals

Denying a vulnerable group of clients an intervention or service solely for the purpose of creating a control group is generally not acceptable to an IRB, and such a strategy will often raise concerns from agency-based personnel.

There are several alternative strategies that include locating a naturally occurring control group for the study.

Evaluating different programs or ways of delivering an intervention without denying services may require considerable creativity, compromises, or adaptations that will affect one's confidence in the study's conclusions.

Designing the evaluation also requires attentiveness to issues of social justice. Funding and other supports for evaluation efforts reflect a political process and often depend on private or governmental sponsorship. This may shape or limit the interventions, programs, or questions that are pursued. When there are decisions that result in resources being engaged in a differential manner, the evaluation team needs to consider if there are inequities that result in advantages or harm for certain participants or programs. Does the evaluation purposefully or unintentionally include or exclude certain populations? For example, in constructing a sample or selecting a program for study, are there certain neighborhoods, types of programs, or populations that are overrepresented or underrepresented in the study? Are certain language groups, such as Spanish-speaking clients, excluded from the study? Is the sample of participants to be studied primarily male? If the findings from the study will result in better services, increased protections, or enhanced resources, the issue of who is included in the study and who informs the study is a central consideration. If some programs are overlooked and not evaluated, this may raise concerns about fairness, particularly if some agencies or locations receive a disproportionate amount of attention and resources devoted to program improvement. Data and findings from studies with vulnerable populations can also be interpreted or reported in a manner that harms the population that is being studied (Grinnell, 1997).

Concerns may also be expressed if participation in the research study interrupts services, inconveniences clients or workers, or distracts workers from the time needed to devote to their work rather than a study (Grinnell, 1997). In identifying these challenges, Grinnell concluded, "Increased knowledge must never be obtained at the expense of human beings" (p. 59). Approaches to evaluation that are perceived to be harmful will not and should not gain or sustain agency support.

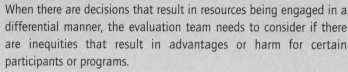

Checking Vitals

When there are decisions that result in resources being engaged in a differential manner, the evaluation team needs to consider if there are inequities that result in advantages or harm for certain participants or programs.

If some programs are overlooked and not evaluated, this may raise concerns about fairness, particularly in some agencies or locations that receive a disproportionate amount of attention and resources devoted to program improvement.

Getting Started

Concurrent to the construction of the structure of the evaluation, the evaluator will need to deepen his or her knowledge and competency in relation to the agency's program and purpose. Evaluators should have the competency required for the project, practice within the limits of their knowledge and experience, demonstrate cultural competency, and seek to improve their knowledge and skills (AEA, 2004). Building competency in relation to the field of practice under study may begin with library research—a "search of the relevant literature, filling in your knowledge of the subject and learning what others have said about it" (Rubin & Babbie, 1993, p. 365). In addition to library research and reading agency literature, building competency may be facilitated by using key informants—that is, other people who have studied the organization or the areas of practice and policy addressed by the agency. It may be helpful to begin by asking to meet members of the organization to gain background information and their viewpoints on the agency, its programs, and the broader context. However, there are some risks inherent in these early conversations and meetings. For example, the persons involved in these initial conversations may have an ongoing relationship and role in the evaluation, so the evaluator should strive to make an initial constructive impression and set the foundation for a positive and productive relationship nature. Another issue for the evaluator is to recognize that these exploratory and preliminary conversations provide a mixture of facts and the key informant's point of view. Evaluators can gain additional perspectives through observing agency life or even participating in agency activities to gain their own perspective on the organization, program, or area for study (Rubin & Babbie, 1993).

Checking Vitals

Evaluators should have the competency required for the project, practice within the limits of their knowledge and experience, demonstrate cultural competency, and seek to improve their knowledge and skills (AEA, 2004).

In addition to library research and reading agency literature, building competency may be facilitated by using key informants—that is, other people who have studied the organization or the areas of practice and policy addressed by the agency.

Evaluators can gain additional perspectives through observing agency life or even participating in agency activities to gain their own perspective on the organization, program, or area for study (Rubin & Babbie, 1993).

In most organizations and evaluation processes, the researcher will be introduced by an agency leader or key stakeholder. In fact, this introduction is important to reduce the potential perception of being spied on or deceiving the participants about one's identity. This introduction may take place in a large staff meeting, a meeting with select agency staff members, or simply through a broadcast memo or e-mail. Typically, the goal is to inform the organizational members about the study, including the personnel conducting the study, in order to facilitate an initial rapport to boost the level of participation and cooperation with the study.

Example

The evaluation team met with the agency managers for the first time to present the intended study. Hoping to get started with the right spirit of cooperation, the team presented the value of the study—both the process and outcome—for the agency and for the managers. The team communicated

(Continued)

(Continued)

that it cared about the project and the agency and would do their best to understand the perspective of the agency, which was one of the reasons why they needed the managers' assistance. The team recognized the multiple pressures and demands on agency time and energy and would be respectful of that time in conducting the study. The team indicated that gaining clear evidence about the effective functioning of the program would have benefits for the persons served by the agency and for the agency itself. The team approached the project with a sense of commitment, care, and openness. The team hoped that this initial meeting would set a positive tone, begin to build trust, and make the evaluation process at least somewhat enjoyable. After setting the tone and affirming the value of the study and the approach of the evaluators, specific information about the design, activities, and timetable were shared with the group. This same approach would be used with individual participants as the study progressed. (Bloom, Fischer, & Orme, 2003)

This introduction will require the evaluator to give a clear, concise, and plausible explanation for the purpose of the research:

Here again you face an ethical dilemma. Telling them the complete purpose of your research might lose their cooperation altogether or importantly affect their behavior. On the other hand, giving only what you believe would be an acceptable explanation may involve outright deception. Realize in all this that your decisions may be largely determined by the purpose of your study, the nature of what you are studying, observations you wish to use, and other such factors. (Rubin & Babbie, 1993, p. 366)

Rubin and Babbie (1993) note that one's involvement with the agency as a researcher might result in people being flattered. To conduct a study communicates a sense of importance, and the process of being studied and having one's work or viewpoints solicited or listened to can be empowering. This researcher interest may also lead to worries about one's performance, a sense of being judged or blamed, and a wariness that could result in the passive-aggressive or outright ostracization of the researcher.

This engagement process should include the researchers talking with the organization about the strengths of the study as well as the limitations and shortcomings associated with the design and other elements of the approach. While identifying limitations and potential weaknesses, the researcher should also talk about how these limitations will be addressed in the study. The researcher's assumptions, values, theories, and evaluation methods, and other elements of his or her approach, should also be disclosed in these initial conversations and throughout the evaluation process. The source of the request for the evaluation and the source of funding should also be disclosed (AEA, 2004).

The process of building a relationship with an agency and the participants in a study can get complicated. In addition to dealing with negative responses, the researcher might find that the positive trusting relationship invites a range of complications. When interviewing workers, participants may turn to the evaluator for advice, counsel, and supervision. Participants may ask an evaluator for assistance with a range of personal and professional issues. The evaluator might be asked to advocate for the workers by voicing employee dissatisfactions to and with senior management. The organization's administration may ask or expect the researcher to speak on its behalf to internal audiences, external audiences, and funding bodies. The person conducting the evaluation may feel a duty to help and respond to some of the suffering that is being identified and documented. The researcher needs to maintain a clear sense of his or her role, responding politely and genuinely while maintaining boundaries and managing this professional relationship. Seeking consultation and supervision with regard to if or how to respond to persons in distress is essential.

Checking Vitals

This engagement process should include the researchers talking with the organization about the strengths of the study as well as the limitations and shortcomings associated with the design and other elements of the approach.

The researcher's assumptions, values, theories, and evaluation methods, and other elements of his or her approach, should also be disclosed in these initial conversations and throughout the evaluation process.

The researcher needs to maintain a clear sense of his or her role, responding politely and genuinely while maintaining boundaries and managing this professional relationship.

CONCLUDING THE STUDY

In professional practice, endings are a time of particular challenge. What happens when the study is concluded? To maximize the benefit of the study and to fulfill an explicit or implicit promise to the study participants, a debriefing plan should have been agreed to early in the evaluation planning process and then implemented. However, this can go awry in a number of ways:

1. The organization and the evaluator may have failed to address dissemination and reporting back when designing and approving the study.

2. The dissemination plan may have been noted in a general manner, "when we are done, we will report back to the participants," but no details were identified or agreed to at that time.

3. The circumstances may have changed during the study such that an initial plan is either not helpful or impractical.

4. The dissemination and reporting back plan was not reviewed during the course of the study to update or adapt based on the evaluation experience and process.

5. The reporting back is delayed for some time; for example, the analysis may be time-consuming, there may be an elongated period of clarification and negotiation about the content of the final report, or some aspects of the study may be completed long before other ones are done. The evaluators may have multiple projects or have moved on to another project before the reporting is completed. This timing in reporting back is further complicated when the study involves longitudinal data collection or follow-up data collected months or years after an intervention has ended. Also, some large agencies may have cumbersome approval processes for releasing information, and such decisions may be low priority.

6. There may be some elements of the final report that are critical of the agency or key individuals, and there may be reluctance on the part of the organization or others to share the findings.

7. The ability to protect the confidentiality of respondents may have been a bigger challenge than anticipated, and crafting and delivering a report may further heighten one's worries about protections for participants.

8. Due to agency turnover, many of the participants may not be on the scene by the time the report is ready to be shared. For example, in one

evaluation study, the time period reviewed spanned several years. By the time the final report was ready to be shared, the evaluator was one of the few people who had been present in the early days of the study.

9. The funding for the project may have been exhausted before the study was completed or only sufficient to cover the actual study without sufficient funds for the travel, time, and publications that might be needed for dissemination.

10. The agency or organization may want to suppress the findings because the findings are negative, or because the findings will provide an opportunity for new criticism or a competitive advantage for other agencies in the same social service market.

11. The researcher may be reluctant to acknowledge all of the limitations of the study as these may lessen the value of the study or give the impression that the findings are not trustworthy or useful (Grinnell, 1997).

Finishing a study is full of challenges. To maximize the study's potential to help others and to fulfill a promise to the participants, evaluators and agencies should take the following steps:

1. Explicitly make a commitment with regard to reporting back and the dissemination of findings at the onset of the study. Gain this agreement in writing as many of the principals in power at the beginning of the study may not be there by the time the study concludes.

2. Detail a dissemination plan, including content, audience, format, and timing: "Within 3 months after submitting the final report, the evaluation team will meet with all agency staff members at a regular monthly staff meeting and present an overview of the evaluation process, the findings of the study, and recommendations for action based on the study. In addition to this verbal report, a 3-page executive summary will be provided to all agency employees."

3. Intentionally review the dissemination plan during the study to assure that it is accurately detailed and will be helpful, allowing for adaptations in content or timeline as needed.

4. Incorporate funding for the reporting back and dissemination of findings. If there are insufficient funds in the budget, identify a mechanism for disseminating results through cost-effective means, such as an agency newsletter, broadcast e-mail, or letter to employees to provide at least some feedback.

5. Strive to provide such feedback in a timely manner by establishing time-lines for reporting. These timelines may need to incorporate administrative review such that the agency and the evaluator need to be vigilant and committed to this conclusion.

6. Aim to be honest about the study design, implementation, limitations, and findings, while reporting results in a manner that respects the confidentiality of participants.

When reporting results, the evaluation team needs to protect the confidentiality of participants by reporting data in aggregate form and/or by omitting identifying information. Reporting results should be done accurately, even if those results are negative. Reporting accurately does not require one to be impolite or unduly harsh and disparaging. The participants' right to know the results of the study should be weighed with potential harm, and harm is frequently minimized by careful and respectful reporting. In verbal presentations and written reports, the evaluation team should acknowledge and properly credit persons responsible for the study and its reporting (Reamer, 2001).

The ability to widely disseminate the results of the evaluation through peer-reviewed journal articles, professional newsletters, professional conference presentations, and other means should have been identified at the early stages of the evaluation process. In fact, the value of these efforts may not become clear to an organization until later in the evaluation process. Such exposure may also require a measure of mutual trust that is not always present in the early stages of an evaluation, as relationships are in the formative stages. Consequently, initially an agency may be reluctant to approve or support presenting the study to a wider audience; however, this should be revisited as the process progresses. Should one write an article or make a presentation without agency support? It may be legal to do so, but one should weigh the potential benefit of advancing knowledge versus maintaining a relationship with the agency. One should ask, what action will advance the best interests of the persons being served by the agency, rather than prioritizing that action that will advance my career? One also should inquire about the potential for harm. When one's self-interest is involved in a decision, the potential for rationalizing one's choices increases. It is best to get supervision and consultation when addressing ethical dilemmas.

An evaluator's institutional review board will have requirements with regard to storing data from a project. These requirements will address safety and confidentiality as well as length of storage time. There may be reasons for revisiting the study at some future date. This revisiting of the data may require an additional review process, depending on the purpose of the inquiry.

Checking Vitals

When reporting results, the evaluation team needs to protect the confidentiality of participants by reporting data in aggregate form and/or by omitting identifying information.

The participants have the right to know the results of the study, and its reporting should be careful and respectful to minimize potential harm.

The ability to widely disseminate the results of the evaluation through peer-reviewed journal articles, professional newsletters, professional conference presentations, and other means should be identified at the early stages of the evaluation process.

IN CONCLUSION

In summary, evaluators should take steps to ensure that ethical considerations are overtly identified and that one's knowledge of ethical issues informs and shapes the entire evaluation plan and process:

1. Craft an initial evaluation plan that includes an identification of participants (pay close attention to fairness and justice issues), a methodologically sound process, and a reporting and dissemination plan.

2. Identify and review the institutional review board requirements for one's own institution as well as the requirements or guidelines that are associated with an agency or organization involved in the evaluation.

3. Address the policies and procedures required for the protection of human subjects and for informed consent. If a governmental or institutional body is not involved in this study, the obligation to maintain ethical practices is still in effect for research professionals.

4. Submit the evaluation plan and procedures to an agency board for review and approval.

5. Build on preliminary discussions with the relevant organization, and take the first steps to present and explain the nature of the evaluation and to seek their cooperation in the implementation of the study. Even if the evaluation is a requirement of a governmental or funding body, presenting the study and gaining cooperation is valued.

6. Ensure that the clients understand that their receipt of services is not contingent on their participation in the study. Employees may be required to participate, but inform all participants about privacy protections.

7. Report to relevant stakeholders.

The process and outcomes of program evaluation have considerable opportunities to help or harm vulnerable persons served by social service organizations, members of those organizations, and the general public. In addition, the conduct of an evaluation confronts the evaluator and participants with issues of autonomy and privacy and justice. Consequently, program evaluation is extensively and intricately an ethical process.

As an activity with ethical considerations and dimensions, a program evaluation needs to address the central questions of the protection of human subjects and informed consent, as well as a broad range of challenges that are identified by adherence to professional codes of ethics. There are a number of areas for an evaluator to examine in designing, conducting, and concluding an evaluation. This requires strong attention to the realities of field-based evaluation.

REVIEW AND REFLECT

Big Ideas

• The protection of human subjects is of paramount importance in conducting agency-based evaluations, and steps should be taken to assure voluntary participation and safety.

• Each stage of the evaluation process poses challenges and potential ethical complications. How you start and finish the evaluation process need particular attention.

• An evaluation process needs to consider the well-being of the evaluation participants. When there is the potential for harm, an ethical assessment and plan are needed.

Discussion Questions

• What qualities or characteristics might compromise a person's ability to make a voluntary choice to participate in an evaluation?

- What does "evidence-based practice" mean, and how do you build and contribute to evidence-based practice?

- What are some of the factors that would build an effective and ethical research relationship with an agency and its constituents?

Activities

- Draft a cover letter to potential research participants that describes the evaluation project and is respectful of their rights and potential risks.

- List the "Top 10" ways to conduct an evaluation in an unethical manner.

- Take an evaluation study described in a journal article and prepare a brief PowerPoint presentation for the agency in which you report the results of the study.

Resources

- *Glossary of program evaluation terms.* (n.d.). [Includes definitions of key terms in relation to ethics, as well as other evaluation definitions.] Retrieved from Western Michigan University Web site: http://ec.wmich.edu/glossary/prog-glossary

- *OHRP informed consent frequently asked questions.* (n.d.). Retrieved from Office for Human Research Protections (OHRP), U.S. Department of Health & Human Services Web site: www.hhs.gov/ohrp/informconsfaq.html

- *Tips on informed consent.* (n.d.). [U.S. government and American Psychological Association guidelines on informed consent. Includes brief discussion of Web-based research and sample consent forms.] Retrieved from www.socialpsychology.org/consent.html

CHAPTER 5

*Agencies
and Academics*

The Social and
Political Context
of Program Evaluation

I would like you to read my seminal work on the epistemological ontology
of knowing and then you will begin to understand my ideas about how to
evaluate your program.

B ased on the rationale presented earlier in this book, the case for program
evaluation has been successfully presented and accepted by the agency
leadership. The value of examining agency practice and programs has been
affirmed. In addition to the practical considerations involved in satisfying a
funding source or an external audience, the agency genuinely needs to know
what is working and what is not working in order to successfully achieve its
desired outcomes.

With a commitment to evaluation, the agency needs to determine how to proceed—that is, if an agency wants a program to be evaluated, how does one go about getting this done? The beginning mechanics of program evaluation typically result in engaging one of several potential sources of evaluation capacity and expertise: (1) internal, agency-based evaluation resources; (2) external evaluation resources associated with a university department, school, or institute; or (3) a consulting firm that specializes in evaluation. Each of these organizational options presents strengths and challenges in conducting an evaluation; the initial decision about who will conduct the evaluation is perhaps the most important decision facing an organization after determining that an evaluation has merit.

In addition to making evaluation implementation decisions, the process of planning and conducting the evaluation takes place in the context of financial, historical, and political dynamics. These dynamics are shaped by the decisions regarding the conduct of the evaluation. An awareness of these dynamics and potential issues is important for evaluator and agency alike.

INTERNAL AGENCY-BASED EVALUATION TEAMS

An agency-based internal team of professionals presents a number of strengths for an organization. A successful evaluation process requires *knowledge of the intervention* or program that has been implemented and now needs to be examined. An agency-based evaluator may have the greatest ease in understanding the evaluation target. This insider status provides knowledge of the broader agency culture and workforce, and either direct knowledge of the program to be evaluated or easy access to the key providers and stakeholders.

A successful evaluation process requires some measure of *agency cooperation and support*. For example, case records may need to be identified and read. Workers may need to be interviewed or focus groups conducted. Persons served by the program may need to be interviewed or surveyed. Agency data may need to be reviewed, and data collection may need to be modified to suit the purposes of the evaluation. Some agencies when beginning an evaluation process may encounter organizational ambivalence or resistance by some members of the workforce due to perceived impositions and demands on their time. Some agencies may lack the commitment to participate or prefer not to be evaluated. Some agencies may have concerns about the outcome of the evaluation and the repercussions associated with the findings. An internal evaluator, implementing an evaluation launched by the agency, will know where to locate data and relevant information, have the relationships to gain needed levels of assistance and cooperation, and know the agency leaders whose endorsement and direction will facilitate the evaluative work in a timely manner.

A successful evaluation effort will result in the generation of knowledge that helps assess the impact and value of an intervention or program. This knowledge should be expressed in terms that are *understandable to the agency* and that *provide direction and clear implications and recommendations* for the agency in relation to the program. This analysis, organization of the findings, translation for the agency leadership and stakeholders, and reporting may be facilitated by an internal evaluator. This agency-based evaluator understands the organization, its purposes and mission, and the audiences who need to be included in the initial and concluding presentations and reporting out of the evaluation findings. An agency could benefit from the internal capacity to conduct an evaluation of its pilots and programs and to have this feedback come from knowledgeable, connected evaluation professionals who can effectively communicate with the organization. This internal capacity may encourage the conducting of program evaluation activities.

Checking Vitals

A successful evaluation process requires knowledge of the intervention or program that has been implemented and now needs to be examined.

A successful evaluation process requires agency cooperation and support.

A successful evaluation effort will result in the generation of knowledge that helps assess the impact and value of an intervention or program.

There are also a number of challenges associated with designating an agency-based evaluator to examine an agency program. First, many agencies may not even have this as an option. How many agencies have internal capacity and expertise to conduct evaluations? The agency may not have *sufficient funding* to dedicate staff members to evaluation. The staff members who have responsibilities in relation to quality assurance and program outcomes may be principally focused on compliance, with standards and specifications from a funding organization or assuring that certain types of reporting to address accreditation or other audit and monitoring functions are successfully completed. These professionals may not have the skill set for program evaluation, and gaining such staff may be beyond the financial capacity of the agency, particularly if the agency has a relatively small staff or budget. For some agencies, program evaluation may be an infrequent activity that does not merit developing and maintaining the internal capacity to conduct program evaluation.

In addition to not having sufficient funding or trained program evaluators on the staff or having their efforts directed to compliance and monitoring functions, there are other *workforce challenges*. Having an evaluator on staff does not guarantee that this person has knowledge of the program to be evaluated, particularly in large, multifaceted organizations. An evaluator on staff may not have the networks and relationships with program staff or agency leadership that are required for the successful conduct of the project. The requirements of the evaluation may take the evaluator to a range of unfamiliar audiences and stakeholders outside of the agency. The persons to be interviewed, surveyed, or engaged in the evaluation may perceive that the agency-based evaluator has a stake in the outcome of the evaluation and has agency relationships that may be perceived by others as complicating the evaluator's clarity of purpose and objectivity. In fact, familiarity with the program and program staff may complicate the evaluator's ability to gain information from internal and external subjects. The evaluator may face an objectivity challenge, particularly if relationships and knowledge of the program are an integral part of the evaluator's work life. If there is the perception of self-interest or self-involvement in the evaluation, the credibility of the process and findings are seriously jeopardized.

The internal evaluator also may face challenges in being either too close to or too distant from the program. The evaluator may be subject to *internal political pressure,* in addition to one's own attempt to maintain a measure of objectivity and distance in conducting the evaluation and reporting its findings. The agency leadership will most likely have a stake in the outcome of the evaluation. An innovation, intervention, or program that someone in the agency leadership has identified or championed may have come under some scrutiny, requiring an evaluation. The judgment of the administrator who championed the program may be questioned, such that engaging in an evaluative process to implement accountability associated with the effective use of agency resources will produce expectations and hopes for specific outcomes. Some persons with power in the agency will be looking for a successful outcome in relation to their investment. Other persons with power may be less enthusiastic and may benefit from a negative evaluative outcome. The internal evaluator will be in a position that is subject to the mixed perceptions of the participants in the study and the political pressures associated with the champions and critics of the program under review.

Checking Vitals

Challenges with designating an agency-based evaluator:

> The agency may not have sufficient funding to dedicate staff members to evaluation.

> Having an evaluator on staff does not guarantee that this person has knowledge of the program to be evaluated, particularly in large, multifaceted organizations.

An evaluator on staff may not have the networks and relationships with program staff or agency leadership that are required for the successful conduct of the project.

The evaluator may be subject to internal political pressure, in addition to one's own attempt to maintain a measure of objectivity and distance in conducting the evaluation and reporting its findings.

UNIVERSITY-BASED EVALUATION TEAMS

In recognition of the challenges with regard to objectivity and of the subtle, and not-so-subtle, pressures in the conduct, findings, and reporting of an evaluation, and to remove concerns about the credibility of the evaluation, using an evaluator or evaluation team external to the agency is a valued strategy. Some funding bodies may require this external perspective. In many communities, the college or university that is proximate to the agency or that serves a region or state is a source of evaluation assistance and capacity. Through official announcements and embedded in their missions, universities frequently invite such consideration through the affirmation of their research capacity, commitment to the advancement of knowledge, and valuing community outreach and engagement. This can turn out to be a complicated invitation.

Oftentimes, upon first examination, the university appears to be an asset to the agency and a resource for the evaluation process. With its faculty dedicated to the advancement of knowledge, with its curriculum that includes research and evaluation coursework, and with a supply of students to serve as either inexpensive labor, research assistants, or team members, agencies may perceive that the university can provide the people and expertise needed to conduct a successful evaluation project. This can be a reasonable expectation or at least a viable option if there is an accurate assessment by the agency and the university.

University-based evaluators provide a number of positive attributes for an agency. Faculty members, particularly if the university has research as a prominent mission, have been trained in research methods, and a number of faculty members will have evaluation methods expertise. The university is a source of professionals with evaluation and research expertise and may have knowledge about a relevant field of practice. The university is external to the agency and can provide the disinterested objectivity that will enhance the conduct of the evaluation and the credibility of the findings. University faculty members may be expected to be engaged in the community and to apply their research skills to promote relationships with the community, goodwill, and public service. Faculty members may be encouraged to be involved in projects that generate some measure of external funding for the university. Along with the equipment, student workforce, and other resources needed to successfully conduct an evaluation, many universities have the mission and purpose to support such involvement.

Checking Vitals

Positive aspects of using a university evaluator:

Faculty members, particularly if the university has research as a prominent mission, have been trained in research methods, and a number of faculty members will have evaluation methods expertise.

The university is external to the agency and can provide the disinterested objectivity that will enhance the conduct of the evaluation and the credibility of the findings.

A university-agency partnership, however, may face a number of challenges with regard to conducting a program evaluation. First, there is a *financial challenge*. Agencies may expect that a university can provide staff to conduct an evaluation because faculty members will be motivated by an intrinsic interest in the topic and that conducting such research is an integral part of a faculty member's role. The agency may present the request almost as if the agency is presenting an opportunity to the faculty member, even an opportunity that would be generous and helpful to the faculty member. Likewise, the agency may see its evaluation project as a great opportunity for students to learn about the evaluation process. Like the faculty member, the student will benefit from this experience that the agency is offering. The value of this experience and performing one's duty as a faculty member may seem from an agency viewpoint to be sufficient compensation for this effort. While potential opportunities may have tremendous value to faculty members and students, these opportunities may not substitute for the need for financial support to allow faculty members to dedicate their time to this effort. Plus, students may not be able to afford to dedicate the time to such a project, despite its potential for learning. Most often, faculty members, students, and their administrative units will require financial compensation (including university overhead expenses) for program evaluation activities.

An additional challenge for an agency-university evaluation plan may be the *nature of the university workforce.* University faculty members with content expertise might not have evaluation expertise. The ability to teach research courses required for a professional degree program may not encompass program evaluation methods and strategies. Faculty members who have program evaluation knowledge may be able to teach this in the classroom but may have limited experience in program evaluation in an agency setting. A faculty member with evaluation knowledge and experience may not be familiar with a certain field of practice or the programs that need to be evaluated. This may not be an obstacle to a university faculty member's involvement, as some faculty members can comfortably apply evaluation methods to a variety of settings, but the faculty member will need to be willing to engage in some measure of self-education about the target programs and field of practice. A faculty member with evaluation expertise and knowledge may require additional staff support to conduct an evaluation, but team members from the faculty or graduate student population might not be available. Finally, the alignment of faculty expertise and knowledge, knowledge of a field of practice or programs, ability to operate in an agency setting, and the availability of additional team members may be difficult to achieve.

Checking Vitals

Challenges for a university-agency evaluation plan:

Most often, faculty members, students, and their administrative units will require financial compensation (including university overhead expenses) for program evaluation activities.

University faculty members with content expertise might not have evaluation expertise.

A faculty member with evaluation knowledge and experience may not be familiar with a certain field of practice or the programs that need to be evaluated.

With sufficient funding and with appropriate faculty and staff members, *political considerations* could still affect an evaluation process. For example, faculty members may have a conflict of interest if they have a past or present relationship with the agency and its leadership. In addition, faculty members may have a conflict of interest because the agency is a field education site for the university, and maintaining a positive relationship with the agency may make it difficult to deliver less than positive findings about the program being evaluated. The professor evaluator may have some other stake in the survival, growth, or elimination of an agency program and its funding. In rural or other small communities, the likelihood of multiple and dual relationships may be unavoidable. Political considerations, shaped by an academic culture, could include complicated expectations and requests from agency management including the following:

1. *Time.* University faculty members may have time and workload assignments for a significant time span into the future. For example, a teaching schedule and other university duties may be determined an entire academic year ahead of time. These schedules combined with the faculty member's other commitments to students (e.g., advising and working on doctoral student committees) and already existing research projects may affect the faculty member's availability. Due to grant funding or other contingencies, an agency may determine that it needs an evaluation plan and an evaluation to be started with minimal advance notice and preparation. Faculty members may not have the time to launch such a plan and research endeavor that is congruent with the agency's time frame.

Example

The agency's initial funding for the pilot program did not include any funding for evaluation. Yet it became evident to the program managers that to sustain the program's funding, the managers would need to be able to demonstrate some level of effectiveness beyond consumer testimonials. Fortunately, they were able to identify unspent funds near the end of the fiscal year that could be directed toward a modest evaluation effort. They called the university and asked if a faculty member could begin an evaluation and spend the funds within the current fiscal year before the year ended. The faculty member with evaluation and content expertise had a full teaching schedule and was already committed to work on another project. She had to decline but announced the opportunity on the faculty e-mail list seeking another faculty member. There were no responses to the request for assistance.

2. *Perspective.* A university-based researcher may have thorough knowledge of evaluation and research methods, but these may not fit the reality of agency practice. Pure and cleanly conceptualized designs and methods may be difficult to craft in the real world of an agency. The circumstances under which an evaluation is conducted may further complicate this commitment to appropriate design and implementation. The reality of agency practice and the challenges of studying program effectiveness when services are delivered in a changing and stressful environment can pose elements that potentially frustrate the university-based evaluator and the agency.

Example

With no internal evaluation resources, the program managers approached a local university and requested assistance with an evaluation of a pilot program. The purpose of the pilot program matched areas of interest relevant to a select faculty member. The university evaluation faculty member indicated an interest in the pilot program and its effectiveness. The university evaluator agreed to design and conduct an evaluation, particularly when the program managers assured the evaluator that program data had been collected and was readily accessible. Although the evaluator was aware of the complications that could arise in agency-based evaluation projects, she was committed to learning from and supporting best practices in agency settings. However, this commitment would be sorely tested when she learned that the program model had been unevenly implemented in the eight sites, had relatively few participants so the sample size would be small, involved a retrospective study that looked back over 3 years of implementation, and required that the full study be completed in 6 months. The agency's restricted budget for the evaluation limited the size of the research team and resulted in running out of funds before the final report was written. Because the agency and the university worked together on other projects and were partners in the community, the university subsidized the completion of the evaluation.

3. *Teamwork.* In addition to the challenges in starting an evaluation project, university faculty members may face challenges in relation to assembling a team. The fact that a faculty member is available to be engaged in a project does not assure that student assistants are available to assist with data collection, analysis, and other project requirements. University staffing patterns are

arranged so that the institution can accomplish its primary educational mission and research purposes. These patterns are often planned in advance, commit students to a range of specific duties, and are time-consuming. A faculty member serving as an evaluator may have difficulty dedicating his or her own time to the project and locating appropriate, available team members.

4. *Imprecision and ambiguity.* The rigorous, structured, and carefully crafted design of an evaluation, which may be taught in a classroom, may not suit the purposes of an agency-based evaluation. The commitment to a controlled and circumscribed process that would allow for some definitive statements about program effectiveness may not match agency circumstances. The university researcher, agency-based evaluator, or both, may want to make a confident statement about success or failure. However, such clarity may be difficult to achieve, and mixed results from an evaluation may conflict with the agency's desire to herald the success of a new program that is under scrutiny.

Example

The agency's new program had been implemented in a number of states and was viewed positively based on worker and client feedback. There had been no rigorous evaluations or sustained scrutiny of program effectiveness. The agency wanted a strong affirmation of the effectiveness of the program. To justify the adoption of this new program model and to anticipate its expansion beyond the initial five pilot sites, a university-based evaluator with expert knowledge of the program was engaged within the first year of program implementation. The use of a random sample, or a controlled experiment with a control group and experimental group, was rejected as no sites wanted to withhold treatment and all sites were trying to recruit enough participants to have sufficient service numbers to warrant funding and continuation. It was difficult to design an evaluation that would produce the definitive statements of success desired by the agency.

In addition to the difficulty in crafting or conducting an evaluation study or group design method that matches textbook conditions, the process of conducting an evaluation can introduce a range of complications and opportunities that affect the conduct of the evaluation. The university-based evaluator may need to adapt to the realities of the practice environment and the needs of the agency in the overall conduct of the evaluation.

> ### Example
>
> A number of measures of satisfaction and the use of program data (and changes over time in key outcome measures) were determined to be the primary basis for understanding the effectiveness of the program. The evaluator began to collect information on various aspects of the process of implementation and the usefulness of various program features. While learning about implementation, the evaluator realized that some of the agency forms and surveys used with families needed to be modified to address their intended purpose. This feedback was communicated to the program leaders, who agreed and modified the forms.
>
> On a quarterly basis, the evaluator reported back to the program leaders and the program staff from all sites with regard to initial findings. Based on these reports, workers modified their behavior and refined program policies to better serve clients. This communication and consequent modifications continued for the 3 years of the evaluation. Program leaders indicated that this continual feedback helped them to improve the program and implement the model. This feedback loop reduced the evaluator's ability to gain a clear assessment of the program's effectiveness as to some extent the program was continually modified. This also introduced a consultative approach to the evaluator's role and added frequent reporting requirements. Consequently, the evaluator became less distant and more engaged in the project. The ability to remain somewhat aloof and then pronounce some measure of effectiveness or failure at the end of the 3-year evaluation period may have been tested by this continuous feedback, program modification, and consultation. Although this may have complicated the evaluator's ability to judge program effectiveness, program managers appreciated the process evaluation and modifications. The evaluator also appreciated the communication and engaged process and the opportunity to affect program improvements, but the improving program presented a moving target for the evaluation. The need for a rigorous, controlled evaluation continued.

A number of strengths are associated with university-based evaluators, including expert knowledge, some measure of objectivity and an external perspective, and a mutual commitment to advancing knowledge about best and promising practices. However, the differences in work cultures and environment, including sense of time and methodological rigor, may require an identification of issues to negotiate and may make it challenging to work together. The university researcher may not be prepared for the complicated environment and pressures of agency practice, and the agency's desire for a talented and inexpensive resource may make these arrangements frustrating for all involved parties.

Checking Vitals

Challenges:

Faculty members may not have the time to launch such a plan and research endeavor that is congruent with the agency's time frame.

A faculty member evaluator may have difficulty dedicating his or her own time to the project and locating appropriate, available team members.

A university-based researcher may have thorough knowledge of evaluation and research methods, but these may not fit the reality of agency practice.

The university researcher may want to make a confident statement about success or failure, but mixed results from an evaluation may conflict with the agency's desire to assess a new program that is under scrutiny.

EXTERNAL EVALUATION ORGANIZATIONS

To gain the expertise needed to conduct a thorough evaluation, an agency may choose to engage a consulting firm or private company that specializes in research. In addition to competency, this may gain the agency an evaluator with the ability to respond to a request in a timely manner and to meet the time frames and requirements associated with funding and agency decision making. A private consulting organization provides an external review and reasonably objective viewpoint that can support the credibility of the process and findings. However, there are a number of issues to consider in using a research firm.

Research firms may not be readily available, particularly to agencies in less populated communities. When a firm is available, it may not have experience or expertise in social science evaluation, or the principals may not have sufficient knowledge of the field of practice and would have to begin by learning about the agency and its programs. When available and knowledgeable, a private firm may be very expensive. The research infrastructure and staff required for an evaluation and its reporting may result in too many billable hours and be prohibitively expensive. The expense associated with an evaluation may be modified when the agency has preexisting approaches and templates that have been applied in previous studies. However, this may impose a process and structure that does not fit the agency need or program. The program and its elements may be construed to conform to the approach of the evaluator and may be less adaptable when faced with various agency pressures. In some locations, the consulting firm may be an integral part of the professional community such that the personnel and involvements of the firm may complicate a perception of objectivity. This perceived "involvement" could cause some concerns if the firm desires an ongoing relationship with the agency. However, engaging a research firm from outside of one's community may significantly increase the expense and pose some challenges for customizing and communicating about the evaluation.

In addition to a private research firm, there may be a research center or institute associated with a university that is equipped to conduct evaluations. These entities may have the advantages of a university—skilled staff members and an external perspective—without some of the drawbacks related to time and availability. However, these university-based centers may also present some of the complications associated with private firms—such as cost and customization of an evaluation.

Checking Vitals

Considerations for using an external evaluator:

It provides an external review and reasonably objective viewpoint that can support the credibility of the process and findings.

A private firm may be very expensive, and the research infrastructure and staff required for an evaluation and its reporting may result in too many billable hours and be prohibitively expensive.

The consulting firm may be an integral part of the professional community such that the personnel and involvements of the firm may complicate a perception of objectivity.

OTHER POLITICAL CONSIDERATIONS

The nature and number of complicating factors in an evaluation are influenced by the nature of the evaluation and the decision with regard to the evaluation team. Some additional issues also transcend the type of evaluation or evaluators.

The timing of the evaluation process may be driven by agency considerations with political implications.

Example

Although the university-based evaluator was appreciative of the value of being engaged in the evaluation process from the very conception of the new program, gathering data in the first weeks and months of program implementation resulted in negative findings. The workers were not meeting time frames for engaging families, for building caseload size and program participation, or for case decision making and moving toward successful outcomes. Workers often seemed confused about the program elements—attempting to remain faithful to the model but encountering situations that did not look like anticipated scenarios. The findings at the end of the first 6 months were mixed at best. The evaluator thought that the workers were still learning the model and program elements. Training and supervision was just beginning to address the variations encountered in the field. Agency leaders needed evaluation information and pressed for early findings despite the evaluator's feedback that the program was not ready for such scrutiny.

The evaluator feared that the success of the program and its innovative approaches would be judged to be a failure when, in fact, the workers' early adoption and practice of core principles and values was shaky at best.

In addition, the evaluation process may be influenced by issues that affect the workforce. The climate and culture of the agency may support worker retention or result in workforce instability. These conditions have potentially helpful or complicating affects on the evaluation process.

Example

This was an interesting innovation and pilot program introduced by the agency. The program managers were eager to describe the program, its implementation, and the immediate and intermediate outcomes associated with the program. Funding had been tight for any new programs, including this one, despite agency enthusiasm for its potential. As a result of financial limitations, workers recruited for this program were paid at a lower rate than workers in other agency programs. This resulted in a high degree of initial enthusiasm by workers, attracted by the creativity and potential of the service, but many quickly left the program to earn more money in other agency programs or other agencies altogether. The constant turnover required the university-based evaluator to continually reintroduce the evaluation process and procedures, particularly with regard to data collection. It seemed that workers left before they fully understood or gained veteran experience in the program, and the impact of this turnover would be reflected in the program outcomes and shaped the ability to achieve success.

These issues that are political in nature can also be laced with ethical considerations:

1. *Conflict of interest and objectivity.* The validity of the evaluation process and findings will be strengthened or compromised by perceptions and realities with regard to the connections between the evaluation team, the agency, funding considerations, and contextual concerns. If the evaluator is the personal friend of the agency executive director who is requesting the evaluation, the neutral stance and open-mindedness of the evaluation process may be called into question. If the evaluator depends on the agency for additional business or other types of consultation and employment, the validity of the study and the methods and findings of the study may be perceived as constructed in a manner to assure future business. Avoiding conflicts of interest in rural areas or areas with few evaluation resources may be difficult, but identifying potential conflicts of interest, examining these conflicts, and setting up some system for scrutiny and accountability would be advantageous to support the validity of the study.

2. *Honesty*. When there is a conflict of interest or a dual relationship between the evaluator and the agency, an honest reporting of the results of a study may be challenging. If those findings suggest that a prized project, initiative, or agency emphasis is less effective than promised or desired, presenting these adverse results may not be welcome. A commitment to an accurate accounting of the data and findings should be affirmed early on before any complications might arise. Similarly, it is possible that an evaluation may be very negative, causing the findings to have undue negative consequences for a program. The evaluation process should identify the limitations of the methods used, the information sought or reported, and any features of the analysis that may lead to certain outcomes. Acknowledging the limitations of an evaluation and providing a context for understanding the findings is needed to support the proper interpretation of the results. There is the potential to understate negative findings or to overstate negative findings based on political and social concerns and methodological limitations. The evaluation process should build in some checks and balances, team review and reporting, and proper modesty in presenting one's conclusions.

3. *Confidentiality*. The evaluation process exposes an agency to the scrutiny of others. This scrutiny includes not only the data and subjects that are studied but also the processes and behavior of the agency in a broader context. The evaluation team observes a range of agency behaviors and practices. Evaluators have an obligation to not unnecessarily expose agency processes, particularly those that are tangential to the evaluation. This respect for the privacy of the agency encourages the examination of practice and the evaluation of programs. Embarking on an evaluation process introduces an organizational vulnerability that the evaluation team needs to treat in a respectful manner.

These issues and others are discussed in greater detail in Chapter 4, on ethics and evaluations.

Checking Vitals

Identifying potential conflicts of interest, examining these conflicts, and setting up some system for scrutiny and accountability will be advantageous in supporting the validity of the study.

The evaluation process should identify the limitations of the methods used, the information sought or reported, and any features of the analysis that may lead to certain outcomes.

Evaluators have an obligation to not unnecessarily expose agency processes, particularly those that are tangential to the evaluation.

IN CONCLUSION

The value of an evaluation process extends beyond the ability to make a pronouncement about the effectiveness or features of an intervention or program. The ability to be open to examination, commitment to best or promising practices, and a willingness to change and be self-reflective and oriented toward continual improvement are features and values supported by program evaluation. In looking for an organizational model that will build and serve the social service workforce and be congruent with the agency mission and purposes, some agencies have incorporated principles of a "learning organization." These principles have included (1) the concept of systems thinking; (2) a commitment to and capacity for learning; (3) challenging one's own thinking and incorporating new learning and other viewpoints; (4) creating a shared vision and picture of the future; and (5) supporting the development and learning of teams (Senge, 1994). This learning environment—and the challenges that come with it—are the motivation and organizational determination that informs and promotes evaluation.

Recognizing that program evaluation takes place in a social and organizational context that includes dynamics of change and power, it is important to bring political awareness in addition to one's evaluation knowledge. This awareness is needed by both the agency involved in the evaluation and the evaluator conducting the evaluation.

In summary, here are some guidelines for agencies to consider when implementing an evaluation program:

1. After deciding to conduct an evaluation (and this evaluation may not be optional given the funding source or other requirements), the next most important decision is who will conduct the evaluation.

2. Determining who will conduct the evaluation will be shaped by the availability of an internal agency evaluation capability and the need for actual and perceived objectivity.

3. If there is no internal capacity to conduct an evaluation or if the desire and need for an external review are high, identifying and selecting an external evaluator should be approached in a deliberative manner.

4. The primary external evaluators will be university faculty members, a university-based evaluation and research institute, a consulting firm that has evaluation capacity, or an independent contractor. These options might not exist in one's community and may require hiring from afar. Each option poses strengths and limitations.

5. Factors in considering an evaluator include (1) knowledge of evaluation and research methods; (2) experience in conducting evaluation projects in real-world settings; (3) ability to balance rigor and reality; (4) limited conflict of interest, dual relationships, or other complicating relationships that affect the perception and experience of objectivity; (5) some content knowledge of the program under scrutiny or the ability to gain sufficient background to understand program elements, data to be collected and its meaning, and processes and outcomes; (6) approach to the evaluation and the degree to which feedback about process elements and outcomes is desired; (7) expenses; and (8) commitment to ethical practices.

6. Engage the evaluator as early as possible in the process when implementing a new or pilot program.

7. Recognize that with new programs, the first months may involve a period of time for workers to learn the program and its values, and this may complicate the ability to understand the impact and success of the program. Begin early, but set aside a period of time that is a reflection of training and gaining proficiency with a model of practice, rather than an evaluation of the model's effectiveness.

8. Determine a schedule for receiving feedback that matches the evaluation's goals. If the intent is to improve practice, a process evaluation and continual feedback may be desirable. If the purpose is to build knowledge about best or promising practices and address program effectiveness as required by external funders or skeptical administrators, a less collaborative approach seems warranted.

9. Be as realistic as possible about timelines and funding. Typically, insufficient time and insufficient funds are allocated for evaluation. Match the evaluation design, data collection, and agency expectations to the realistic time frames and funding available.

10. Establish a protocol for completing the evaluation that includes the nature and outline of a written report and supports a process for reporting back to relevant agency stakeholders, as appropriate. An evaluation can be an opportunity to support the elements of a learning organization with a positive effect on agency morale.

Guidelines for university-based evaluators:

1. Evaluation knowledge and competency is a desirable quality for a faculty member because this type of knowledge and skills needs to be transmitted

to professional students (so they can conduct or cooperate with evaluations in their professional work life). These are skills that promote faculty member engagement with the community. The faculty member with competency in evaluation methods can potentially advance knowledge about best and promising practices.

2. Keep evaluation skills current and engage in activities that test and expand one's knowledge of field-based research and evaluation.

3. Consider agency requests for evaluation services. These may provide an opportunity to advance practice, gain experience for future projects, gain funding, strengthen partnerships and external relations, align with the university's mission, and/or provide funding and training for students. It is important to understand the value to your program and the university (i.e., will the university provide additional support? Are evaluation activities valued and considered in university merit, promotion, and tenure decisions? To what extent does agency-based and community-based work match the mission of the school or university?).

4. Weigh the benefits with the costs—your time and time frames, funding, other potential uses of your time, and availability of students. Assume time and cost overruns—at least, do not be surprised.

5. Be prepared to be flexible. Balance rigor with reality. Know your limits—you may have to set the project boundaries based on skill, time, and resources.

6. Identify conflicts of interest, dual relationships, and contextual and political factors.

7. Respect the agency's and the workers' confidentiality.

8. Make a commitment to honesty, and identify and acknowledge the dynamics that may shape or influence project choices, outcomes, and reporting.

9. Follow through with the project, as the agency members' experience with you will shape future openness to conduct and participate in research and evaluation.

10. In your work with agency personnel, increase their capacity to understand, use, and conduct evaluations.

Some of the most complicated aspects of an evaluation may have little to do with data or methodology. The evaluation process and its findings have the potential to upset a steady state within an agency. Agency activities and programs are the result of past decisions and preferences of agency personnel, and the evaluation may bring these decisions and the direction of the agency into question. The agency should make a careful choice about the evaluation team, and evaluators need to be aware of the political context in which they will operate during the evaluation.

REVIEW AND REFLECT

Big Ideas

• The conduct of program evaluation is a political process that is shaped by the nature of the organization and the dynamics that the agency is experiencing.

• The selection of the evaluator is one of the most significant decisions that can be made in conducting a program evaluation. There are a number of alternatives each of which presents strengths and potential limitations.

• It is helpful to recognize the challenges that face the evaluation process up front and to make a plan that addresses the issues posed by the political process and the type of evaluation team.

Discussion Questions

• Is it possible to conduct an evaluation that is free from the influence of political and organizational considerations?

• Given their strengths and potential limitations, what type of evaluation team would you prefer to engage if you were an agency administrator—internal evaluator, university-based faculty member, or research center affiliated with a university or research company?

• To what extent should an evaluator compromise in the use of evaluation methods to be responsive to agency demands or needs?

Activities

• Design a brochure advertising your services as an independent evaluator.

• Construct a budget for an evaluation project. Look at it two ways: Begin with a set amount of funding and break down line items in that budget that will add up to the total amount of funding available to you, or construct an ideal budget (accounting for major budget items such as personnel, supplies and services, travel, equipment, and other expenses) and propose the costs for evaluating a program that you identify.

• Role-play a negotiation between an agency administrator and an outside evaluator in which you list all of the topics that you need to discuss before the evaluation begins.

Resources

• Hasenfeld, Y. Z., Hill, K., & Weaver, D. (n.d.). *A participatory model for evaluating social programs.* Retrieved from http://www.irvine.org/assets/pdf/pubs/evaluation/Eval_Social.pdf

• Rutnik, T. A., & Campbell, M. (2002). *When and how to use external evaluators.* Retrieved from http://www.irvine.org/assets/pdf/evaluation/when_how_external_evaluator.pdf

CHAPTER 6

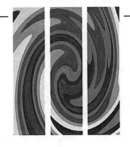

Cultural Competency and Program Evaluation

with Toni Johnson

Acme family services found it difficult to get the diverse clientele to complete the comprehensive family assessment tool.

The process of program evaluation does not take place in a social and cultural vacuum devoid of gender, race, ethnicity, and other considerations. Cultural competency and respect for diversity and inclusiveness is as essential for a researcher or person involved in program evaluation as it is for a clinician, community organizer, or program manager. The evaluation process requires an awareness of cultural attributes and processes and their impact on the people and programs under examination. The commitment to consider diversity and the knowledge of the consequences of entering a system increase the probability of an accurate and culturally sensitive evaluation. It is necessary to recognize that even though one is an outside evaluator, may employ a range of research methods and processes, and may strive toward objectivity, one's own background, experiences, and training influence the evaluation process. Cultural competence can result in more accurate findings, properly interpreted dynamics and impacts, facilitation of the relationships that support the study, and benefits to the participants.

In program evaluation, this required competency includes understanding the cultural context in which services are provided and the cultural factors that have an impact on the evaluation, including methodological and evaluation implementation considerations. Some programs explicitly identify cultural features as an explicit outcome of the program or intervention that is subject to evaluation. Effectively working across multiple cultures by evaluators is the goal, and traditional methods may not always be effective or relevant (Rodgers-Farmer & Potocky-Tripodi, 2001).

Before exploring the application of cultural competency to program evaluation, it is important to note that in addition to the cultural factors presented by programs and persons served by those programs, agencies also have a culture. In addition to considerations of culture related to the ethnicity, race, gender, and other features of the evaluator, the agency and program, and the clients served, various other features related to the culture of the agency should also be identified, incorporated into the evaluation process, and to some extent addressed. As noted in Chapter 5 on political factors and evaluation, understanding this culture of the organization is another challenge for the evaluator. Although this chapter will focus on traditional cultural factors, understanding the nature of bureaucracies and the artifacts, rituals, and values of an agency present another type of cultural competency that is needed to succeed.

Checking Vitals

Cultural competence can result in more accurate findings, properly interpreted dynamics and impacts, facilitation of the relationships that support the study, and benefits to the participants.

In addition to considerations of culture related to the ethnicity, race, gender, and other features of the evaluator, the agency and program, and the clients served, various other features related to the culture of the agency should also be identified, incorporated into the evaluation process, and to some extent addressed.

BACKGROUND

Evaluators, in general, and outside evaluators, in particular, face a number of cultural challenges for conducting a program evaluation, primarily due to historical discrimination, harm, and oppressive actions by researchers and supporting organizations. For example, with the African American experiences in the Tuskegee experiments, the Native American tribal experiences with boarding schools, and the exclusion of Spanish-speaking participants and women from study populations, sensitivity to race, ethnicity, and gender are warranted. Consequently, cultural competency in evaluation has been increasingly highlighted in the evaluation and research process (see Resources, at the end of this chapter).

Defining Cultural Competency

For the evaluation process, similar to a clinical or organizational context for practice, a number of attributes are associated with culturally competent work. These attributes include the following:

1. *Awareness and acceptance.* The person who is conducting an evaluation of a program is aware of the diversity within the staff of the program being studied; the agency sponsoring the program; and the clients, consumers, or customers being served by the program. This awareness includes an acceptance of persons from diverse backgrounds and with diverse characteristics so that all persons are treated in a respectful manner and not prejudged as to their ability, performance, and competency (Goode, 2004).

2. *Self-awareness.* The person who is conducting the evaluation is knowledgeable of his or her own attributes and the ways in which these have shaped his or her personal and professional life, approach to work and evaluation, and pattern and styles of relationships. Consequently, the evaluator needs to have the skills and ability to at a minimum self-identify, examine, and control and hopefully change assumptions, false beliefs, and stereotypes. Dr. Lydia Prado, of the Mental Health Corporation of Denver, noted,

> People feel passionate about their own experiences and want evaluators to understand that their experience of the world is different from yours. They expect you to be respectful and to acknowledge the rules you are operating by. People appreciate an attitude of "learning from" rather than "learning about"—an attitude that validates and values multiple perspectives. (Colorado Trust, 2002, p. 3)

3. *Dynamics of differences.* The person who is conducting the evaluation is knowledgeable of the dynamics associated with differences between persons from a variety of historical and cultural backgrounds. These dynamics include historical experiences and resulting messages transmitted through generations about safety, respect and relationships, risks and threats, and positive regard. This also includes an understanding of power and how one's attribution and sense of power or powerlessness will affect the delivery and the receipt of services, including one's response to an evaluator. An evaluator's understanding of a position of privilege may serve to underscore a sense of humility and openness to learning about another person's perceptions. Experiences with multiple forms of discrimination and the fear of or experience of oppression and harm will also shape the responses of persons with whom the evaluator is working or from whom information is sought. The evaluator may also have to examine dynamics related to empathy, assumption of familiarity, and personal attribution when studying or working with persons similar to or different than themselves.

4. *Knowledge of individual cultures.* The person conducting the evaluation may need to be familiar with specific, individual cultural groups or communities in order to understand the program being evaluated, the agency in which the program is embedded, the persons who serve as key informants, and the persons who are served by the program. For example, a research study was conducted on marital communication involving a coding system that observers used to record conflicts in couples' interactions. Observers who were not of Asian heritage observed there were "no conflicts" among Asian couples. However, an observer brought into the evaluation from an Asian community perceived numerous indications of conflicts that persons from outside the culture were not able to detect (Colorado Trust, 2002). The evaluator may have to identify and use resources that will assist in this educational process, including the study of specific cultures and employing cultural translators.

5. *Adaptation of skills.* The person conducting the evaluation will need to consciously determine if her or his methods and approaches are culturally syntonic or respectful of the persons and programs that are subject to evaluation. The evaluator may approach her or his work with a preferred set of methods, steps, or templates, but cultural competency requires flexible thinking and potentially redesign (Cross, 1997).

In addition to viewing cultural competency as a set of attributes, there are a number of overarching definitions of cultural competency. For example,

Cultural competence is the capacity to work effectively with people from a variety of ethnic, cultural, political, economic, and religious backgrounds. It is being aware and respectful of the values, beliefs, traditions, customs, and parenting styles of those we serve, while understanding that there is often as wide a range of differences within groups (e.g., Native Americans) as between them. It is being aware of how our own culture influences how we view others. (Practice Notes, 1999)

Cultural competency is a set of attributes and a respectful approach characterized by self-reflection, humility, and openness. Building on knowledge about diverse populations served, a collaborative approach increases the likelihood of sensitive work and reinforces cultural competency. A number of considerations and steps shape the development of an evaluation plan and process to reflect the evaluator's competency and sensitivity. Twelve considerations are identified to support this sensitive and successful evaluation process.

Checking Vitals

Outside evaluators in particular face a number of cultural challenges for conducting a program evaluation, primarily due to historical discrimination, harm, and oppressive actions by researchers and supporting organizations.
    Attributes of cultural competency:

Awareness and acceptance

Self-awareness

Dynamics of differences

Knowledge of individual cultures

Adaptation of skills

Building on knowledge about diverse populations served, a collaborative approach increases the likelihood of sensitive work and reinforces cultural competency.

Designing a Culturally Responsive and Sensitive Evaluation Plan

There are a number of factors to consider (and steps to take) that can shape the development of a culturally sensitive evaluation plan and process. These include the following:

1. Review the study plan and procedures to assure that the evaluation is inclusive and nondiscriminatory with regard to the sample/population characteristics.

For example, a study might be set up to examine the experiences of only one race, ethnic group, or gender when the program serves multiple persons. This may be a de facto exclusion based on geographic location—only looking at rural or suburban programs—when the program serves a variety of geographical sites. The exclusion of various linguistic groups also limits the inclusivity of the study.

2. Review methods to assure that the evaluation is inclusive with regard to language (non-English speaking), literacy, and/or data collection strategies (e.g., telephone surveys or mailed questionnaires that will overlook or leave out persons without an address or telephone number).

For example, during a large group study focusing on attitudes toward persons with disabilities, Huer, Saenz, and Doan (2001) determined the need to translate the questionnaire into Vietnamese. To ensure equivalence in research protocols, the document was translated into one language and then translated back into the original language (back translation). These repeated translations of the same document are intended to assure that any culturally specific concepts of the English language version are either effectively translated into the target language or eliminated, resulting in documents that are equivalent (Brislin, 1993; Matsumoto, 1994; Huer & Saenz, 2003).

Researchers involved in this study on differing abilities first sought two individuals who had extensive experience with the Vietnamese culture and both languages (English and Vietnamese). One individual identified had previous service with the South Vietnamese army and was a Vietnamese-to-English translator during the Vietnam War. The second, a former professor in Vietnam, held a master's degree in education from an American university, and taught English as a second language in American public high schools. One person translated the survey into Vietnamese and the other did the back translation. The translation was not considered complete until both persons agreed on the final translated version (Huer et al., 2001).

With regard to language, removing persons from a study who speak languages or dialects other than English could leave out key program participants and limit the generalizability and value of the study. In addition to having questionnaires, surveys, interview schedules, and other materials reviewed by linguistic and cultural experts so that these tools include relevant colloquialisms and accurately reflect meaning, evaluators can demonstrate linguistic sensitivity by taking the following actions:

a. Learning key words in the relevant language so that you can communicate a greeting and acknowledge the person's language and culture.

b. Providing written or recorded materials describing the research project in the languages of potential consumers and respondents.

c. Using certified/trained interpreters when this level of assistance is required. Due to availability and expense, the evaluator may be inclined to use students as translators; however, particularly if the student is not a native speaker, one needs to assess the student's linguistic and cultural proficiency. Similarly, using children or other family members to translate for their parents or other relatives during an interview may be a more readily available option than contracted interpreters. However, given the nature of the evaluation, this may be complicated at the very least, if not harmful, and should be avoided.

d. Remembering that limitations in English proficiency are not a reflection of limited intellectual functioning. Understanding the dominant culture's language has no bearing on the person's ability to effectively communicate in his or her own language (Goode, 2004). For example, after an interview conducted in English with an immigrant from Mexico, the interviewers described the fellow as quiet, interesting but lacking passion in regard to the subjects of the interview, and tending to be a bit nervous and deliberate in his communications. A second interview was conducted with the same fellow in Spanish. He was described as energized, outgoing and highly motivated, interested, and committed to the issues under discussion, and passionate and persuasive in his knowledge of the subject.

3. Review the evaluation process to assure that diverse persons are consulted with regard to gaining an understanding of the nature of the program, the design of the program evaluation, and other evaluation strategies.

A research team studying the effects of the "wrap-around process" used in a project serving families with emotionally disturbed children sought to increase the number of Latino and African American families involved in the evaluation process and to decrease the potential for cultural mistrust that researchers often encounter in communities of color. During the planning stages of the research project, the team developed an advisory group that included Latino and African American family members who were ineligible for or uninterested in participation in the study but accurately reflected the demographic characteristics of individuals sought for the study. This group became an integral part of the research plan, and their feedback was sought and included in all phases of the project. The principal investigator developed a successful argument for including the advisory group in the budget and was able to provide a small stipend and meals for the advisory group members.

4. Educate yourself about the persons being served and evaluated by the agency. Be aware of their history and levels of acculturation and, to the extent possible, discover their experiences with regard to interaction with agencies, authority, and academia. Do not rely on the clients or the agency staff to be the primary source of education about the individual cultures. Identify relevant sources of information for learning about specific and individual cultures, including relevant books, Web sites, training materials, key informants, and other formal and informal educators. (For more information, see Public Health–Seattle & King County, GLBT, Web site).

For example, a small research project in a southwestern state prepared to start an investigation seeking to understand the lives of Native American/First Nations' families affected by Native American women infected with the AIDS virus. The study team was encouraged by colleagues of color to take time to get to know the community as a prerequisite to the study. The principal investigator was not of Native American heritage or from Indian country* but had extensive knowledge about the HIV/AIDS virus and had lost a family member and several friends to AIDS. Before starting the project, the principal investigator sought ideas from community members on books, articles, and videos that allowed him to increase his knowledge about Native American people. He was careful not to burden individuals with his ignorance but did not avoid those persons eager to share their pride in their heritage by sharing stories of their childhood. The principal investigator spent several months reading and learning about Native Americans and Native American history from books, articles, individual conversations, and educational media. He further narrowed his information gathering to focus on the specific individuals and groups sought for the study. He stated that he

*Indian Country is a term that has multiple meanings that historically has been used to designate a geographical area or destination, used as a legal term, and as a cultural concept that encompasses the past, present, and future of First Nations' people (Oswalt, 2002).

used Isajiw's (2000) approach to working with cultural groups and concentrated on increasing his knowledge in two areas: (a) understanding the concept of ethnicity and ethnic development, and (b) understanding each specific tribal group, including customs, history, religion, language, acculturation level, and general practices. He set aside time during the planning and developmental phase of the project for each research assistant to read and digest the materials that he had gathered. Although several members of their research team were Native Americans, they were from different tribal nations; the reading and research assignments were a requirement for all team members. During the process of seeking materials, the principal investigator identified and relied on three community members to help verify the teams' understanding and interpretation of materials. This level of education and preparation was necessary to be able to accurately seek, identify, and understand behaviors observed or reported during the study. For example, what does anger look like in Native American youth? How does this compare with European Americans? How should one interpret expressions of anger (Inouye, Yu, & Adefuin, 2005).

5. Consider the customs and needs of the persons being served by the programs that are being evaluated. The effective inclusion of the customs and needs of persons being served in the evaluation best occurs during the planning stage but should be considered throughout the evaluation or research process.

In the study investigating the effects of the wraparound process with families of emotionally disturbed children, parents were recruited and trained to work with the research assistants in the data collection process (Haynes, Sullivan, Davis, & Yoo, 2000). Parents involved in an advisory capacity with the research project informed the evaluator and the research team that parents recruited for the research study may be more inclined to participate in a lengthy interview (that included personal questions) if presented with an opportunity to be matched with a person conducting the data collection who resembled them in ways important to them. For example, some preferred to have someone of the same race, while it was important for others to have someone of the same gender.

All of the parent advisory board members supported the idea of training parents to be data collectors. The evaluation philosophy, a document that guided the evaluation process, specified parent involvement at all levels and provided the foundation necessary for the investment of the time and energy required to identify, recruit, and train parent data collectors.

Checking Vitals

Culturally sensitive evaluation planning:

Review the study plan and procedures to assure that the evaluation is inclusive and nondiscriminatory with regard to the sample/population characteristics.

Review methods to assure that the evaluation is inclusive with regard to language (non-English speaking), literacy, and/or data collection strategies (e.g., telephone surveys, or mailed questionnaires that will overlook or leave out persons without an address or telephone number).

Review the evaluation process to assure that diverse persons are consulted with regard to gaining an understanding of the nature of the program, the design of the program evaluation, and other evaluation strategies.

Educate yourself about the persons being served by the agency and evaluated.

Consider the customs and needs of the persons being served by the programs being evaluated.

6. Identify and discuss the characteristics and strengths of the program and persons served.

In preparing a report detailing the evaluation of a school-based program serving teen children of prisoners, the evaluation team was cognizant of the number of negative descriptors that teachers used to describe the (primarily) African American population. The largely negative descriptors appeared to be generalized to the group and included gangbangers, uneducable, destined for prison, dope dealers, resource drains, and community menace. The evaluation team was careful to report the teachers' perspectives as given but made a conscious decision to avoid applying a deficit model during the analysis and interpretation of the project. The data collected included strengths, and positive characteristics of youth were also investigated and reported (Johnston, 2002).

7. Include appropriate questions and areas of inquiry in relation to culture, such as demographic information or identifying culturally related practices and behaviors that are addressed by the program or have an impact on the program.

For example, a demographic data sheet was developed for use in the evaluation of the school-based program for adolescent children of prisoners. Among other items, the data sheet asked the youth to state whether or not they belonged to a religious group and if so to specify which group (Johnston, 2002). This question was included in the data collection process because the evaluator was aware of the importance of religious beliefs and practices to African Americans in general but, early on, became aware of the importance of religion and spirituality in this particular African American community. Findings indicated that 9 out of 10 youth directly interviewed expressed a religious preference and stated that they relied on their faith to sustain them during difficult times. Throughout the yearlong ethnographic study, references to religion surfaced frequently with the teens, their families, and the teachers, and in the community.

During the evaluation, the primary evaluator noted that the executive director of the program, who was Irish American and had reported to the evaluation team that she felt that she was a victim of religious abuse in her early life, frequently expressed a strong disdain for organized religion and voiced her views during individual and group meetings with the youth. The evaluation uncovered the fact that the youths' fondness for the executive director and their desire to support her made them reluctant to openly express their religious beliefs or encourage peers, during support group meetings, to use religion or spirituality as a coping mechanism. When the evaluator met with the executive director to share preliminary information, the executive director was very surprised to hear that her views on religion presented a conflict for many of the youth who held a deep and abiding respect for religion. Even more important, the information was used to consider ways of strengthening the youths' existing coping skills, including their religious beliefs.

In this example, the executive director's failure to appreciate the role of religion was uncovered by an evaluator who had some knowledge of the population served and listened to and elicited information from youth. In some cases, it is the evaluator who has incomplete knowledge of the population, misses certain cultural content, or even has an unexamined bias that may shape the questions and areas for inquiry in the evaluation data collection process. Also, sometimes when the questions are asked, they are asked in a manner that does not yield the richest and most useful information. For example, a demographic question might ask for "Latino" or "Hispanic" backgrounds but miss the opportunity for more precision by identifying "Puerto Rican," "Chicano/a," "Central American," or "Cuban." With religion, asking simply "Christian" may not provide helpful information. Even "Catholic" or "Protestant" or "Orthodox" may be categories that are less helpful. One might want to ask Protestants to identify a denomination or other information, such as identification as an "Evangelical" or "Charismatic/Pentecostal," or complement religious identification with a question about religious behaviors (e.g., frequency of worship attendance).

In another example, the consultant met with the Native American women, and after a long period of silence one of the women voiced the concern of the group. It seems that the person working with their tribe viewed Native Americans as a singular cultural group. She was unhappy that the distinctions between Cheyenne tribal life and Arapaho tribal practices were not recognized by persons outside of these groups.

8. Behave in a respectful manner and recognize that how respect is communicated and conveyed is culturally defined and determined.

This attentiveness to respect may include simple ways in which an evaluation project is organized. For example, taking an aggressive approach to data collection with the intention of completing a research study in the shortest period of time possible may be viewed as disrespectful in many cultures.

Parette, Brotherson, and Huer (2000) described an approach to doing focus groups with Mexican American families that yielded useful data and was undertaken in a respectful manner. Family stressors and needs, such as lost wages, child care, and transportation, were considered when families were identified and recruited for focus group meetings. The focus group moderator set aside a full 8-hour day to have refreshments and social interactions before and after data collection activities. Research team members made sure that groups were kept small and took place at a location that was convenient and familiar to the families. Research team members knew in advance that many participants would take the day off from work and would interrupt their typical activities and meals to participate in the research. Consequently, refreshments were provided, as well as frequent breaks with sufficient food for all participants. In addition, the families were provided a small stipend as a token of appreciation for their participation. The families viewed the research as a way of helping their children but also saw the focus group meetings as a social occasion (Parette et al., 2000).

9. Identify and appreciate any special vulnerabilities, as well as strengths, in relation to the culture of the persons in the program or served by the program. Appreciation for potential disapproval, discrimination, recrimination, or stigma may include carefulness in recruitment and identification of participants, data collection logistics, debriefing and reporting, and participant recognition.

There may be a number of vulnerabilities for persons within the organization or served by the organization that require special attentiveness and sensitivity.

This could include persons who are members of stigmatized groups, such as Muslim and Islamic persons after September 11. Another example of vulnerability is program evaluation involving services to gay, lesbian, bisexual, and transgendered persons. Certain traditional roles, for example, or an authoritarian orientation may make women particularly reluctant to participate or at risk when asked to express their views. Children may be expected to remain silent as a sign of respect to their elders. Other vulnerabilities may be introduced by color, age, economic dependency, or lack of social status.

10. Demonstrate a high respect for confidentiality throughout the evaluation process. Attentiveness to confidentiality and privacy should be considered at each stage of the evaluation plan, not just when reporting results.

In one study, for example, the public library was chosen as a data collection site for a research study seeking to identify the needs of African American and White children of prisoners and their parents and caregivers. Research participants were told to look for the signs ("University Research Study") posted throughout the library. No public documents identified the research participants or the study focus. Two hours after the data collection process started the room was filled with adults and teenagers completing documents and children playing with each other and research assistants. At the 3-hour mark, a middle-aged man walked in and loudly asked what the study was about. Several of the adults stopped working and the room became quiet. The evaluation leader went over to the gentleman and informed him that the study was of a confidential nature and gently escorted him to the door.

Two of the African American research participants later told the research assistant of their appreciation of the precautions being taken with confidentiality. One stated that her initial concerns about confidentiality almost prevented participation. Although she needed the small stipend that was promised, she was more concerned about being judged by others, having information about her family "given to the wrong people," or adding to the shame that her children had already experienced. Ultimately her desire to obtain help for herself and her children, as well as her intention to provide support for families in the same circumstances, caused her to participate. She said, "When I saw the respectful and compassionate way that myself and other parents and children were treated, I felt very good about my decision to be in the study." In retrospect, it may have been possible to create signage that still provided direction but was even less identifying than "university research."

11. Consider the value gained from the evaluation and its potential benefit to the participants/community. Participants are often invited to join and engage

in the evaluation process in the hope and with the implied promise that the results of the evaluation will have benefits for the participants or for future persons served by the program under evaluation. To the extent that these benefits can be realized, this implied promise is satisfied and the potential for some help for future recipients of services is honored.

For example, the innovative program that was evaluated included components that explicitly identified extended family and close family friends as key participants in the intervention process. This approach to working with families was particularly welcomed by the Native American families who incorporated many members, not all of them blood relatives, into family decision making. The nonadversarial and inclusive nature of the intervention was perceived as beneficial to the families and community served. The evaluation was attentive to this broad range of participants, and the positive results of the evaluation were shared with a number of policymakers to support the maintenance and replication of these programs (Pennell & Anderson, 2005).

12. Identify and delineate any advocacy implications (individual, agency, or broader policy) from the research or in the process of conducting the evaluation. The evaluation process and its findings can intentionally or unintentionally contribute to the identification of positive change. It might also discover examples or patterns of discriminatory behavior.

One evaluation study discovered that some of the workers seemed to be particularly effective in helping clients. These clients reported high satisfaction with the services they received, and the families and workers could detail positive behavior changes and progress toward successful completion of the program. Among other traits, the workers were particularly well-educated and attentive to the cultural backgrounds and communication styles of their clients. The evaluation highlighted the positive attributes of the workers and the connection to program success. This made sense to the program leadership who instituted additional training and elevated some of the skillful workers to serve as casework consultants and trainers for the agency.

As the data collected for the evaluation was compiled, now over a number of years, it appeared that persons located in some communities were receiving a more extensive array of services than those in other communities. It appeared to the evaluators that the number of available services in differing communities was similar, but families in one community were gaining more agency connections and services than another community. Recognizing that there may be some variables they were unaware of yet not wanting to ignore this pattern, this observation was included in the evaluation debriefing with program leadership.

Checking Vitals

Culturally sensitive evaluation planning:

Identify and discuss the characteristics and strengths of the program and persons served.

Include appropriate questions and areas of inquiry in relation to culture, such as demographic information or identifying culturally related practices and behaviors that are addressed by the program or have an impact on the program.

Behave in a respectful manner and recognize that how respect is communicated and conveyed is culturally defined and determined.

Identify and appreciate any special vulnerabilities, as well as strengths, in relation to the culture of the persons in the program or served by the program.

Demonstrate a high respect for confidentiality throughout the evaluation process.

Consider the value gained from the evaluation and its potential benefit to the participants/community.

Identify and delineate any advocacy implications (individual, agency, or broader policy) from the research or in the process of conducting the evaluation.

In summary:

1. Have we constructed a sample or scope of study that is inclusive of diverse people served?

2. How have we addressed language and literacy to assure accuracy and inclusiveness in our study?

3. Have we engaged a consultant(s)—formal or informal—to help understand the program and provide feedback on our evaluation design and plan?

4. What material resources have we identified and reviewed to educate ourselves about the agency and persons served?

5. Are there actions or steps that we can take to increase the sense of comfort or safety for evaluation participants?

6. Have we identified key descriptors and outcomes in an accurate manner that avoids negative stereotypes and includes program and participant strengths?

7. Have we inquired about demographic and culturally related information for participants to identify factors that help understand their experience?

8. Are there specific ways that we can sensitively convey respect for people's efforts and time commitment while they are participating in the study?

9. Have we been sufficiently sensitive to the potential stigma or vulnerabilities experienced by evaluation participants?

10. In what ways have we been attentive to confidentiality at each stage of the evaluation?

11. Are there ways in which the study process and findings can actually provide benefits to the present or future recipients of services?

12. Have we discovered information that can and should inform advocacy efforts?

In addition to raising a series of questions about conducting a culturally responsive and sensitive evaluation, the stages of the evaluation process can be examined for guidance on cultural awareness and competency.

Implications for Methodology and the Evaluation Process

At each stage of the evaluation process, there are decisions and strategic actions that should be guided by a culturally competent perspective on one's work.

1. *Problem identification/research questions.* The assumptions made by the agency and the persons leading and evaluating the programs shape the ways problems and programs are studied and how challenges and successful outcomes are defined. For example, the study might be conceptualized in a manner that focuses on the weaknesses and problems of minority groups or women. Assumptions about other races, cultures, or genders may be based on overgeneralizations and skewed and unrepresentative experiences and prior research. The formulation of the research questions might be overly determined by the evaluator's own viewpoints. Incorporating the perspectives of evaluation participants in the approach and design of the study may reduce such bias. The evaluation should be framed in a manner that accurately reflects the experiences of diverse participants and makes their perspectives visible (Rodgers-Farmer & Potocky-Tripodi, 2001).

2. *Evaluation design: Sampling.* Sampling allows the opportunity to include a rich variety of experiences and to gain an accurate description of those experiences—if the study is using precise criteria—rather than comparing persons based on a single broad dimension of diversity. To address diversity and promote more accurate descriptions of the persons being served and the program outcomes, it is helpful to identify a wide array of demographic information. For example, as noted earlier, it may be more helpful to inquire about Chicanos, Puerto Ricans, Cubans, Central Americans, and Caribbean and South American identities rather than "Latino" or "Hispanic." These descriptions might also include such variables as place of birth, legal status, acculturation, and language dialect and use. Similarly, it is more helpful to identify participants as Korean, Japanese, Chinese, or Vietnamese, rather than simply "Asian." It may make sense in some circumstances to be even more precise: Okinawan, North or South Korean, Chinese regional populations, or Vietnamese of Chinese ethnicity. This precision extends to religion (as noted earlier), gender, and other forms of self-identity. Within cultural and ethnic groups there can be considerable heterogeneity based on age, gender, acculturation, education, socioeconomic conditions, religion, and multiple other factors. As noted in the problem identification stage, an evaluator also needs to be attentive to sampling strategies that create an inaccurate and overly negative perception of diverse populations. For example, interviewing gay and lesbian adults in a barroom setting could result in a description of alcohol use in the gay, lesbian, bisexual, and transgender (GLBT) community that does not reflect general practice. (For more information, see Public Health–Seattle & King County, GLBT, Web site.)

In addition to precision in sample definition, two potential decisions and strategies pose risks for the evaluation. One risk comes from looking at the program implementation and impact on segregated sections of the population. For example, a study may look only at the impact on men or only on women, or a study may exclude all persons who speak Spanish. This evaluation will present a distorted or skewed picture of the program impacts. Conversely, to include all and only minorities may imply that the services are designed only for minority populations or that only minority persons have a set of problems that are addressed by the program. The challenges of balancing cross group and special group characteristics and balancing majority and minority inclusion require the evaluator to planfully approach sample decision making within the boundaries of the program design and implementation. This may include questioning the sample that is provided to the researcher by the agency.

Checking Vitals

Sampling:

To address diversity and promote more accurate descriptions of the persons being served and the program outcomes, it is helpful to collect a wide array of demographics.

The challenges of balancing cross group and special group characteristics and balancing majority and minority inclusion require the evaluator to planfully approach sample decision making within the boundaries of the program design and implementation.

3. *Evaluation design: Data collection.* The data collection and evaluation design process can be enhanced by collaboration with the project's target population. Asking the right questions—through interviews, surveys, and questionnaires, or record review protocols, for example—can be enhanced through discussion with key informants rather than assuming program and participant knowledge. This definition of evaluation questions at the outset with community member input can help assure accuracy and sensitivity to meaning.

Data collection should include information on language, race, gender, socioeconomic factors and ethnicity, religion, and other key variables as identified by the evaluation team.

In data collection, gaining access to the population of interest may be challenging because of historic complications and mistrust of research. There may also be the experienced injustice of "one-way" research as families and communities feel exploited for their knowledge but perceive no benefit or engagement in their participation. Gaining access and buy-in are key tasks for the evaluation team. Strategies for engaging minority community member engagement include (1) gaining the sponsorship of a respected and well-known ethnic agency; (2) explaining the purpose of the research and stating the evaluation's goals and how these goals align and compare with the goals and aspirations of the persons participating in the study; (3) describing fully how the information will be used; (4) conducting evaluation activities, such as interviews and focus groups, in comfortable and safe locations (such as tribal buildings for Native Americans, or neutral community sites rather than at a social service agency or government building); (5) enlisting community members to serve as advisory board members; and (6) training indigenous personnel to serve as interviewers or in some other staff capacity, including leadership roles (Rodgers-Farmer & Potocky-Tripodi, 2001; Colorado Trust, 2002).

It may be helpful to conduct preliminary studies using focus groups, consulting with community members and professionals, and conducting sufficient pilot tests as a genuine and helpful strategy for producing data collection resources that are valid and reliable across multiple contexts (Thyer, 2001b). Also, these pilot experiences provide an opportunity for the community to have a first-hand experience with the evaluation team prior to a major study to assess the team's credibility and sensitivity.

Data collection also raises questions about the identity of the person seeking and gathering information: Should the researcher be of the same background as the subjects? Is cultural and gender matching important to gain valid information? As in social work practice in general, one of the goals for the profession could be to increase the number of minority and women researchers, particularly encouraging diverse persons to design, lead, and implement program evaluation activities.

In addition to deciding who should collect the data, how the data is collected is also an area open for consideration. Can one locate and use culturally appropriate measures that have been applied to diverse populations? Instruments that have been constructed and validated using one population (e.g., White middle-class clients) may introduce subtle inaccuracies. Using linguistically congruent tools is also important (Rodgers-Farmer & Potocky-Tripodi, 2001).

Methods for collecting data also need to be considered. For example, in a study of health risk behaviors, researchers used an established telephone surveillance system to conduct surveys. However, this strategy did not collect enough data from non-White and Hispanic respondents to generate reliable prevalence estimates or trends for tobacco use. A focused telephone survey to assess multiple tobacco-related factors in all state counties collected more information, but with a significant response bias; plus, conducting a focused survey proved to be very expensive. A geographically targeted system, offered in both English and Spanish, was piloted as an approach to fill the information gap among non-White groups. A pilot of the survey among minority populations generated more responses, inclusion of traditionally uninvolved Hispanics, and stronger estimates that allowed for subgroup analyses within specific groups. A question to assess sexual orientation was also added to the demographic information collected by this tailored survey (Dilley & Boysun, 2003).

At times, minority populations need to be not only represented but prioritized for data collection. For example, in one study, the smoking behaviors of particular minority groups were the primary focus of the study (due to the targeting of these groups by the tobacco industry's marketing campaigns). Culturally sensitive patterns and identifying culturally distinct groups was an important part of the study. The primary system for identifying persons for surveys covered a broad geographic area but insufficiently included some of the groups targeted for marketing by the tobacco industry. To promote inclusion of these key groups in the targeted state, researchers employed a number of strategies, including (1) using telephone lists that focused on specific populations in the community or state (e.g., use of a survey of the GLBT community); (2) creating in-language surveys (in this tobacco study, including language surveys of Chinese, Korean, and Asian Indian communities); (3) using mapping techniques and regional stratification inclusive of communities of interest; (4) developing culturally and linguistically appropriate survey instruments that included culturally sensitive item content and acculturation measures, with extensive testing of instruments to ensure validity and reliability; and (5) involving community groups in survey development and implementation and verifying existing data sources. Taking culture, language, geographic, and socioeconomic characteristics into consideration is needed to ensure representative and valid estimates, particularly when culturally diverse groups are prioritized in the study (Schumacher et al., 2003).

Checking Vitals

Data collection should include information on language, race, gender, socioeconomic factors and ethnicity, religion, and other key variables as identified by the evaluation team.

Strategies for engaging minority community member engagement include the following:

Gaining the sponsorship of a respected and well-known ethnic agency;

Explaining the purpose of the research and stating the evaluation's goals and how these goals align and compare with the goals and aspirations of the persons participating in the study;

Describing fully how the information will be used;

Conducting evaluation activities, such as interviews and focus groups, in comfortable and safe locations (such as tribal buildings for Native Americans, or neutral community sites rather than at a social service agency or government building);

Enlisting community members to serve as advisory board members; and

Training indigenous personnel to serve as interviewers or in some other staff capacity, including leadership roles.

Methods for collecting data also need to be considered (Rodgers-Farmer & Potocky-Tripodi, 2001; Colorado Trust, 2002).

4. *Evaluation design: Methodology.* The use of different group designs or methods may have some relevance in considering culturally responsive research. In addition to the advantages and disadvantages of between-group designs and comparisons, cultural considerations may further complicate using some designs, such as an experimental design that withholds treatment, and pose particular challenges, such as the construction of culturally valid pre-tests and post-tests. Some methods may be of particular interest because of their sensitivity to the complexity of variables and their ability to tell an in-depth story.

Ethnographic interviews allow for this detail in description but also pose a number of challenges for evaluators. In a qualitative, narrative approach, the use of self-awareness of one's biases, thorough exploration of context, appreciation of the client's perspective, and acknowledgment of different cultural realities and patterns are crucial considerations. Maintaining a non-judgmental attitude, self-reflection, and the process of self-monitoring are also essential (Lowery, 2001, p. 321). The evaluator's ability to learn the culture is important so that the search for patterns and interrelationships, and the identification of themes and processes, is culturally accurate (Lowery, 2001).

5. *Dissemination and reporting.* Finishing up the evaluation and reporting back on a study pose a number of issues for cultural competency. Preceding the reporting, interpreting the results requires some care. Data can be presented in a fairly straightforward manner, but the interpretation should avoid a deficit model—presenting differences as deficiencies. The results should also be interpreted in a manner that reflects the lives of the people studied. A culturally

competent person knowledgeable of the population(s) should review the data. When results are presented, the evaluator should solicit feedback and verification: Do the findings match the experience and perceptions of the participants and stakeholders? Do the results make sense given the data presented? Is the analysis and interpretation clear, accurate, respectful, and valid? The goal is accuracy and recognition that interpretations and the presentation of findings can be presented in a manner that is respectful of the population.

As with all program evaluation, it is important to provide timely feedback. This feedback should be in a clear and useful format through culturally appropriate methods. This may necessitate an oral presentation rather than simply a written report. It may be important to prioritize a written report designed for the public rather than a scientific article that will be slow in becoming available and inaccessible to most audiences. A draft of the report may be reviewed by key cultural informants for sensitivity to language, and the dissemination strategy could be proposed to and shaped by these same stakeholders. The evaluator might ask: What is the timeliest, clearest, and most accessible means for reporting back to concerned participants, stakeholders, and community members?

Not only is timeliness and accessibility important, but the content of what is reported needs to be examined to assure accuracy, carefulness, and usefulness. For example, there are risks in reporting information with small and potentially identifiable groups of respondents. So if reporting on a project with a small number of Native Americans participating in the study, one might want to combine this data with another category to protect the identities of respondents. However, aggregating data has risks as well. In combining categories, some of the nuances and precision of the study might be compromised, and data should only be aggregated if the responses are similar enough to each other to convey accurate and useful information. The overgeneralization from one's study to broader populations and groups should be avoided.

The evaluation may have an implicit or explicit goal of providing information and advancing knowledge that can influence policy and practice. At its simplest, an evaluation that demonstrates the success of a program provides support for the program's advocates or, conversely, shortcomings provide evidence for the program's critics. The evaluation process may have an explicit goal of educating and empowering program participants by having research respondents assist in the conduct of the evaluation, including helping to define the focus of the project, adapting or crafting an evaluation methodology, and having a role in the interpretation of the results and any applications. Promoting multiple and contrasting viewpoints may be encouraged to assist in constructing a responsive and well-informed study. The ultimate goal of some evaluations and research projects is to shed light on the experience of participants and to lessen oppression (Rodgers-Farmer & Potocky-Tripodi, 2001).

Checking Vitals

Methodology:

In addition to the advantages and disadvantages of between-group designs and comparisons, cultural considerations may further complicate using some designs, such as an experimental design that withholds treatment, and pose particular challenges, such as the construction of culturally valid pre-tests and post-tests.

Dissemination and reporting:

Data can be presented in a fairly straightforward manner, but the interpretation should avoid a deficit model—presenting differences as deficiencies.

A culturally competent person knowledgeable of the population(s) should review the data.

The goal is accuracy and recognition that interpretations and the presentation of findings can be done in a manner that is respectful of the population.

Feedback should be in a clear and useful format through culturally appropriate methods.

IN CONCLUSION

Cultural competency is a goal for program evaluation and evaluators. This competency can be acquired through the thoughtful consideration of a number of factors that shape the evaluation process. In addition to general principles to promote cultural sensitivity, the evaluation team should examine the stages of the evaluation process for opportunities to build in culturally responsive strategies. The evaluator's objectivity is displayed in the context of personal and professional qualities that should encourage self-reflection, consultation with others, and a commitment to accuracy and understanding in the conduct of the evaluative process.

Cultural competency is a goal for evaluators, just as it is for clinicians and organizational leaders. Such competency is developed through thoughtful work and reflection. The evaluator's understanding of cultural competency is much broader than identifying racial or ethnic or gender differences. This competency is required throughout the stages of an evaluation.

REVIEW AND REFLECT

Big Ideas

• Cultural competency is a goal and value for evaluation just as it is for clinical and organizational practice.

• There are a number of guidelines that can increase the evaluator's responsiveness and sensitivity to culture and diversity.

• Sensitivity to culture and diversity should be manifest at each stage of the evaluation process.

Discussion Questions

• How would you approach the challenge of learning about a specific cultural group or diverse population?

• In the example in the chapter, when a university research study is conducted in a local library, critique this setting and setup with regard to privacy concerns and confidentiality, and create guidelines for safe settings for data collection.

• How does a researcher's need for or experience with cultural competency differ from that expected of a clinician or program manager? And how should an evaluator approach a study if he or she is of a different gender, race, religion, ethnicity, or sexual orientation than the population being studied?

Activities

• If you were constructing an "evaluation philosophy"—guiding principles that you would use to shape the decisions that you make with regard to the evaluation process—what would be the key statements in your evaluation philosophy with regard to culture?

• Create a demographic section for a questionnaire in which you gain the information you need to understand the sample population you are studying.

• Write a job description for a person to be a cultural consultant to work with your evaluation team.

Resources

• *Guidelines for research in ethnic minority communities.* (2000). Council of National Psychological Associations for the Advancement of Ethnic Minority Interests. Washington, DC: American Psychological Association.

• Harris, J. L. (1996). Issues in recruiting African American participants for research. In A. G. Kamhi, K. E. Pollock, & J. L. Harris (Eds.), *Communication development and disorders in African American children* (pp. 19–34). Baltimore: Paul Brookes.

• Langdon, H., & Cheng, L. R. (2002). *Collaborating with interpreters and translators.* Eau Claire, WI: Thinking Publications.

• Reich, S. M., & Reich, J. A. (2006). Cultural competence in interdisciplinary collaborations: A method for respecting diversity in research partnerships. *American Journal of Community Psychology, 38,* 51–62.

• Sue, S. (1999, December). Science, ethnicity and bias: Where have we gone wrong? *American Psychologist, 54,* 12.

CHAPTER 7

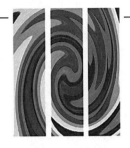

Program Definition

Using Program Logic Models to Develop a Common Vision

Purpose of Information/Referral Program

With most evaluation projects, one of the first things to address is the way the program is supposed to operate. Who are the intended clients? What services should they get? How will those services help them? At the beginning of an evaluation project, it is fairly standard to ask a variety of stakeholders, people with an interest in the program (more about this later), about the program. These interviews are typically informal and unstructured and usually include a series of basic questions that encourage stakeholders to tell the evaluator about the more significant aspects of the program from their point of view. Also, it gives the person doing the evaluation a chance to meet some of the folks associated with the program in a safe and nonthreatening environment.

Checking Vitals

In doing a program evaluation, you must first address the way the program is supposed to operate:

Who are the intended clients?

What services should they get?

How will those services get to them?

Interview stakeholders:

Use informal interviews.

Give a series of basic questions that encourage stakeholders to tell the evaluator about the more significant aspects of the program from their point of view.

Consider the situation where a residential program for delinquent children was about to be evaluated. These are some of the comments that came up in informal conversation: One staff member spoke in great detail about the physical surroundings of the facility, saying that for many of the children, it was the first time they had a safe place to sleep and good nutrition in years. Another staff member was fixated on the educational program. He stated that children who had not attended school in years were able to attend school regularly, achieve academic success, and catch up with their age-group. Yet a third person spoke about the group treatment model. She saw the therapeutic process helping these historically violent youth find ways to negotiate with each other in a constructive manner and resolve conflict productively. Finally, a fourth person, a referral source outside the program, praised the program for giving kids a safe place to stay.

It is interesting to note that people, very knowledgeable about this program, working side-by-side on the same program, have very different viewpoints about the most important part of the program, as well as its purpose. In the example above, two different staff people thought that group therapy was the key to the program. When asked about the key element of this program component, one of them felt the structure provided by the group process was the key, while the other person felt the experienced and trained staff was the factor that made the difference.

All of the discussants in this exchange are most likely correct. Social work programs do some amazing things, so it is likely that one program could conceivably accomplish all of the above. Additionally, it is common for two co-workers who have worked together for years to have very different points of view about a specific program. As you would expect, a number of factors contribute to this.

The role of persons with respect to the program has a major impact on their perspective. A group worker will probably have a different view than a family worker. Additionally, personal and professional factors will influence this perspective. A person with years of experience will see the program differently than a newly hired employee. Professional training, life experience, individual experiences with the program, and many more things have an influence on one's perspective. The organizations where programs reside are also subject to program expansion/cutbacks, changes in leadership, philosophical shifts, and other dynamics that impact a program's intentions. Most likely, the program will have multiple purposes based on the perspective of the person describing the program. In order to get the most complete description of the program, you must include people with many different viewpoints.

Checking Vitals

The relationship of practitioners and other constituents with respect to the program has a major impact on their perspective.

Professional training, life experience, individual experiences with the program, and many more things have an influence on one's perspective.

The organizations where programs reside are also subject to program expansion/cutbacks, changes in leadership, philosophical shifts, and other dynamics that impact a program's intentions.

In order to get the most complete description of the program, you must include people with many different viewpoints.

Undoubtedly, this primary task of clarifying a program's intent is complicated with a range of views and different key actors. One way to address the multiple points of view surrounding a program is to develop a program logic model (PLM). The development of a program logic model accomplishes a number of purposes:

Stakeholders are allowed to articulate their views about the program.

Stakeholders are allowed to hear and appreciate the views of other stakeholders.

Divergent views about the program are synthesized in a collaborative process.

An integrated model is developed with stakeholder ownership.

The integrated model is scrutinized publicly for feasibility.

The model serves as a solid reference for program management decisions.

The model is used as an organizing tool for evaluation.

The model can be used as a promotional tool for the program.

The model can be employed to support program proposals for grant activity.

In this discussion, PLMs will be the common reference; however, there is a little baggage around the name at the onset of the process. It reeks a little bit of jargon. Often the term "logic model" connotes some type of computer programming reference that makes many practitioners a little nervous. In some cases, the term "program model" is used as an effective replacement. A student aware of this concern suggested using "happy program description." As the process continues, this detail becomes irrelevant as the respective rendition is known as the hospice program model or the diversion program model. The investments made by practitioners to describe the model create an investment that provides ownership, and this concern, in effect, goes away. Prior to advancing and illustrating this approach, the historical development of this approach should facilitate a deeper understanding of its original intent and reinforce its utility.

BRIEF HISTORY OF PROGRAM LOGIC MODELS

Logic models were first introduced during the 1960s and 1970s to evaluate large federal social programs. A process called evaluability assessment that involved utilizing program logic models was introduced as an alternative to the standard large-scale evaluation process, which would often take years to complete. The traditional process included sending an evaluation project proposal to possible consulting firms, reviewing and accepting a proposal, conducting the evaluation, and finally, reporting the findings. From start to finish, this process would take months and sometimes years from requesting proposals to receiving information. Obviously, this process did not lend itself to collection of useful and timely program information. The key questions would often change as would the key actors invested in specific questions (Horst, Nay, Scanlon, & Wholey, 1974; Nay, Scanlon, Graham, & Waller, 1977). Logic models were a critical part of this expedited evaluation process that would focus initially on getting the program's intended functioning clarified (Rutman, 1980; Wholey, 1983, 1994). The use of logic models has enjoyed significant popularity since that time (Alter & Egan, 1997; Alter & Murty, 1997; Hartnett & Kapp, 2003; Kapp, 2000; McLaughlin & Jordan, 2004; Savas, 1996). One of the authors of this book had the good fortune to work with Joe Wholey in the mid-1980s. As a result, much of our experience is inspired and informed by his work.

BUILDING A PROGRAM LOGIC MODEL

The process of constructing a program logic model provides an extensive amount of information for the evaluator. Additionally, it provides some very productive initial exchanges that allow the evaluator and the program people to get acquainted. One of the first steps in developing the program logic model is deciding who to interview.

Whom Do You Interview?

The term "stakeholder," as stated earlier, is used to describe individuals who may have some investment in the program. See Table 7.1 for a list of potential stakeholders.

While the list is long, it is useful to be as inclusive as possible. Additionally, efforts should be made to include different points of view. It may also be useful to consult with your contacts in the agency about critical interviewees who may represent divergent views or key actors who need to be supportive of the evaluation process. For example, with a hospice program, the interview group might include the clinical director, the medical director, the social worker, the bereavement counselor, the nurse, the local hospital staff, a financial staff person, and a representative of a funding source. This group would most likely offer different perspectives about the process. In another project, one of the authors was developing a multi-program logic model, a model of juvenile justice services within a judicial district, and all the different service providers were included: probation, diversion, detention, intake, and assessment.

Table 7.1	Stakeholder Groups

Clients	Children, adults, partners, spouses, relatives, friends, clergy, community members
Direct service staff	Educational staff, family therapists, group workers, direct care staff, intake workers, information/referral staff
Supervisory/management staff	Team leaders, program managers, clinical supervisors
Executive staff	Executive directors, associate executive directors, regional managers
Board of directors	Members of the agency board
Funders	City, state, and federal funders, United Way, foundation funders
Community partners	Juvenile court, child welfare offices, probation office, mental health center, law enforcement, job centers, religious groups, youth center personnel

However, the evaluator did not include local legislators serving on a juvenile justice advisory committee, which proved to be a faux pas on the evaluator's part as these stakeholders held distinct views and were quite influential. In retrospect, it would have been beneficial for their input to be included in developing the model. In hindsight, the evaluator should have spent more time investigating key stakeholder groups with the members of the evaluation team.

Checking Vitals

One of the first steps in developing the program logic model is deciding who to interview.

Considerations when choosing stakeholders:

It is useful to be as inclusive as possible.

Efforts should be made to include different points of view.

Consult with your contacts in the agency about critical interviewees who may represent divergent views or key actors who need to be supportive of the evaluation process.

The Interview Process

After deciding who to interview, one needs to decide what questions to ask (see questionnaire in Table 7.2, adapted from Wholey's [1983] exemplar). A list of straightforward questions provides a sound structure for collecting the information needed to construct a program logic model. While the questionnaire format works nicely in individual interviews, it can be adapted to the setting.

In some cases, there may be an evaluation team or a project team that will continually work together. On occasion, the authors have used the interview guide to facilitate a discussion among a group. A group interview can facilitate discussion among members that may lead to more refined input into the model.

Table 7.2	Logic Model Questionnaire

Eco-Structural Family Program IW Guide

1. How is the program staffed and organized?

2. What components are involved with the program other than staff?

3. Can you describe the major activities of the program?

4. What resources are devoted to these activities?

5. What are the main objectives of the program? What is the program trying to accomplish?

6. What accomplishments is the program likely to achieve in the next 2 to 3 years? What would you expect?

7. How will the activities undertaken by the program accomplish these results?

8. What kinds of information do you have on the program?

9. How do you use this information?

10. What kinds of information do you need to assess program performance?

11. How would you use this information?

12. What measures or indicators are relevant to the program?

13. What problems face the program?

14. What factors are likely to influence the program over the next 2 to 5 years?

Source: Adapted from Stroul et al., 1980; Wholey, 1983.

If a group discussion seems to support the ongoing evaluation process, it may be important to give members a set of questions to answer privately and then share with the group—particularly when some of the group members may be more talkative or dominant. Each individual team member can talk about answers to specific questions as the initial part of the group's discussion. The evaluator can then attempt to compare and contrast the individual feedback.

Checking Vitals

A list of straightforward questions provides a sound structure for collecting the information needed to construct a program logic model.

A group interview can facilitate discussion among members that may lead to more refined input into the model.

If a group discussion seems to support the ongoing evaluation process, it may be important to give members a set of questions to answer privately and then share with the group.

DEVELOPING THE INITIAL PROGRAM LOGIC MODEL

The completed interviews, group or individual, will give the evaluator an extensive amount of detail about the program functioning. The information is then organized around the structure provided in PLM #1. Using this structure, a logic model is developed which describes the program's resources, activities, program processes, and immediate, intermediate, and long-term outcomes. Although the input is often varied, this format allows the inclusion of many different programs. It is flexible enough to include a variety of perspectives. Additionally, it is the evaluator's job to present the program in a logic model that represents the perspectives offered during the interviews. While the evaluator makes every effort to organize the information in the most concise manner, this is not the time for the evaluator to select or filter the information. The task at this point is to present a program logic model that reflects the program ideas reflected in the interviews. A variety of different models are presented at the end of the chapter. Some of these are single program models and some are examples where a logic model was constructed to represent a group of programs. This is often useful when grouping services together is useful for funding or planning purposes.

Evaluator has a lot of power if they do not choose to "follow the rules" or interpret correctly. they can filter, not represent views correctly. Put it in a diff. order that d/n make as much sense

Program Logic Model

PLM #1

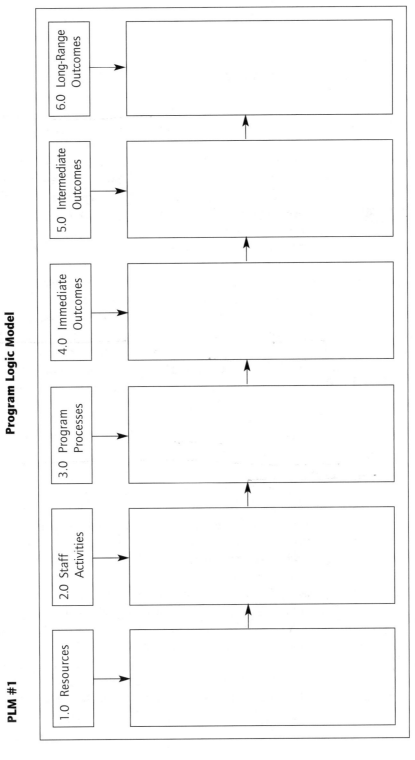

What Is in a Logic Model

In our experience in developing logic models, jargon is used in many different ways; therefore, some basic clarification may be useful. While everyone may not agree with our definitions, the following may help to make them more explicit and hopefully clear up some of the confusion. PLM #1 is a blank logic model that includes the column headings in the model. The first column identifies the "Resources" that are invested in the program to make all the good things happen. If you look at the other PLMs, you will see things listed like staff, clients, and facilities—not that surprising. Some other models also include collaborative partners in the community or the organization like the committees listed in PLM #3 (Juvenile Justice Service Programs) or the agency partners listed in PLM #4 (Homework Hotline Project Logic Model), and others. Additionally, some models include less concrete things that are still viable resources, like the best practices reference in PLM #3 and positive relationships with the "Community" in PLM #8 (Non-Custodial Parent Program Logic Model).

The "Staff Activities" column usually includes broader groupings of the significant program components (service and those that support service). When it is made clear that this is a broader rubric than is refined in the next column, much of the confusion usually subsides. PLM #9 (Hospice Program Logic Model) lists the different aspects of a hospice program. PLM #3, a multi-service model, lists the different juvenile justice services available in the respective counties.

The next column lists the key processes associated with service delivery. We usually ask program people to think of the key things that need to get completed for effective service to occur. In PLM #4, for example, it is imperative for students to contact the "Hotline" before any support can be offered. PLM #8, on the other hand, lists different service pieces: assessment, referrals, mediation, and so forth. Additionally, a one-to-one relationship between "Staff Activities" is not necessarily needed. In some cases, certain activities are more important than others. In addition, some service components are more fully developed than others. In PLM #5 (Resident Treatment Program Project Logic Model), two things are notable: (1) Family therapy is more developed because there are two more specific processes listed than in the other service areas; and (2) having therapy-focused services, especially during aftercare, is essential to the success of the program.

The remaining three columns list program outcomes separated by timing. "Immediate Outcomes" are those that are intended to be accomplished toward the end of service. This distinction is very concrete in residential programs where clients tend to leave the program and less discrete when services are continuous.

In those cases, efforts are often made to describe this part of the program as the early parts of discharge from the facility. Intermediate outcomes focus on the idea of clients adjusting to the ongoing adjustment to life in the community. These outcomes tend to occur at a later point in time and also represent a more advanced level of accomplishment. In PLM #5, it is one thing to place youth in less restrictive settings (Immediate Outcome), but in the intermediate outcome, youth are expected to be maintaining that status.

The last level of outcomes looks at a longer time frame. Continuing with PLM #5, the youth are integrating the behaviors listed previously into their long-term lifestyles. Additionally, a type of ripple effect is often implied. When the earlier outcomes are accomplished, broader undertakings are intended to take place. For example, in PLM #3 the long-range outcomes expected as a result of a range of individual youth-oriented outcomes focus more on societal phenomena, like the crime rate and family violence rates decreasing.

Reviewing the Program Logic Model

The initial model is then presented to the project team or stakeholder groups. It is best if the review of the model is somewhat structured. First, make sure the stakeholders understand the presentation of the model; that is, what is represented in each of the boxes. Second, ask the members to look for surprises; that is, things they did not expect to see that were included and program aspects that were excluded. The final step of this initial review is to ask for revision ideas.

This may include presenting the model in a different fashion. For example, in a presentation of an initial model of school social work to school social workers, the social workers felt the model looked entirely too linear; so it was modified to its form as shown in example PLM #2. The resources, activities, and program processes all appear to contribute to all of the outcomes, as opposed to a more sequential order that is presented in a traditional logic model. In another example (see PLM #3, a logic model of juvenile justice services), the project team decided that outcomes should be organized by the recipients: youth and families, and communities. The revisions suggestions are then integrated into the model and presented to the team with a preference toward consensus agreement on the model, or at least a version of the model with which all parties can live. While it may seem impossible to develop a model

this step helps of balance some of the "power" but not the concerns, all

PLM #2   **School Social Work Program Model**

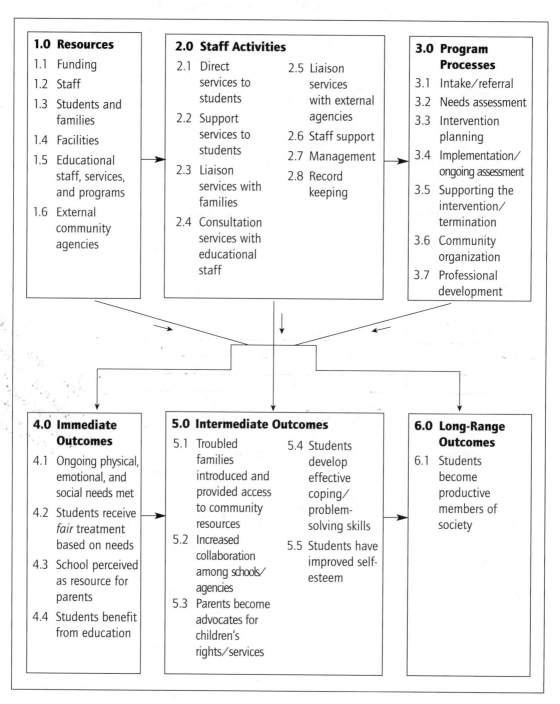

1.0 Resources

1.1 Funding

1.2 Staff

1.3 Students and families

1.4 Facilities

1.5 Educational staff, services, and programs

1.6 External community agencies

2.0 Staff Activities

2.1 Direct services to students

2.2 Support services to students

2.3 Liaison services with families

2.4 Consultation services with educational staff

2.5 Liaison services with external agencies

2.6 Staff support

2.7 Management

2.8 Record keeping

3.0 Program Processes

3.1 Intake/referral

3.2 Needs assessment

3.3 Intervention planning

3.4 Implementation/ongoing assessment

3.5 Supporting the intervention/termination

3.6 Community organization

3.7 Professional development

4.0 Immediate Outcomes

4.1 Ongoing physical, emotional, and social needs met

4.2 Students receive *fair* treatment based on needs

4.3 School perceived as resource for parents

4.4 Students benefit from education

5.0 Intermediate Outcomes

5.1 Troubled families introduced and provided access to community resources

5.2 Increased collaboration among schools/agencies

5.3 Parents become advocates for children's rights/services

5.4 Students develop effective coping/problem-solving skills

5.5 Students have improved self-esteem

6.0 Long-Range Outcomes

6.1 Students become productive members of society

PLM #3

Juvenile Justice Service Programs

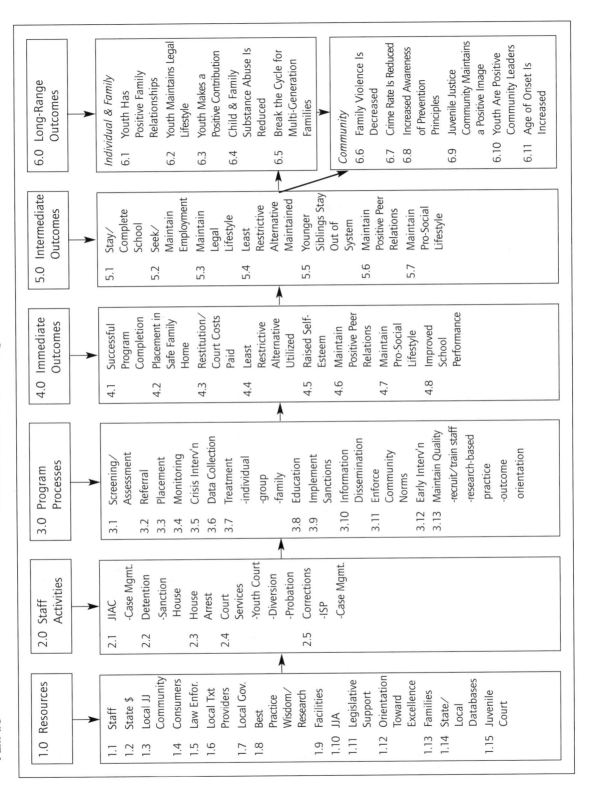

1.0 Resources	2.0 Staff Activities	3.0 Program Processes	4.0 Immediate Outcomes	5.0 Intermediate Outcomes	6.0 Long-Range Outcomes
1.1 Staff	2.1 JIAC	3.1 Screening/ Assessment	4.1 Successful Program Completion	5.1 Stay/ Complete School	*Individual & Family*
1.2 State $	-Case Mgmt.	3.2 Referral	4.2 Placement in Safe Family Home	5.2 Seek/ Maintain Employment	6.1 Youth Has Positive Family Relationships
1.3 Local JJ Community	2.2 Detention	3.3 Placement	4.3 Restitution/ Court Costs Paid	5.3 Maintain Legal Lifestyle	6.2 Youth Maintains Legal Lifestyle
1.4 Consumers	-Sanction House	3.4 Monitoring	4.4 Least Restrictive Alternative Utilized	5.4 Least Restrictive Alternative Maintained	6.3 Youth Makes a Positive Contribution
1.5 Law Enfor.	2.3 House Arrest	3.5 Crisis Interv'n	4.5 Raised Self-Esteem	5.5 Younger Siblings Stay Out of System	6.4 Child & Family Substance Abuse Is Reduced
1.6 Local Txt Providers	2.4 Court Services	3.6 Data Collection	4.6 Maintain Positive Peer Relations	5.6 Maintain Positive Peer Relations	6.5 Break the Cycle for Multi-Generation Families
1.7 Local Gov.	-Youth Court	3.7 Treatment	4.7 Maintain Pro-Social Lifestyle	5.7 Maintain Pro-Social Lifestyle	*Community*
1.8 Best Practice Wisdom/ Research	-Diversion	-individual	4.8 Improved School Performance		6.6 Family Violence Is Decreased
1.9 Facilities	-Probation	-group			6.7 Crime Rate Is Reduced
1.10 JJA	2.5 Corrections	-family			6.8 Increased Awareness of Prevention Principles
1.11 Legislative Support	-ISP	3.8 Education			6.9 Juvenile Justice Community Maintains a Positive Image
1.12 Orientation Toward Excellence	-Case Mgmt.	3.9 Implement Sanctions			6.10 Youth Are Positive Community Leaders
1.13 Families		3.10 Information Dissemination			6.11 Age of Onset Is Increased
1.14 State/ Local Databases		3.11 Enforce Community Norms			
1.15 Juvenile Court		3.12 Early Interv'n			
		3.13 Maintain Quality			
		-recruit/train staff			
		-research-based practice			
		-outcome orientation			

PLM #3a

Juvenile Justice Service Programs–Youth Version

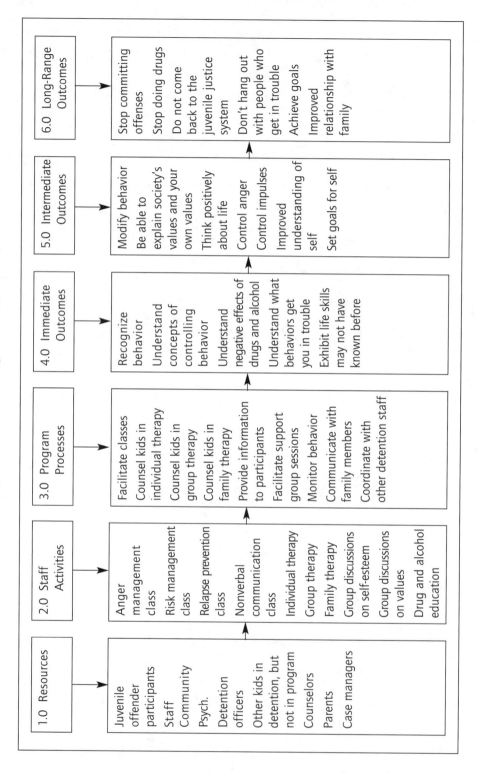

1.0 Resources	2.0 Staff Activities	3.0 Program Processes	4.0 Immediate Outcomes	5.0 Intermediate Outcomes	6.0 Long-Range Outcomes
Juvenile offender participants	Anger management class	Facilitate classes	Recognize behavior	Modify behavior	Stop committing offenses
Staff	Risk management class	Counsel kids in individual therapy	Understand concepts of controlling behavior	Be able to explain society's values and your own values	Stop doing drugs
Community Psych.	Relapse prevention class	Counsel kids in group therapy	Understand negative effects of drugs and alcohol	Think positively about life	Do not come back to the juvenile justice system
Detention officers	Nonverbal communication class	Counsel kids in family therapy	Understand what behaviors get you in trouble	Control anger	Don't hang out with people who get in trouble
Other kids in detention, but not in program	Individual therapy	Provide information to participants	Exhibit life skills may not have known before	Control impulses	Achieve goals
Counselors	Group therapy	Facilitate support group sessions		Improved understanding of self	Improved relationship with family
Parents	Family therapy	Monitor behavior		Set goals for self	
Case managers	Group discussions on self-esteem	Communicate with family members			
	Group discussions on values	Coordinate with other detention staff			
	Drug and alcohol education				

that integrates a number of divergent perspectives, our experience is that a few revisions usually produce a model that is almost always supported. Also, the logic models are not presented as final; it is more palatable to describe the models as susceptible to revision at a later date, as works in progress, much like the programs they represent.

Checking Vitals

Make every effort to get the stakeholders to understand the presentation of the model, that is, what is represented in each of the boxes and the overall model.

Ask the members to look for things they did not expect to see that were included and program aspects that were excluded.

Ask for revision ideas.

Revision suggestions are then integrated into the model and presented to the team with a preference toward consensus agreement on the model, or at least a version of the model with which all parties can live.

Different Points of View

There has been extensive discussion around the different points of view that can exist for the same program. To highlight that point, we would like to compare and contrast two different program logic models about the same program. PLM #3 and PLM #3a focus on the juvenile justice services for youth in a specific county. PLM #3 reflects the perspective of program managers of different services. PLM #3a is based on the input of youth in detention about the juvenile services offered in that jurisdiction. One difference is the specificity of the youth model; as expected, the youth describe things very concretely. The resources describe individuals that a youth might meet in the context of services. The description of the service provided by the youth in the activities and processes boxes are surprisingly similar. There is a difference in language that reminds those in the position of constructing program logic models to avoid as much jargon as possible to make it easy for all audiences to use.

Obviously, the description forwarded in PLM #3 is more detailed, but the portrayal offered by the youth (PLM #3a) can be distinguished when you compare both models. We find it fascinating to look at the different specifications of the program

(Continued)

(Continued)

outcomes between the two models. The youth model has "Intermediate" and "Long-Range Outcomes" that are listed in the three levels of outcomes offered by the other model. However, the youth model adds a level of detail related to intermediate outcomes. Interestingly, the youth model describes these outcomes with more of a clinical focus, specifically, on the types of things that would be in individual youth treatment plans. This example illustrates that there are many vital and viable points of program viewpoints often associated with the different program perspectives, which in this case is defined by a managerial point of view versus a client's point of view. If the client perspective were excluded, an important aspect of the program would have been most likely underrepresented. This example hopefully illustrates the unique and useful points of view held by different parties and the value of being as inclusive as possible.

Checking Vitals

There are many credible points of program viewpoints often associated with the different program perspectives.

It is important to be inclusive and to value the views held by different parties:

Example: The case above is defined by a managerial point of view versus a client's point of view. If the client perspective were excluded, an important aspect of the program would have been most likely underrepresented.

Assessing the Program

The next phase is to use the program logic model as a tool to critique the program. The material about using the logic model to assess the program comes from the evaluability assessment process mentioned earlier (Rutman, 1980; Wholey, 1983). Wholey (1983) describes this phase as a "plausibility analysis" (p. 48). At this point, the evaluation team is asked to critique the theory behind the program as described. In other words, if the resources are invested and the activities/processes occur, is it realistic that the outcomes will occur? In one case, one of the authors was evaluating a tutoring program where children call an 800 number to get help with their homework (see PLM #4). Initially, the logic model described outcomes that focused on the young participants' grade point

PLM #4

Homework Hotline Project Logic Model

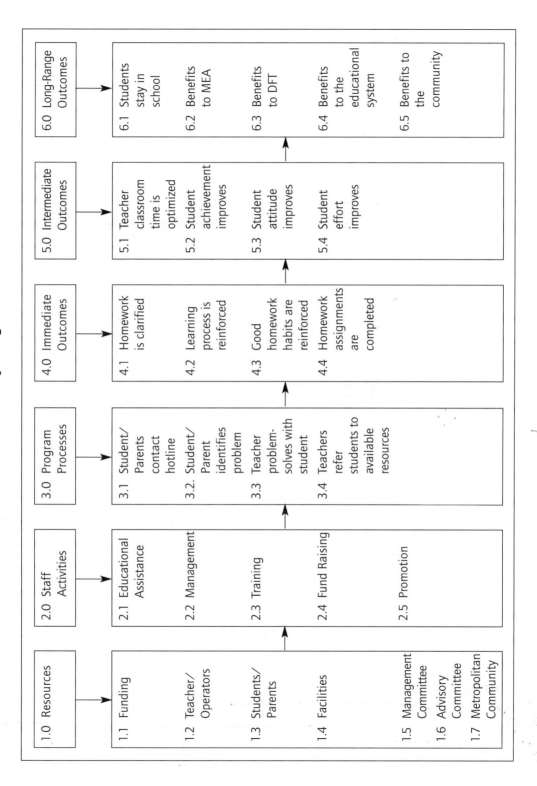

1.0 Resources	2.0 Staff Activities	3.0 Program Processes	4.0 Immediate Outcomes	5.0 Intermediate Outcomes	6.0 Long-Range Outcomes
1.1 Funding	2.1 Educational Assistance	3.1 Student/ Parents contact hotline	4.1 Homework is clarified	5.1 Teacher classroom time is optimized	6.1 Students stay in school
1.2 Teacher/ Operators	2.2 Management	3.2. Student/ Parent identifies problem	4.2 Learning process is reinforced	5.2 Student achievement improves	6.2 Benefits to MEA
1.3 Students/ Parents	2.3 Training	3.3 Teacher problem-solves with student	4.3 Good homework habits are reinforced	5.3 Student attitude improves	6.3 Benefits to DFT
1.4 Facilities	2.4 Fund Raising	3.4 Teachers refer students to available resources	4.4 Homework assignments are completed	5.4 Student effort improves	6.4 Benefits to the educational system
1.5 Management Committee	2.5 Promotion				6.5 Benefits to the community
1.6 Advisory Committee					
1.7 Metropolitan Community					

averages, graduation rate, college choice, and so forth. In this phase of the discussion, the program staff agreed that these outcomes were overly ambitious, and the more likely goals were to help kids complete their homework and promote the collaboration among the teachers' union who were staffing the project. The model was adjusted to include the more realistic outcomes.

Another aspect of this process is assessing the program in light of the clear vision forwarded by the program logic model. In one case, a group of practitioners were reviewing the program logic model for a residential treatment program (see PLM #5), with a special focus on the program's actual implementation. The team of managers and practitioners came to the conclusion that the program's aftercare was not being implemented and this was having a severe impact on the program's intermediate outcomes. Administrative attention and resources were invested in a more complete implementation of the aftercare services. In these cases, positive program improvements focusing on outcome were forwarded by simply viewing the program through the fresh perspective offered by the logic model.

Checking Vitals

Use the program logic model to critique the program:

> If the resources are invested and the activities/processes occur, is it realistic that the outcomes will occur?

> Is the implementation of the program achieving the desired outcome?

Can we make positive program improvements that will help us achieve the desired outcome?

IDENTIFYING INFORMATION NEEDS

A program's information needs can also be assessed using a program logic model. While many evaluators use the program logic model as a sort of roadmap for the evaluation design, Wholey (1983) was one of the earliest to suggest this option. One of the central questions in any evaluation is what aspects of the program require some type of evaluative attention? The logic model can be used to facilitate that discussion. Program staff can sit around a

helps crit. thinking

PLM #5

Residential Treatment Program Project Logic Model

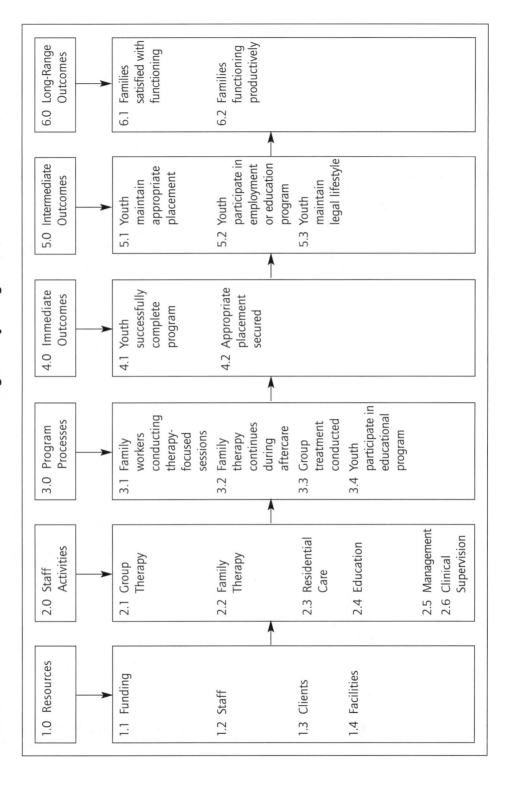

1.0 Resources	2.0 Staff Activities	3.0 Program Processes	4.0 Immediate Outcomes	5.0 Intermediate Outcomes	6.0 Long-Range Outcomes
1.1 Funding	2.1 Group Therapy	3.1 Family workers conducting therapy-focused sessions	4.1 Youth successfully complete program	5.1 Youth maintain appropriate placement	6.1 Families satisfied with functioning
1.2 Staff	2.2 Family Therapy	3.2 Family therapy continues during aftercare	4.2 Appropriate placement secured	5.2 Youth participate in employment or education program	6.2 Families functioning productively
1.3 Clients	2.3 Residential Care	3.3 Group treatment conducted		5.3 Youth maintain legal lifestyle	
1.4 Facilities	2.4 Education	3.4 Youth participate in educational program			
	2.5 Management				
	2.6 Clinical Supervision				

table and circle areas on the logic model that represent key information needs. The result of this discussion is an inventory of what critical information is available and what needs to be collected. PLM #6 includes a logic model where the information needs for an Eco-Structural In-Home Family Support program have been circled. Table 7.3 describes the area of the program, its respective

Table 7.3	Eco-Structural In-Home Family Support Program Information Needs

Program Component	Indicator	Information Source
1.3 Family and community service worker	% of family and community service worker positions filled	Quarterly human resources staff roster reports
3.2 Intake and family assessments	# of intake and family assessments completed each month	Program manager intake reports
4.2 Improve family attachment	% of families classified as balanced on the Circumplex Family Typology	Faces II research forms completed at program completion* (Olson, Russell, & Sprenkle, 1983)
4.4 Improve social support	% of families with an increase in social support	Change in reported social support scores from intake to program completion, using the Social Support Inventory* (Tracy, Whittaker, Pugh, Kapp, & Overstreet, 1994)
6.2 Communities maintain resources for child and family development	% of families that report involvement in community resources	3-month follow-up survey with parents*
6.3 Families and communities interact to improve quality of life for residents	% of families with at least one family member participating in pro-social community activity	3-month follow-up survey*

*original data collection

PLM #6

Eco-structural In-Home Family Support Program

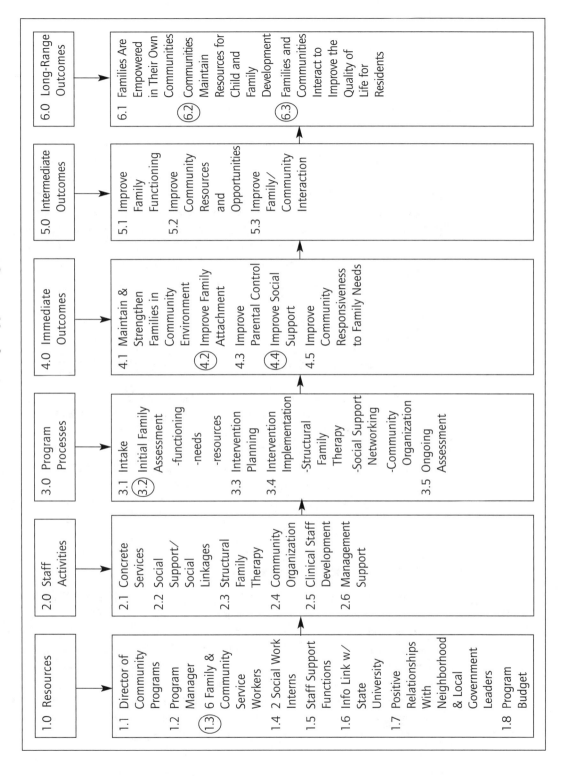

1.0 Resources	2.0 Staff Activities	3.0 Program Processes	4.0 Immediate Outcomes	5.0 Intermediate Outcomes	6.0 Long-Range Outcomes
1.1 Director of Community Programs	2.1 Concrete Services	3.1 Intake	4.1 Maintain & Strengthen Families in Community Environment	5.1 Improve Family Functioning	6.1 Families Are Empowered in Their Own Communities
1.2 Program Manager	2.2 Social Support/ Social Linkages	(3.2) Initial Family Assessment -functioning -needs -resources	(4.2) Improve Family Attachment	5.2 Improve Community Resources and Opportunities	(6.2) Communities Maintain Resources for Child and Family Development
(1.3) 6 Family & Community Service Workers	2.3 Structural Family Therapy	3.3 Intervention Planning	4.3 Improve Parental Control	5.3 Improve Family/ Community Interaction	(6.3) Families and Communities Interact to Improve the Quality of Life for Residents
1.4 2 Social Work Interns	2.4 Community Organization	3.4 Intervention Implementation -Structural Family Therapy -Social Support Networking -Community Organization	(4.4) Improve Social Support		
1.5 Staff Support Functions	2.5 Clinical Staff Development	3.5 Ongoing Assessment	4.5 Improve Community Responsiveness to Family Needs		
1.6 Info Link w/ State University	2.6 Management Support				
1.7 Positive Relationships With Neighborhood & Local Government Leaders					
1.8 Program Budget					

indicator, the measure used to assess that aspect of program performance, and the source of that information. In this example, the logic model functions as a centerpiece for the design of the program evaluation. The evaluation plan for this program includes using some available information like the *human resources rosters of clinical staff* (1.3) and *program manager intake reports* (3.2). Original data collection is required to access program performance on outcomes, *improve family attachment* (4.2), and *improve social support* (4.4). These outcomes will be assessed using existing clinical measures. The remaining outcomes will be assessed in a follow-up survey with parents, developed by the agency, which will look at their involvement in community services and community activities. Starting with the logic model, the team is able to develop a plan to address the program's information needs by tapping existing information and doing some additional original data collection.

Checking Vitals

A program's information needs can also be assessed using a program logic model.

A program logic model can be used to facilitate a discussion that leads to identifying which parts of the program need evaluative attention.

The result of this discussion is an inventory of what critical information is available and what needs to be collected.

The program logic model allows teams to develop a plan to address the program's information needs by tapping existing information and doing some additional original data collection.

A Few Words About Measurement

Another source of confusion in working with practitioners is the difference between a process and an outcome. We hope this will help to clear that up, or at least our approach to this may provide a strategy. The different program logic models illustrate that a process is the implementation of a key program component; as in PLM #8, when a client is interviewed or referred for service, a legal review is conducted or in PLM #6 when a family assessment is completed. These are key events in the delivery of the service. Oftentimes, program managers will simply count the number of occurrences. This is called a process measure. For example, a process measure might include the number of legal reviews that were completed.

Outcomes, on the other hand, are results that occur when program processes are effectively implemented. For example, when the services included in PLM #6 are completed, then accordingly child support payments should increase. The outcome measure would include the number or percentage of clients whose child support payments increased.

Checking Vitals

A process is the implementation of a key program component:

Example: the number of legal reviews that were completed.

Outcomes are results that occur that are directly linked to program processes:

Example PLM #6: If the stated services are completed, then child support payments should increase.

The outcome measure would include the number or percentage of clients whose child support payments increased.

Promoting the Program

Social workers often struggle to promote their programs. Some social workers feel their efforts should be devoted to providing services and not self-promotion. Promoting their own work is not client-centered; these efforts are not perceived as helping the service recipients. Additionally, social workers are not accustomed to describing their work to audiences outside of their profession. This is due to the complex nature of their work and inexperience in this type of activity. While some social workers may prefer to bypass this type of activity, it is becoming increasingly necessary for social workers to describe their services in a manner that can be clearly understood. Program services are being forced to be more accountable to funders about the quality of services. Social workers also practice in a diverse set of arenas with professionals who are products of very different training, which often requires the clarification of many basic assumptions and ideals. In addition, social workers often compete with other professions for their jobs. In this example, the services provided by school social workers were questioned by the administration of all specialized services. Lacking a firm grasp of their work, the administration wondered why the work had to be completed by a social worker and not a psychologist or other school professional. In some cases, as funding dwindled, superintendents were considering hiring paraprofessionals to work with special needs children and did not see the need to hire trained social workers at a higher salary.

One of the authors was invited to work with a school social work department to help them develop a clear model of practice (see PLM #2). The assistant superintendent had the highest respect for school social workers as he knew them personally to be very dedicated workers. However, he was unclear about what a school social worker actually did. To address this need, the department worked with one of the authors to develop a program logic model and disseminate the model. A review of the model highlighted some of the ambiguities of their practice and led to the development of new procedures.

When the model was presented to the assistant superintendent, he changed his attitude about the services. He not only felt the model helped to clarify and justify school social work, he partnered with the department to present the model and new procedures to principals and superintendents throughout the district. In this case, a key actor in the school district had been converted from a skeptic to a champion of school social work services by the development and presentation of a program logic model accompanying new procedures.

Checking Vitals

Social workers need to have the ability to describe services in a manner that can be clearly understood.

Program services are being forced to be more accountable to funders about the quality of services.

Logic models can help clarify ambiguities and can lead to the development of new procedures.

Logic models can help clarify and justify social work positions in the competitive workforce.

USING PROGRAM LOGIC MODELS IN GRANT PROPOSALS

Funding for social service programs continues to be competitive and often scarce. As a result, social work programs are becoming more reliant on public and private grants. One of the keys of a good grant proposal is a clear presentation of the service and accompanying plan to evaluate the services. It is often difficult to describe a program—especially a new or non-existing service—in a narrative format. The logic model is a great tool to assist in that process.

All of the features of a logic model can be applied to a new program in the grant proposal process. First, a logic model can facilitate a critical review of the planned service prior to submitting it for funding. Additionally, the discussion of the program via a logic model provides a natural flow between the evaluation plan and the program. Finally, the logic model is a very clear way to present a complex service entity with many program components and multiple levels of intended outcomes. More and more funding sources are requiring the inclusion of logic models in the proposal. The United Way and many federal grants mandate the inclusion of a program logic model.

PLM #7 was developed to complement a proposal for an integrated service model that includes both family court and services for victims of domestic violence. The logic model was critical for helping the planning team actually visualize what components would need to fit together. The development of the model forced discussions about how the pieces would fit together. This discussion helped the planners to discover pieces of the program that were left hanging, especially areas where the systems would be integrated and/or left separate. This brought clarity to the proposal and made for a stronger grant proposal.

shows the practical need

Checking Vitals

Funding sources are beginning to require the inclusion of logic models in the grant application process.

The United Way and the federal government mandate the inclusion of a program logic model.

The features of a logic model can be applied to a new program in the grant proposal process.

A logic model can facilitate a critical review of the planned service prior to submitting it for funding.

The discussion of the program via a logic model provides a natural flow between the evaluation plan and the program.

The logic model is a clear way to present a complex service entity with many program components and multiple levels of intended outcomes.

PLM #7   Integrated Family Court and Domestic Violence Program Logic Model

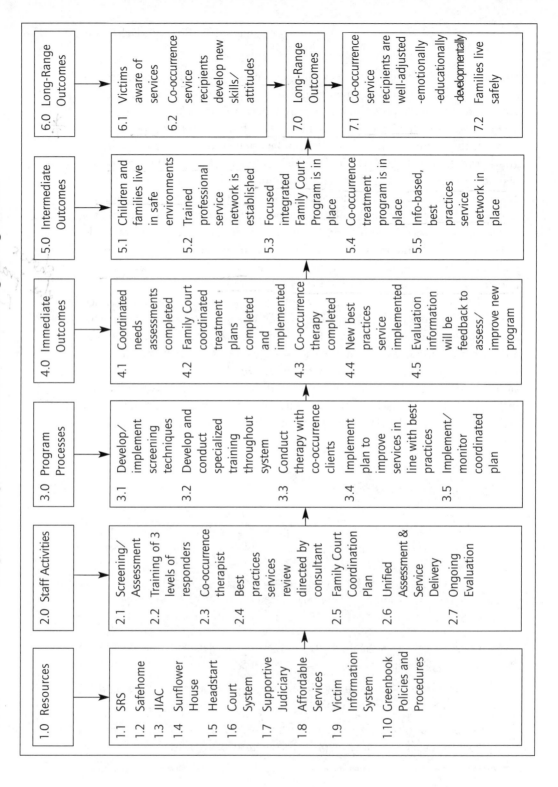

PLM #8

Non-Custodial Parent Program Logic Model

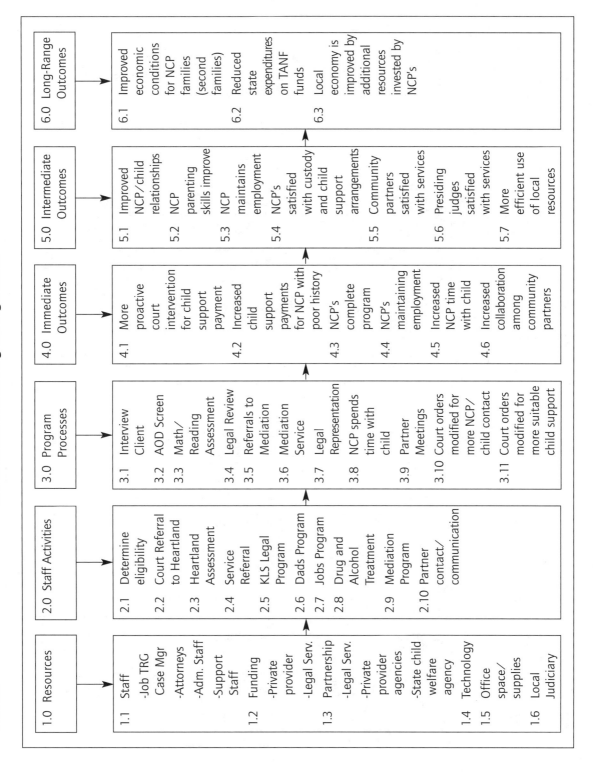

1.0 Resources	2.0 Staff Activities	3.0 Program Processes	4.0 Immediate Outcomes	5.0 Intermediate Outcomes	6.0 Long-Range Outcomes
1.1 Staff -Job TRG Case Mgr -Attorneys -Adm. Staff -Support Staff	2.1 Determine eligibility	3.1 Interview Client	4.1 More proactive court intervention for child support payment	5.1 Improved NCP/child relationships	6.1 Improved economic conditions for NCP families (second families)
1.2 Funding -Private provider -Legal Serv.	2.2 Court Referral to Heartland	3.2 AOD Screen	4.2 Increased child support payments for NCP with poor history	5.2 NCP parenting skills improve	6.2 Reduced state expenditures on TANF funds
1.3 Partnership -Legal Serv. -Private provider agencies -State child welfare agency	2.3 Heartland Assessment	3.3 Math/Reading Assessment	4.3 NCP's complete program	5.3 NCP maintains employment	6.3 Local economy is improved by additional resources invested by NCP's
1.4 Technology	2.4 Service Referral	3.4 Legal Review	4.4 NCP's maintaining employment	5.4 NCP's satisfied with custody and child support arrangements	
1.5 Office space/supplies	2.5 KLS Legal Program	3.5 Referrals to Mediation	4.5 Increased NCP time with child	5.5 Community partners satisfied with services	
1.6 Local Judiciary	2.6 Dads Program	3.6 Mediation Service	4.6 Increased collaboration among community partners	5.6 Presiding judges satisfied with services	
	2.7 Jobs Program	3.7 Legal Representation		5.7 More efficient use of local resources	
	2.8 Drug and Alcohol Treatment	3.8 NCP spends time with child			
	2.9 Mediation Program	3.9 Partner Meetings			
	2.10 Partner contact/communication	3.10 Court orders modified for more NCP/child contact			
		3.11 Court orders modified for more suitable child support			

PLM #9

Hospice Program Logic Model

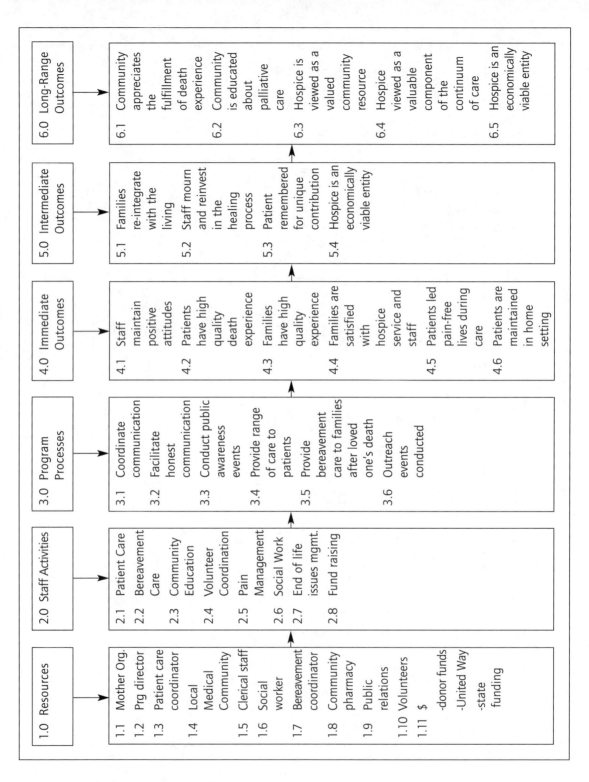

1.0 Resources	2.0 Staff Activities	3.0 Program Processes	4.0 Immediate Outcomes	5.0 Intermediate Outcomes	6.0 Long-Range Outcomes
1.1 Mother Org.	2.1 Patient Care	3.1 Coordinate communication	4.1 Staff maintain positive attitudes	5.1 Families re-integrate with the living	6.1 Community appreciates the fulfillment of death experience
1.2 Prg director	2.2 Bereavement Care	3.2 Facilitate honest communication	4.2 Patients have high quality death experience	5.2 Staff mourn and reinvest in the healing process	6.2 Community is educated about palliative care
1.3 Patient care coordinator	2.3 Community Education	3.3 Conduct public awareness events	4.3 Families have high quality experience	5.3 Patient remembered for unique contribution	6.3 Hospice is viewed as a valued community resource
1.4 Local Medical Community	2.4 Volunteer Coordination	3.4 Provide range of care to patients	4.4 Families are satisfied with hospice service and staff	5.4 Hospice is an economically viable entity	6.4 Hospice viewed as a valuable component of the continuum of care
1.5 Clerical staff	2.5 Pain Management	3.5 Provide bereavement care to families after loved one's death	4.5 Patients led pain-free lives during care		6.5 Hospice is an economically viable entity
1.6 Social worker	2.6 Social Work	3.6 Outreach events conducted	4.6 Patients are maintained in home setting		
1.7 Bereavement coordinator	2.7 End of life issues mgmt.				
1.8 Community pharmacy	2.8 Fund raising				
1.9 Public relations					
1.10 Volunteers					
1.11 $ -donor funds -United Way -state funding					

This chapter has illustrated a process for taking on the first task in most evaluation activities; that is, getting the stakeholders to specify the program. Through the use of program logic models, the initial task is completed in a manner that facilitates other key evaluation activities: a clear vision is forwarded and supported; the design of the program is scrutinized from a fresh point of view; an evaluation plan can be laid out with a focus toward program outcomes; and a tool is in place to use for promoting the program to internal and external constituents as well as possible funding sources.

REVIEW AND REFLECT

Big Ideas

• Program evaluation questions and designs need to be considered and developed within an informed concept of an existing program.

• Program logic models provide a great opportunity to flesh out varying perspectives, combine a range of ideas, and synthesize those program notions into an agreed-upon model.

• Program logic models can be used to critique existing theories about program function/operation, succinctly promote programs to diverse constituencies, and identify program information needs that drive evaluation designs.

Discussion Questions

• How can practitioners working with the same program have different points of view about its functioning?

• Why is it necessary to have multiple points of view when developing a program logic model?

• What was one of the benefits of the logic models over the traditional model of evaluation?

• How can a program logic model be used to critique an existing program?

• How do the authors suggest a program logic model is used to develop a list of information needs?

Activities

• Pick one of the models and identify the different viewpoints that may be associated with that program.

• Pick one of the models listed in the chapter. Identify the clearest aspects of the model, then the vaguest, and then decide if you think the model as proposed is actually feasible.

• A more traditional approach to program evaluation would be to develop a research question based on the opinion of a researcher and an upper-level administrator. Contrast and compare this model with the approach to developing information needs based on a logic model. What are the potential benefits and drawback of each approach? If you were king or queen of a specific evaluation project, which option would you choose and why?

Resources

• Center for What Works. (n.d.). *Performance measurement toolkit for nonprofits and funders.* Retrieved from http://www.whatworks.org/display common.cfm?an=1&subarticlenbr=13%20

• Hatry, H. P., Morley, E., Rossman, S. B., & Wholey, J. S. (2003, May). *How federal programs use outcome information: Opportunities for federal managers.* Retrieved from Urban Institute: http://www.urban.org/publications/ url.cfm?ID=1000484

• James Irvine Foundation. (n.d.). *Evaluation: Tools and resources.* Retrieved from http://www.irvine.org/evaluation/tools-and-resources

• McNamara, C. (1997–2008). *Basic guide to outcomes-based evaluation for non-profit organizations with limited resources.* (Adapted from: *Field guide to nonprofit program design, marketing and evaluation.*) Retrieved from http://www.managementhelp.org/evaluatn/outcomes.htm

• United Way. (n.d.). *Outcome Measurement Resource Network.* Retrieved from http://www.liveunited.org/outcomes/index.cfm?

• W. K. Kellogg Foundation. (n.d.). *Evaluation toolkit.* Retrieved from http://wkkf.org/Default.aspx?tabid=90&CID=281&ItemID=2810002& NID=2820002&LanguageID=0

CHAPTER 8

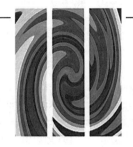

Program Description

Evaluation Designs Using
Available Information

What am I going to tell the board? I have no information
that will reflect how our programs are doing!

The research design content covered in most social work program evaluation courses ranges from descriptive studies to experimental and quasi-
experimental designs to single-subject approaches. Although it is prudent for
these courses to be taught from a survey perspective that covers the gamut of
possible research designs, it is our perspective that the vast majorities of

evaluation projects are descriptive in nature and rely on existing data sources. The more sophisticated designs are labor-intensive and require higher levels of research design expertise that are not practical in many agency settings. Additionally, the implementation of most group designs requires close research project supervision and monitoring to maintain the integrity of the study. Finally, the requisite oversights for these studies warrant resources that are uncharacteristic of most agency studies.

Studies of these types also often present ethical controversies to agency practitioners. The research design may require a control group that is often perceived as depriving individuals of services. In turn, program evaluators argue that the most appropriate way to assess the effectiveness of the program is to employ this type of methodological rigor. Consequently, these types of designs are complex and difficult to sell in agency-based projects and are not employed frequently. The details of these challenges and some possible strategies for implementing this type of research design are described in Chapter 10 (Evaluation Design: Group Designs and Methods).

This chapter describes what we feel are more common evaluations; those methods that are conducted without interfering with the service process. These types of evaluations do not employ complex research designs; the evaluators and relevant program staff usually identify the key information needed within the context of the service and develop methods for collecting that data. These evaluations have often been referred to as naturalistic evaluations (Posavac & Carey, 2007).

Rehr (2001) discusses the barriers of experimental and group designs from the perspective of an administrative and clinical practitioner. Additionally, she references Schön's (1983) work related to reflection in action. Agency-based practitioners have ongoing questions related to their interests in improving service. Not only do group designs require intrusion into service; their implementation, as stated, requires extremely complex management. Rehr prefers the untapped potential of existing data sources within the agency. Epstein (2001) elaborates about evaluation models that rely on existing data sources. He distinguishes between research-based practice (RBP) and practice-based research (PBR). While both approaches seek to advance the understanding of service delivery, their orientations are very distinct. In the former, research methods are fundamental. In the latter, the practice setting is the centerpiece, and evaluative activity is conducted in a manner that is complementary to service processes and activities.

The evaluation design approach centering on the logic model in the preceding chapter is definitely consistent with naturalistic and PBR models where the program is the focus and the evaluation evolves with the program and its relative information needs in mind. These types of evaluation often draw on available data sources that are collected for other purposes, clinical or administrative.

Checking Vitals

In research-based practice (RBP), research methods are fundamental. In practice-based research (PBR), the practice setting is the centerpiece, and evaluative activity is conducted in a manner that is complementary to service processes and activities (Epstein, 2001).

Often, the first reaction of an evaluation team is to engage in some type of original data collection as they have been taught in their research and evaluation courses. Examples might include a survey of consumers or a focus group with community constituents. If an evaluation team is considering conducting some original data collection, they can either adapt an existing instrument or develop their own. While the development and implementation of survey instruments is often useful, there are many challenges associated with finding a suitable match between an existing survey and the actual information need (Epstein, 2001). "Growing their own" instrument, developing a customized measurement tool specific to a particular information need, may fit the current information needs more closely, but this a lengthy and complex process. Before taking on this endeavor, it is prudent for evaluators and practitioners to turn to the agency's existing data sources.

Most agencies are likely to collect information for other purposes that have great value for evaluation. These sources of data should be examined and exploited prior to entertaining new data collection. Two primary questions should be addressed in the early stages of evaluation design: (1) What are the key information needs? and (2) Do available sources of data exist to address these information needs? The first question can be addressed by having an open discussion focused on the vital information needed to manage the program; this can easily be centered on the logic model as exemplified in Chapter 7 (Program Definition: Using Program Logic Models to Develop a Common Vision). The second question is the centerpiece of this chapter. This discussion will start with some ideas for identifying existing sources of information and some consideration of possible data sources.

Checking Vitals

Evaluators and practitioners must identify existing agency data sources before adapting or developing a new instrument.

Two primary questions should be addressed in the beginning stages of the evaluation process:

What are the key information needs?

Do available sources of data exist to address these information needs?

TAKING INVENTORY OF AVAILABLE DATA SOURCES

Available data sources are numerous and can be very rich. Our experience consistently indicates that the utility of in-house data is often underestimated. One way to heighten the awareness of different sources of available information is to spend some time identifying and describing different possibilities. This type of consciousness-raising about existing agency data can often uncover unknown and viable information.

Sources of data can be divided into three groups: (1) systematically gathered data; (2) treatment documentation; and (3) clinical/administrative judgment (see Table 8.1). *Systematically gathered data* covers a wide range of information that

Table 8.1   Available Data Sources

Source	Description	Examples
Systematically gathered data	Information that is routinely collected on an ongoing basis.	Billing records, which may include client contact hours, salary data from personnel data systems, and client scores on a clinical instrument.
Treatment documentation	Information stored in case files.	Assessments, service plans, case notes, social histories, psychiatric or psychological evaluations.
Clinical/ administrative judgment	Information acquired by observing the service delivery process on a regular basis.	Family worker insights on the supportiveness of job duties related to family contacts, supervisor impressions on treatment team commitment to family-oriented practice.

is currently being collected in the agency in an ongoing fashion to meet existing needs. This can include personnel information (staff qualifications, salaries, etc.); accounting data (which often includes billing records that can be used to track client contacts); and data that is stored in clinical, quality, or other information systems. Systematically gathered information is often stored in automated information systems. While many of these have an administrative focus, it is common for agencies to maintain additional systems intended to inform clinical practice or to respond to specific contractual requirements for quality assurance purposes. The data stored in these entities can be extremely valuable in evaluation projects. Another advantage of this source of data is that it is typically stored in some type of electronic format, such as a spreadsheet or database application, where it can be cleaned, manipulated, or analyzed for the evaluation project. In short, data entry may not be needed for this source of data.

Checking Vitals

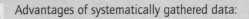

Advantages of systematically gathered data:

Systematically gathered information is often stored in automated information systems, and this can be extremely valuable in evaluation projects.

The source of data is typically stored in an electronic format, a spreadsheet, or database application, which allows it to be cleaned, manipulated, or analyzed for the evaluation project.

Treatment documentation includes a wealth of valuable data that is usually stored and routinely updated in the case files. This includes vital pieces of information often referred to as routine paperwork (initial assessment and ongoing service planning documentation, social histories, discharge reports, incident reports, etc.). Critical information about the operation of the program almost always resides in the case files. Although effort is usually required to retrieve and process this source of information, such resources are minimal when compared with original data collection efforts, but the potential payoffs are high.

Checking Vitals

Advantages of treatment documentation:

Critical information about the operation of the program almost always resides in the case files and can be used in the evaluation process.

A third source of information—*clinical and/or administrative judgment*—is often ignored in the evaluation process because of its idiosyncratic and personalized nature. Our experience is that judgments of this type are prevalent, and it serves all parties to address this source of information in a purposeful and open manner. Clinical and administrative judgment is informed by practice wisdom that has been gleaned from observing agency or service practices. While some scholars have developed more exclusive and rigorous definitions that include knowledge of practice methods, practice experience, or their integration (Dybicz, 2004; Klein & Bloom, 1995), this definition is purposefully conceived to be inclusive of multiple forms of knowledge and observation but exclusive to those derived from intimate exposure to agency practice.

This last category is tricky to put your arms around, but it is usually working in the minds of those who are interpreting data and making decisions, so we have found it useful to acknowledge this source of data and encourage practitioners to recognize this information and talk about it openly as part of the process. Program evaluations often focus on key program processes and, although clinical/administrative judgment is not necessarily documented in the routine collection of that data, it often has a latent and powerful influence on the interpretation of information and should not be summarily dismissed. It is not only a valuable source of insight; oftentimes practitioners are making judgments based on this type of information, and it is more helpful to openly bring that information into the light and include it openly in discussions about program performance.

For example, reimbursement, program management, and supervisory attention are customarily focused on the number of contacts and the amount of time direct service staff spend with clients and consumers. Although there is usually reasonable quantitative data around the number or length of contacts made by each worker, the discussion of this process usually goes deeper into the organizational structure, the styles of workers and managers, and various work routines. It is helpful not only to give practitioners permission to consider this information but to encourage them to examine different aspects and bring them forward for discussion. Obviously, this process requires some clear arrangements about the process for identifying and considering this information. Hopefully, some examples from our practice will help to highlight the various sources of data as well as the operation of those data sources.

Checking Vitals

Advantages of clinical/administrative judgment:

It often has a latent and powerful influence on the interpretation of information.

It is a valuable source of insight. Practitioners are often making judgments based on this type of information; it is more helpful to openly bring that information into the light and include it openly in discussions about program performance.

USING AVAILABLE DATA SOURCES TO EVALUATE PROGRAMS

Agencies can take a variety of different approaches to using available data sources to evaluate and assess program performance. The following examples will provide an overview of the variety of different questions, agency circumstances, and data sources that can be utilized by exploiting existing data sources.

Examining a Special Interest Question

In this example, an agency was trying to figure out the level of implementation of the aftercare service. Multiple sources of data were used to get to the bottom of this mystery. The administrative and direct service staff at a residential facility for delinquent children were curious about the discrepant findings (from multiple sources of data) surrounding the prevalence of sexual abuse events in their clientele's history. Family contact sheets (systematically collected data) were reporting that aftercare contacts were taking place. Every youth and his or her family was receiving aftercare contacts; most were receiving multiple contacts addressing aftercare. Conversely, when clinical supervisors and program managers discussed the aftercare program, they were somewhat sure that the implementation was sporadic. The program staff and clinical supervisors consulted with the evaluation department, and a small-scale study was conducted using the case files.

The agency selected a small sample of case files (treatment documentation) and then examined the process notes (which described the aftercare contacts). A review of these discussions determined that typically these contacts occurred on the grounds of the facility and not in the home. Additionally, the discussion focused more directly on the child's behavior in the facility. For example, if the child was having a difficulty in the program, the worker would talk with the family about the need for this behavior to stop. If the behavior was not curtailed, the youth would not get home visits. This behavior was also cast as unacceptable to a youth who would eventually be residing in the community, as it would most likely impact the youth's success. In short, both the location and the focus of the contacts were not squarely related to the youth's eventual transition to life in the community.

The clinical supervisors were able to address this issue in two specific ways. They held a training session that reinforced the importance of aftercare and the importance of this intervention to generally occur in the youth's intended home placement at discharge. Additionally, they also highlighted the need to target aftercare energy on the youth's transition to community life as opposed to life in the facility. The program managers reinforced these principles on a daily basis and in supervisory sessions with clinical supervisors. The aftercare contacts began to increase and the proceedings related to each contact were more in the spirit of the original intent. In this example, systematically gathered information provided a perspective that was challenged by the clinical/administrative judgment. An analysis of treatment documentation was used to provide a more complete assessment of what was occurring while confirming the suppositions presented by practice wisdom. The comparing and contrasting of the multiple data sources are often referred to as triangulation (Patton, 2002, p. 93).

Combining Information Sources Across Agencies

After significant statewide budget cuts, a multi-service children and family service agency was examining their entire approach to treating young men and women. One of the principal goals of the agency was for the children in the client families to lead a "legal" lifestyle. As a response, the agency conducted a major study to determine which and how many of their clients eventually ended up in prison as adults. Obviously, this was seen as a key indicator of program performance.

The agency had an extensive clinical information system where they stored a significant amount of information about the clients receiving services (systematically gathered data). However, the agency did not have information available about the eventual imprisonment of their clients. The agency drew on sympathetic colleagues in the adult corrections department to obtain this information.

At the initial meeting to discuss the project, one of us came to the meeting equipped with volumes of computer printouts about hundreds of clients and former clients. The department of corrections sympathizer reported that the information was not automated and that all the names would have to be located manually in a mainframe computer system that did not have a flexible reporting or data extraction facility. After some negotiation, the two parties agreed to focus the study on two cohorts who left the juvenile facility in different years.

The merging of this data and its subsequent analyses led to the identification of a series of factors and non-factors that related to eventual imprisonment. One of the most surprising findings was that the type of service or level of success in the service did not seem to impact eventual imprisonment. For example, youth who successfully completed the residential program did not run a higher risk of imprisonment than youth who did not successfully complete the program. A statistical model identified the following high-risk profile: African American youth with two or more felonies at intake, who did not go to a home setting upon release, were the most likely to be imprisoned at some point after their release. In response to this, the program invested efforts in aftercare services that would support youth in the home communities and support the increased likelihood of home placement and investigate case management services for their clients (Kapp, Schwartz, & Epstein, 1994; Schwartz, Kapp, & Overstreet, 1994).

USING TREATMENT DOCUMENTATION DATA TO STUDY CLIENT TERMINATION

This research project fully exploits the value of treatment documentation to investigate the ways that client termination operates in an adolescent outpatient mental health service program. Epstein and colleagues have been instrumental in refining an approach to practice research that relies on the essentially untapped information in case files to address critical questions about service delivery. Practitioners develop customized research instruments to extract critical information from the case files related to a vital practice issue. The instruments are used to collect data from case files that inform the respective research questions. In addition to refining this process, efforts are made to assess the validity and reliability of these techniques (Epstein, 2001; Epstein & Blumenfield, 2001; Epstein, Zilberfein, & Snyder, 1997).

In this example, a practitioner in an out-patient adolescent center, interested in addressing the gap of information about termination in clinical settings with younger service recipients, designed and conducted a study exploiting case file information. A research tool designed to collect available data from case files was developed and tested targeting some key issues in client termination with adolescents. Some intriguing information was acquired about the termination process.

First of all, in about two-thirds of the cases there was no "acknowledged termination." In addition, clients who might be viewed as more challenging (in denial about their circumstances, less motivated, and more removed from the therapeutic process) were more likely to have a termination experience. These findings raised serious questions about the prevalence of this accepted component of the clinical process. The notion of clinical experiences that neatly begin and end was not supported by this project. Mirabito (2001) proposes a more "open-door" approach to these services, which may be more consistent with the episodic crisis endemic to this developmental stage. This example and other works using this approach illustrate the immense power of exploiting existing treatment documentation to conduct insightful research about the service delivery process.

Checking Vitals

Using treatment documentation to address critical questions about service delivery:

It allows the evaluator or practitioner to conduct insightful research about the service delivery process.

Practitioners develop customized research instruments to extract information from the case files.

The instruments are used to collect data from case files that inform the respective research question.

Efforts are made to assess the validity and reliability of these techniques.

USING ESTABLISHED INFORMATION SYSTEMS
AS DATA SOURCES FOR EVALUATIONS

As we have been discussing, most agencies operate and maintain information systems for a variety of uses from clinical to administrative. Although these data systems often generate standardized reports, many important evaluation questions cannot be answered by a report from these systems. Key service delivery questions can often be addressed by creating datasets from the information systems and organizing them around specific questions.

Although information systems may hold the appropriate data to examine critical service questions, these systems usually are not equipped for data analysis. Information systems are usually managed with database software that is ideal for managing the entry, storage, and reporting of key data elements. Although these software packages typically include the ability to make inquiries of the data within the system, historically those capabilities have been limited. Although these reporting and analysis facilities within database software packages are improving, many program evaluation questions are more comprehensively examined by constructing data files that are organized appropriately for specific service delivery questions.

Some efforts need to be made to organize the data in a manner that allows for the most complete treatment of the evaluation question. In a fashion very similar to the discussion of information needs centered on the logic model, the evaluation team needs to spend time considering the questions as clearly as possible and plotting a strategy for gathering the data from the various sources in a manner that exploits the data sources with the question in mind. Elements of this discussion obviously include a clear delineation of the exact data needed. The timing of the data needs to be considered with the overall purpose of the analysis in mind. In some cases, it may be important to construct a dataset that includes client outcome at the end of the service, along with treatment process data. This would allow for some data analysis that addresses both the delivery of services and the impact of the service on outcome. So, the defining parameters for the dataset may be clients who completed services within specific time intervals. Some examples of these different strategies will be illustrated in the upcoming section.

In other cases, the outcome data may not be central to the question. Under these circumstances, it may be acceptable to construct a data file using the most recent year's service data. A file like this would allow data analysis that looks specifically at service delivery without looking at client outcomes, more specifically, at client contacts over the last calendar year for the entire agency. While data systems include a wealth of data, it is critical to develop succinct evaluation questions prior to investing significant time in the laborious task of file construction. Proper planning can significantly increase the rate of return on the investment of time in collecting and organizing this data.

Checking Vitals

Efforts need to be made to organize the data in a manner that allows for the most complete treatment of the evaluation question.

The evaluation team needs to spend time considering the questions as clearly as possible and plotting a strategy for gathering the data from the various sources.

The timing of the data needs to be considered with the overall purpose of the analysis in mind.

In some cases, the evaluation team may use data from different information systems. In this case, efforts need to be made to make sure the data are compatible. Data on demographics may be organized around individual clients, and service contact data may be organized around the service event. These differences could be remedied by reconstructing the data to reflect the total service contacts of an individual client. Another consideration when merging data sources is the compatibility across systems. One system may have an information system-specific identifier, while another may use social security numbers. In order to get the data across systems to merge on the right individuals, common identification codes must be located or constructed. Once the data file is completed, the data can then be analyzed with one of many statistical software packages that are well suited to this type of comprehensive analysis.

Checking Vitals

Considerations when utilizing and merging data:

Make sure the data are compatible.

Determine whether there is compatibility across systems.

Identification codes can be located or constructed when incompatibility exists.

Once the data file is completed, the data can then be analyzed with one of many statistical software packages that are well suited to this type of comprehensive analysis.

The following are some specific examples of the strategic construction of data from information systems to meet specific needs. In one example, a family service agency for delinquent youth managed a comprehensive information system for direct service staff and administrative staff. Clinical supervisors collected and used family contact data to support the family therapists' skill development. The supervisor and therapist could examine patterns of client contact, such as length and number of sessions, as well as the relationship between these contacts and client characteristics, race, family type, and so forth. This agency also constructed data files annually that could be used to conduct statistical analyses to investigate specific service questions. When these files were constructed, the family contact data—which was summarized for each client—was combined with demographic, service history, and outcome data. These data files were used continuously to conduct data analysis directed at a variety of service questions (Kapp & Grasso, 1993). For example, different patterns of family therapy contacts with delinquent youth and their families were considered with an interest in the most effective and efficient patterns. The results showed that face-to-face contacts were the most effective, but phone contacts also had a positive impact on home placement upon release (Savas, Epstein, & Grasso, 1993).

In another example, a team of evaluators wanted to determine the impact of different demographic profiles and services on the outcome of youth in a statewide mental health system. The outcomes included both consumer satisfaction and more traditional outcome data related to school performance and home placement. In this case, the data came from different places in separate large state information systems and research projects: The demographic and outcome data came from statewide information and were used for a variety of contractual and service monitoring purposes; the service data was collected in a Medicaid billing system; and consumer satisfaction was managed in its own system. The structuring of this dataset proved to be very complicated. The service data needed to be reorganized around individual youth recipients and not the event. Identifiers had to be constructed across the system, based on codes that included date of birth and other common data elements. Finally, a time frame had to be established to locate data for a certain group of youth, based on these common pieces of data.

Once the dataset was constructed, this data file presented the evaluation team with the opportunity to use statistical modeling programs to examine the service experience of children in the state's mental health system. A model was constructed that linked age with worker and overall satisfaction, which in turn were linked with the youth's perceived success. Service intensity was also linked to perceived success. Ultimately, perceived success was tied to positive outcomes for the child. This model set the stage for critical discussion about aspects of the service process and methods for supporting critical aspects of this path toward more effective services (Cheon & Kapp, 2007). Proper planning can be combined with technical ability to exploit data from information systems to address crucial evaluation questions.

OTHER TOOLS FOR APPLYING EXISTING DATA SOURCES IN EVALUATION

Agencies also have mechanisms to organize existing information in a format that is more conducive to addressing questions about service effectiveness. These are referred to as an ongoing monitoring system (OMS). This evaluation tool is designed to facilitate the use of data that is available but not necessarily organized in a manner that facilitates the examination of a program's operation or performance.

Ongoing monitoring systems are usually designed to give an organization more immediate access to key pieces of program performance data. An OMS can optimize key pieces of information from a variety of places for contractual reporting or other administrative purposes. For example, information could come from client files; or an OMS could include treatment documentation or the rate at which key reports are completed. Staff could enter specific data into an OMS, such as client contacts and number and length of sessions. Other support functions in an organization could collect specific data that contributes to an OMS. In some cases, staff are devoted to collecting certain data and putting it into an OMS. The concept of an OMS is the organization of available data in a format to answer questions about program performance.

Typically, a monitoring system includes pieces of information that would be more descriptive and less in-depth than a traditional evaluation (Poister, 2004). One of the key goals of an OMS is reporting information on a timely basis and organizing the information in a manner that would be useful to specific users. For example, a manager would get information about the treatment teams that he or she supervises. Ongoing monitoring systems usually consume significant resources to collect and manage the information while simultaneously generating and distributing reports. Despite the allocation of resources to undergo this task, the use of this data is often very prescriptive. It is rare that the information as packaged in an OMS will be germane to service issues that arise. The potential data in its original form often has difficulties with timeliness and relevance. However, when organized and fed back in a more useful manner, the information can be packaged and reported in a manner that is accessible and valuable.

Checking Vitals

Ongoing monitoring systems (OMS) are usually designed to give an organization more immediate access to key pieces of program performance data.

An OMS can optimize key pieces of information from a variety of places for contractual reporting or other administrative purposes.

One of the key goals of an OMS is reporting information on a timely basis and organizing the information in a manner that would be useful to specific users.

The columns of the program logic model (see Chapter 7) can be examined using data from an OMS. Resource data from an OMS can help managers determine the availability of resources needed to operate the program and inform planning processes. Program process information, a component of the aforementioned logic models, from an OMS can be used to evaluate the implementation of service delivery. Additionally, service impact can be assessed using outcome data from an ongoing monitoring system.

Sometimes OMSs are run by evaluation teams, who invest time in organizing the data for their specific purposes. More recently, software applications have been developed to manage data from large organizations, such as a state social service provider. These applications allow standard and custom report writing capabilities. Data from these large-scale information systems are nearly inaccessible. The systems are often operated on mainframe systems, and their purpose is to generate reports that are used for restricted purposes, such as billing for service or generating canned reports for various types of contractual monitoring.

The report generating applications identify key pieces of data that have relevance for program evaluation. Specific database tables are created to reflect those key data. These tables are then populated with data from the large databases, making the data more easily accessible. Using spreadsheet software that is commonly available and manageable, agency staff can then generate both standard and customized reports. Standard reports might include client profiles, service utilization, or key outcome reports; while custom reports can focus on either process or outcome data, which can be presented over a specified time span by a given level of the organization, such as a program, a supervisor, or a specific worker (Marty & Barkett, 2002; Moore & Press, 2002).

Checking Vitals

Resource data from an OMS can help managers determine the availability of resources needed to operate the program and inform planning processes.

Program process information, a component of the logic models, from an OMS can be used to evaluate the implementation of service delivery.

Service impact can be assessed using outcome data from an ongoing monitoring system.

Assessing Data Quality Using Existing Data Sources

Although the data drawn from existing sources may be easier to access than engaging in an original data collection process, it is risky to make any assumptions about the quality of the data. Efforts need to be made to assess the quality of the data and resolve as many of the issues as possible prior to conducting any analysis. While there are no panaceas for attending to the quality of these data, it is essential that some processes be utilized to verify the data quality. Also, agency staff need to be critical participants in the effort. Agency personnel have the invaluable insights needed about the collection, processing, and overall context of the internal sources of data to assess its quality and to develop plans to correct any difficulties. Additionally, the open process of auditing the quality of the data lends credibility to the data in the eyes of the eventual users of the data. Finally, the active process of assessing data quality with agency partners helps to build investment in the evaluation. Chapter 9 (Evaluation Design: Options for Supporting the Use of Information) will describe some methods for integrating agency personnel into the data integrity process and all other parts of the evaluation process. In this discussion, the emphasis will be on the more technical aspects of the process.

In some cases, the data collected from existing data sources may have systematic biases built in during the data collection process. A programming glitch may exist in the data that will result in nonsensical values. For example, one agency used the number of times a youth had been placed in the facility as a key piece of the unique identifier. It was never anticipated that some youth would be placed in the facility on more than nine occasions. This was problematic given the single column (1–9) assigned to this field.

Oftentimes, practitioners are asked to collect data that seems in their eyes to be detached from practice. For example, one state information system collected information about monthly youth foster care visits. It was common knowledge that supervisory wrath would pursue those who did not complete this field monthly. So workers filled the form out, but this information had no relationship to actual contact with youth in foster care. Time studies are also completed for a variety of reasons. While this data has potential for assessing the amount of time devoted to client contact versus other activities, such studies are completed by staff with an eye toward compliance and usually do not represent the practitioners' routine. Consequently, this data is problematic for evaluative purposes. Only agency staff can pass these kinds of judgments on data quality, and obviously without their point of view some critical mistakes could be made about the choice and eventual use of data sources.

To get a better sense of the accuracy of the various existing data sources, it is essential to audit both the data and the data collection process. Agency staff is a critical element of both processes. An audit of the process is simply a conversation with those intimately familiar with the way the data is collected. In these discussions, the goal is to try to get the staff to think about biases built into the process that would interfere with the accuracy of the data. When data is collected for seemingly no particular purpose, or at least the purpose is unclear to practitioners, busy practitioners often enter data that fills a need for compliance that does not reflect the service situation. On the other hand, the examination of the process may highlight factors that actually contribute to the quality of the data, such as using this data for other vital purposes like supervision or billing. Before making a decision to use one of the many data sources, these aspects of the data collection process need to be considered.

The other side of auditing the data is testing the data for completion and accuracy. Agency staff can also provide vital support in a consultative role. This process may take some intensive study of the data. Agency personnel can help to verify valid data ranges and point out possible data collection flaws that have the potential to impact the quality of the data. It is acceptable for evaluation staff or other technical types to conduct this sort of activity with consultative supports from agency staff.

Checking Vitals

It is essential to audit both the data and the data collection process. Agency staff is a critical element of both processes.

The goal of the audit is to try to get the staff to think about biases built into the process that would interfere with the accuracy of the data.

One critical issue is simply the completeness of the data. The focus of this effort is to make sure all of the fields in the file are complete. Typically, the raw data is listed in a printed or electronic file by specific fields or variables. For example, all the individual variables for date of birth are displayed and inspected to make sure the data is present and is applicable. If you are working with a population of juveniles, then the range of these data would be scrutinized to make sure none of the participants are over 18 or under the age of 10.

Additionally, it is vital to examine the accuracy of the data. In some cases, you may be able to verify all of the fields, but usually the size of the dataset requires some type of sampling for this activity. To accomplish this, take a sample of 20 to 25 cases and verify the information in their records to the degree possible. The verification can be conducted using ancillary sources of data like the case file or the actual staff person who worked directly with the individual.

Demographic, background, service, and outcome information can usually be substantiated by cross-checking the file or with direct service staff associated with respective cases. A small sample will provide a reasonable estimate of the dataset's accuracy. Oftentimes the problems with data can be resolved (Hatry, 2004). Records with incomplete data can be removed. Efforts can be made to retrieve the missing data or to correct the erroneous information.

In consultation with the evaluation team, some decisions need to be made about acceptable levels of error. For example, more tolerance for error may be adequate in a descriptive study that is attempting to identify client needs (a more general topic). However, in an evaluative study where population subgroups are going to be examined, there may be less comfort with error. The task of cross-validating data does not need to be performed by practitioners. It is feasible to train a part-time person to assist with this task under a reasonable amount of supervision.

Checking Vitals

One critical issue is the completeness of the data and making sure all of the fields in the file are complete.

It is vital to examine the accuracy of the data.

In consultation with the evaluation team, some decisions need to be made about acceptable levels of error.

Much of evaluation work is completed using existing data sources within organizations of varying sizes. This chapter has provided some guidance for examining the different sources along with examples and some ideas for evaluating their accuracy. It should be clear that significant and important evaluative work can be conducted by exploiting the power of existing agency data.

REVIEW AND REFLECT

Big Ideas

- Critical evaluation questions can be credibly addressed by relying on data that resides in the various information systems in an agency.

- Sources of data can be divided into three groups: (1) systematically gathered data; (2) treatment documentation; and (3) clinical/administrative judgment.

- These data sources can be used individually, in combination with each other, and across agencies to provide credible and useful evaluation information.

Discussion Questions

- List, describe, and provide an example of each of the types of data sources.

- How can the various types of data be used to complement each other?

- Describe the process of using data sources across agencies and list some of the challenges.

- What are the pros and cons of existing information systems to address evaluation questions?

- Why is it important to conduct some type of audit of the data from internal information systems?

Activities

- What are some of the strengths and weaknesses of each of the different types of data sources?

- Create a list of all the various types of data sources organized by the three categories.

- Pick a project list of enumerated examples of evaluation projects using existing data. Describe what you like about the project and the parts of the project that give you cause for concern.

Resources

- Hatry, H. P., Cowan, J., & Hendricks, M. (2004, March). *Analyzing outcome information: Getting the most from data.* Retrieved from Urban Institute: http://www.urban.org/publications/310973.html

- Hatry, H., Cowan, J., Weiner, K., & Lampkin, L. (2003, June). *Developing community-wide outcome indicators for specific services.* Retrieved from Urban Institute: http://www.urban.org/publications/310813.html

- Morley, E., & Lampkin, L. (2004, July). *Using outcome information: Making data pay off.* Retrieved from Urban Institute: http://www.urban.org/url.cfm?ID=311040

CHAPTER 9

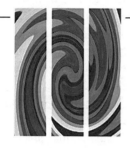

Evaluation Design

Options for Supporting the Use of Information

When Bob, the evaluator, asked his favorite program administrator
what factors influenced his decision making, he was given quite a list.

Evaluation practitioners can invest a lot of time and energy in the technical
aspects of various evaluation research methods. However, it is equally
important to invest in designing and implementing plans to support and promote the use of evaluation information in program decisions and improvement

efforts. While we are not suggesting that the quality of the information is secondary, our experience tells us that regardless of the quality of the evaluation findings, if agency staff is not given adequate support that targets how to use the findings (it is more than just telling how to use it), it is unlikely that the insights gained from the evaluation will influence practice. Agencies are typically inexperienced in the evaluation process, especially in aspects associated with the use of information and decision making. The use of information is rarely driven solely by the quality of the evaluation work; leadership, previous practices, and/or an array of political factors may also be important elements. As a result, it is important for the plan to support agency staff in the use of information needs to accommodate those factors. To be clear, evaluations must be conducted in a manner that provide credible information; however, there also must be a plan to support the *use* of the information. This chapter provides some concrete steps and techniques for evaluators to enhance the likelihood that their findings will influence the operation of the program and improve services.

Historically, the rates of evaluation utilization are very low (Cousins & Leawood, 1986; Taut & Alkin, 2003). Oftentimes, evaluation team members spend their energy on the planning and implementation of the actual evaluation and underestimate the importance of supporting the use of information. Developing a context where evaluation findings are utilized is a complex endeavor.

There has been some significant discussion about different aspects of the utilization process. Patton (1997), in his seminal work on evaluation utilization, is emphatic about investing in the users of the information, which he calls the personal factor. Others have acknowledged the collaborative nature of the evaluation process (Bell, 2004; McNeese, 2004).

In some cases, it is difficult to separate working with evaluation consumers and organizational development work (McClintock, 2004). As we have addressed in this book, the discussion reaches beyond evaluation methods into program operations and the ways services are supported in the agency. Efforts related to information utilization have implications for the agency's mission. Hodges and Hernandez (1999) have found information usage discussions linked closely to an assessment of the agency's client-centeredness. Sluyter (1998) argues that a discussion of information utilization naturally extends to a broader discussion of the importance of service improvement to the agency's leadership.

A variety of ideas have been forwarded to try to promote the use of evaluation findings. Kopczynski and Pritchard (2004) have suggested that an agency volunteer take on the responsibility of facilitating evaluation usage. Patton (1997) offers a set of seven deadly sins to avoid (p. 58). Some other evaluation texts also present tips for promoting evaluation usage (Rossi, Lipsey, & Freeman, 2004; Royse, Thyer, Padgett, & Logan, 2005). The steps for initiating this aspect of the evaluation are usually difficult to determine. We suggest the evaluator conduct an informal assessment of the organization and related political and contextual issues that may inform the development of such a plan. This chapter presents a process for conducting an assessment of the agency's history of using information, some useful skill sets that should suit social workers, and some helpful examples.

CHECKING OUT HISTORY

Each agency has its own unique history with evaluation and using the respective products. When trying to put together a plan to support utilization within an organization, it is important to spend some time looking for critical evidence that can assist in the development of a formidable plan for supporting the use of information; that is, basically, an assessment of evaluation usage potential. This initial step should sound familiar to most social workers. The evidence can include previous evaluation projects and their respective use. When the agency does not have a history of evaluation, information about the organization, some key actors, and its operation in other areas can also be examined to determine ways to support the use of information.

The focus of this assessment process is to seek information that will help in designing a plan to get agency personnel to pay attention to the evaluation findings and to use the insights to improve services. As stated, even when an agency has not engaged in formal program evaluations, there is still available information that will provide insight in the development of a plan to get the evaluation findings into the conversations about improving service delivery. Figure 9.1 shows a list of different aspects to consider as jumping-off points for gathering information about sustaining the use of information. The list is a compilation of factors we have found helpful when planning for the usage of evaluation information. These categories are not exclusive nor inclusive of all concerns in this area; hopefully the list also provides helpful prompts to consider and possibly use to stimulate other issues related to getting the optimal use out of the evaluation efforts.

Figure 9.1	Aspects to Assess When Planning for Information Utilization
Past track record	Has an evaluation been completed previously and how was it received? Did it influence practice in any way? How? Who was involved and in what ways?
Staff point of view	Are current staff open to evaluation activity? Do they have questions on the current approach to service delivery or are things acceptable to them?
Leadership style	Does the agency leadership seem to be open to evaluation? Do they often ask questions that may imply an openness to evaluation, such as "How can we improve this?"
Organizational culture	Is this agency open to examining the way services are delivered or is the status quo acceptable?

Checking Vitals

When trying to put together a plan to support utilization within an organization, it is important to spend some time looking for critical evidence that can assist in the development of a formidable plan for supporting the use of information.

The focus of this assessment process is to seek information that will help in designing a plan to get agency personnel to pay attention to the evaluation findings and to use the insights to improve services.

Even when an agency has not engaged in formal program evaluations, there is still available information that will provide insight in the development of a plan to get the evaluation findings into the conversations about improving service delivery.

Past Track Record

An examination of previous evaluation activity will provide valuable insights about developing a plan to support the use of the upcoming evaluation. One of the first things to consider is the use of a previous evaluation. Was the evaluation used? Who participated in the utilization process? What factors seemed to help with the use of the information? What agency characteristics seemed to support the use of information? If the evaluation was not utilized, try to find out more about its lack of use by asking agency personnel. For example, why do they think the information was not used, and what do they perceive as significant barriers? Are there any ideas about overcoming those barriers?

The motivation surrounding the evaluation can also be telling. Was the evaluation conducted to fit with an agency interest in assessing and improving services; or was the evaluation undertaken to meet an external contractual requirement; or was there another reason for the evaluation? It is also helpful to get different opinions about this topic from a number of different individuals with different organizational histories, based on their tenure and position. For example, direct service staff will have different ideas about this process than program managers whose ideas are likely to differ from the executive leadership.

Checking Vitals

Consider the use of previous evaluations:

Was the evaluation used?

Who participated in the utilization process?

What factors seemed to help with the use of the information?

What agency characteristics seemed to support the use of information?

The motivation surrounding the evaluation can be telling:

Was the evaluation conducted to fit with an agency interest in assessing and improving services?

Was the evaluation undertaken to meet an external contractual requirement or was there another reason for the evaluation?

Staff Point of View

Regardless of the extent of an evaluation history, the insights of the staff involved in planning the project can be very helpful. Engaging agency staff in this process requires educating your colleagues about its intended uses and about what might be important to consider when trying to grasp information that will influence a plan for usage in current and future projects. The description of the evaluation plans will help them understand which types of decisions may be influenced. For example, the evaluation may identify which program components are being fully implemented, or the emphasis may be more related to the factors that seem to contribute to service recipients' successful community integration. When your potential consumers understand the types of decisions that are being targeted by the evaluation, ask them about their thoughts about how they think this will go and what supports might be helpful.

Specifically, if an evaluation focuses on the specifics of therapeutic services to families, these types of questions might provide valuable information:

> What types of decisions might be made about the delivery of family work services (increasing resources or adjusting the job description of family workers)?
>
> Who else might be interested in this question?
>
> What questions might they have?
>
> Who might be opposed to asking this type of question?
>
> Why do you think they might be opposed to this?

Once agency colleagues understand the scope of decisions, then it is often helpful to ask them questions about the context surrounding the use of the evaluation data:

> Who would need to be involved in these types of decisions?
>
> Do you think these individuals in the organization will be open to these types of changes?
>
> What supports would be useful to increase the likelihood that these actors will be accommodating of the types of changes that evaluation information may support?

Checking Vitals

Engaging agency staff in the evaluation process requires educating your colleagues about its intended uses and about what might be important to consider when trying to grasp information that will influence a plan for usage in current and future projects.

It is useful to describe the evaluation process to them and help them understand which types of decisions may be influenced.

Leadership Style

Another consideration is the way that leaders pursue change in the organization. One critical aspect of organizational culture is the role of individual leaders in the evaluation process. How do the key leaders in the organization pursue the kind of change that may be necessary to use evaluation findings to improve programs? Is it more participatory or would it be best described as autocratic? How do you find ways to support them in evaluation-driven change activity? What factors seemed to have been useful in getting their support with various organizational initiatives and decisions?

Once again, even when an organization and its staff appear to be evaluation neophytes with little evaluation history, there are still some valuable insights to be gained by having discussions with invested parties and potential decision makers. Despite a dearth of concrete evaluation experience, you can still learn about an organization by talking to folks who work in that organization. One trick that can possibly yield some useful insights is a visit to your local politico.

Checking Vitals

Consider the way that leaders pursue change in the organization:

How do the key leaders in the organization pursue the kind of change that may be necessary to use evaluation findings to improve programs? Is it more participatory or would it be best described as autocratic?

How do you find ways to support them in evaluation-driven change activity?

What factors seemed to have been useful in getting their support with various organizational initiatives and decisions?

Uncover and Access Local Expertise

There are usually individuals who will know the pulse of the organization. Consider consulting with these individuals about the purpose of the evaluation, whether it is geared to meet the needs of a funder or if the plan is to assess and eventually make changes in programs that will make them better.

Politicos, staff members with an unusual sense of organizational politics, may be members of the evaluation team, or you may have to get your colleagues' help to identify these individuals.

The local politico will usually have a sense of the degree to which this effort will be supported by organizational leadership as well as some ideas to increase the chances of gaining organizational support. The support of a politically knowledgeable actor may be valuable in the identification of organizational impediments and possible ways to address possible obstructions. These internal informants can be crucial to finding key players in the decision process and helping to determine effective strategies for working with them. These insightful players are usually easy to spot, and staff members of an evaluation team or other staff within the organization can assist in locating and helping to engage these individuals.

When engaging in this somewhat tricky practice, it useful to verify your information sources as to who may be likely to help sort through the organizational politics. You are looking for an individual who is known for understanding the politics around the operation, especially the decision-making process of the organization. When looking for this valuable consultant, it helps to verify the avowed reputation with multiple sources from different locations within the organization. For example, one might talk with direct service staff as well as employees from the staff side of the organization, such as accounting or human resources, to find the person who can provide guidance around the decision-making political process.

In one large evaluation project, an initiative that employed a streamline approach for evaluating multiple programs, the evaluators worked closely with the vice president of the program development division, our resident politico, to keep this substantial evaluative effort operating smoothly. A particularly resistant player in the mix was the vice president of program operations, who was deeply embroiled in the details of the daily administration of managing a multitude of services. He viewed the evaluation as an interruption in the ongoing operation. Our politico advised the evaluators to get the department head to support the evaluation project by appealing to his commitment to service quality and effectiveness. As our sage political consultant had advised, once the department head was on board, the vice president of operations, who incidentally reported to this department head, was willing to fall in line and support the evaluation with his blessings and respective staff time.

Checking Vitals

The local politico will have a sense of the degree to which this effort will be supported by organizational leadership as well as some ideas to increase the chances of gaining organizational support.

These internal informants can be crucial to finding the key players in the decision process and helping to determine effective strategies for working with them.

When looking for this valuable consultant, it helps to verify the avowed reputation with multiple sources from different locations within the organization.

Organizational Culture

The discussion of leadership styles and political resources is really the beginning of an informal assessment of organizational culture. Leadership can have a significant impact on organizational culture. While there are some fascinating pieces on organizational culture and service effectiveness (Cooke & Lafferty, 2007; Glisson & Green, 2006; Holt & Lawler, 2005), there is a limited amount of literature to direct someone who is interested in promoting the use of evaluation in an organizational setting. Our experience suggests that leaders that question current practices and are interested in finding better ways to deliver service are receptive to using evaluation information. Poertner and Rapp (2007) compare the use of information in a learning organization to a pilot who constantly examines the instruments in a plane to assess performance. In this type of organizational context, the strategy to engage critical players in the support of evaluation data involves contacting actors from different levels to discuss the potential of the evaluation findings and ways to support their use.

A child welfare agency in Kansas that provides reunification, foster care, and other child welfare services to families, has invested significant time in developing a comprehensive information system that tracks consumer services and outcomes. The staff is continually asked to review the information system to consider changes that would improve direct service as well as policy and program decisions (Moore, Rapp, & Roberts, 2000). This type of agency is clearly open to making changes using evaluation information. They invest significant resources in motivating and supporting the use of data by staff at a variety of levels.

On the other hand, if an organization is more interested in maintaining the status quo and controlling the operation, it is more difficult to find ways to get the evaluation findings into the conversation. In the case where an organization seems to be closed or the decision-making process is more rigid, it is still the evaluator's job to attempt to discern the process for making decisions and a place for evaluation findings in the process. In this type of an organizational environment, the importance of advocating for the use of evaluation findings is oftentimes extremely critical. Evaluation findings are often a rare and critical opportunity for client voices to be heard about the effectiveness of an existing service or the need for additional supports. Under these circumstances, the need to create a venue for the serious consideration of evaluation findings is imperative.

Checking Vitals

If an organization is more interested in maintaining the status quo and controlling the operation, it is more difficult to find ways to get the evaluation findings into the conversation.

In this type of an organizational environment, the importance of advocating for the use of evaluation findings is oftentimes extremely critical.

Under these circumstances, the need to create a venue for the serious consideration of evaluation findings is imperative.

Given the critical nature of this supportive activity and its exploratory nature, some questions have been drawn from previous projects (see Figure 9.2) that permeate a variety of these aforementioned categories. Holding discussions with staff centered on these questions can provide critical information about the history of use; it also can help to stimulate ideas on future use of data. This same line of questioning could be used with "resident politicos." The results of this discussion should give evaluators committed to promoting the results of their work some ideas and strategies for cultivating fertile ground for this type of activity.

Figure 9.2	Use and Support of Information Usage Assessment Tool

1. Can you think of any recent program evaluations that have been completed at your agency?

2. Who did the evaluation work?

3. Why was the evaluation conducted? What was the purpose? (e.g., funder request, internal initiative)

4. Did they involve agency staff? If so, what was their role?

5. Describe the evaluation, including the type of program, research design, data sources, data analysis, and results.

6. How was the evaluation used?

7. Did it impact the operation of services?

8. Did any specific actors inside or outside of the agency play a role in the use of data? What was their role? Were they supportive of the use of data? Were their efforts successful?

9. Was the evaluation completed in a satisfactory manner? Why do you say that?

10. Generally, how would you rate the evaluation? Was it conducted in a credible manner? Were the results used to impact services or policy?

11. What advice would you give someone who might do an evaluation in this agency based on that experience?

12. How are decisions about service made in the agency? Is it a system where a few individuals make the decision? Do the decision makers seek input? Who is given the opportunity for input? Does the input seem to influence the decision?

I AM A SOCIAL WORKER; I AM HERE TO HELP YOU

Hopefully the previous discussion has clarified some parts of the business of helping to prepare evaluation consumers. As stated, there is no foolproof formula for this kind of work. It requires developing a feel for the lay of the land, through observation and inquiry, which informs the development of a corresponding flexible plan. While this aspect of evaluation may be new and ambiguous, social workers are well-equipped to engage in and lead this type of work. The skills, values, and beliefs that social workers acquire in their professional and real-world practice provide an excellent toolkit for this type of work. The skill set is comparable to the types of training suggested in surveys of seasoned evaluation practitioners (Taut & Alkin, 2003). Social workers are at home in agency settings and the accompanying politics that support, or not, the implementation of evaluation and its potential uses.

As a reminder, anyone engaged in this activity must buy the initial premise of this book: The use of evaluation findings has great potential for helping the consumers of service programs. This belief is at the heart of this work. While it is frustrating and tenuous, the risks of investing in these activities are worth the potential payoff of improving the lives of social service clients.

The commitment to the improvement in the lives of service consumers is the foundation of both evaluation work and the social work profession. Although the social worker's efforts are usually directed toward an individual, family, or community, there is a concrete set of skills that is applicable to this work. Social workers are trained to be competent listeners, facilitators, information organizers, advocates, and active consultants. These skill sets are extremely useful in this type of work.

Social workers bring a strong set of complementary interpersonal skills to this work. The set of tasks listed in Figure 9.3 is inherent in the process of supporting the use of information. The social worker's training and experience apply to these tasks. Our previous discussion has focused on understanding the political dynamics of the setting and respective roles of the various actors. In addition to having a firm grip on these aspects of the setting, it is critical to develop a relationship with the actors in the setting. Social workers have the training and experience to support the development and maintenance of these relationships. Social workers in direct service as well as in administrative/supervisory settings are comfortable with sharing both positive and negative results with their colleagues and clients—all helpful when discussing the implementation of the study as well as sharing evaluation findings.

Figure 9.3	Interpersonal Skill Sets Well-Suited to Building a Vital Relationship With Information Consumers

Ability to build relationship based on trust.

Openly communicates good and bad news.

Assesses comfort level with change.

Supports people in the change process.

Identifies and develops resources necessary for change.

Checking Vitals

The skills, values, and beliefs social workers acquired in their professional and real-world practice provide an excellent toolkit for evaluation work.

The commitment to the improvement in the lives of service consumers is the foundation of both evaluation work and the social work profession.

Social workers are trained to be competent listeners, facilitators, information organizers, advocates, and active consultants—all extremely useful skill sets in evaluation work.

One of the strongholds of all levels of practice is the idea of a social worker as an agent of change. Obviously, this process is critical to the use of evaluation insights to make programmatic changes in the interest of better services and happier consumers. As a result, social workers are very familiar with assessing the comfort level with change. The focus of much of the assessment process previously discussed is the readiness of the organization for change. A savvy social worker is well-equipped to determine if the organization and its key actors are interested in making changes based on evaluation. Not too surprisingly, this may be more complex as the level of readiness for change may vary by the level of the agency. For example, oftentimes the administration of an agency does not see the necessity for change. Ironically, we have seen examples where the agency is fiscally sound, but the direct service practitioners are concerned about the well-being of the clients and committed to evaluation-informed change. A trained, experienced social worker is well-suited to assess the varying levels of openness to change throughout an organization.

In any change process, it is paramount to support those enduring the change. Again, social work training and experience provides excellent preparation for this duty. In our experience, we have made the eventually fatal flaw of not staying with evaluation consumers throughout the change process. It is a common mistake to spend the time getting key staff ready to invest in evaluation-focused change and then to leave them unsupported temporarily. Distractions—most commonly pesky data collection and management issues—redirect energy to evaluation implementation and away from the potential information consumers. After resolving the respective implementation struggles, the evaluator returns to reiterate the change strategy discussion only to find the agency actors have reverted to their initial reticence regarding the use of evaluation. In our minds, this common scenario is not a function of the character of the agency personnel but more related to the organizational context.

First of all, agency staff at all levels have extremely full plates and the influence of even the most charismatic, insightful, skilled evaluator will wane immediately when the interest or commitment to evaluation is not routinely nourished with support. In addition, substantial forces within the agency support that status quo. These include but are not limited to staff comfort with a way of doing things; political forces that naturally resist change; and the scarcity of accompanying resources (e.g., staff time, training, etc.) that usually correspond with change. The emphasis on supporting evaluation consumers throughout the change process is vital, especially after some momentum has developed to support change. Change is an uphill battle; therefore, the support of users by the evaluator needs to be ongoing and consistent.

These types of support can range from literally reminding the actors in the agency that they are doing the right thing on behalf of clients to something more active and complex. It may take the form of routine meetings to plan, assess, and strategize the process of implementing and using the evaluation to inform the delivery of services. One of the lessons that we have learned is that the support of the evaluation activity comes in two forms: support of the implementation of the evaluation and support of the users. While there may be overlap between the two, planful efforts need to address both enterprises. Obviously, the evaluation must be implemented in a credible fashion, but the involvement of users needs to continue during the implementation. A temporary lack of involvement can be destructive, as many other competing distractions may derail any momentum toward possible use of the evaluation.

In one case, two distinct units of a juvenile court were evaluating their services. One of the managers was actively involved in the evaluation, while the other manager showed her support by supplying the evaluation resources and not by participating in the implementation. Months later, after the collection of the data, when the evaluation team reconvened to discuss the findings and possible implications, the manager involved in the evaluation was very committed to the use of the data. On the other hand, the manager who only supplied resources and did not participate in the evaluation implementation had lost her enthusiasm for using the evaluation information. Our experience tells us that cyclical involvement in the evaluation (high involvement in planning, low involvement in implementation) often interferes with the eventual use. While it may not be feasible for some decision makers to participate in implementation, they should remain involved through ongoing updates and status reports.

Checking Vitals

A trained, experienced social worker is well-suited to assess the varying levels of openness to change throughout an organization.

The emphasis on supporting evaluation consumers throughout the change process is vital, especially after some momentum has developed to support change.

The support of the evaluation activity must be constant and should not be confused with efforts to complete the evaluation.

Another key is the social workers' ability to ascertain the type of supports that will be useful in the process, locate those resources, and put the resources in place. Obviously, this is more complex in an organization that has little experience using evaluative findings. Resources can take many different forms. It may require political support. For example, in some cases we have had to locate, and sometimes, convert key supporters for the process as well as for the use of evaluation. Funding sources inside or outside the organization can often be converted into evaluation supporters. In some cases, funders have been great supporters of the process and key assets to agency staff with the implementation and use of evaluation. In other cases, we have had to use persuasive efforts to remind the funder of the potential of the evaluation for clients. In addition, funders are often useful for helping to identify sympathizers who can be helpful to those struggling to get the evaluation implemented and used as a source for change.

Other resources may be more concrete. Sometimes it may take more personnel to complete the data collection. It may require staff who are involved in data collection, or it may require additional temporary staff. Part of the process of evaluation is the continual review of organizational readiness change and the accompanying identification/location of respective resources. Social workers are well-equipped to help with the process of locating and cultivating these types of resources.

Funders are not the only viable influence in the process of seeking support for the use of critical information. Staff, supervisors, and managers are also potentially influential in convincing key actors in the organization of the value of using evaluation information to improve services. In some cases, we have found support for the use of information with staff and managers by appealing to their commitment to service effectiveness. This has been fruitful in cases where top-level decision makers have been more oriented toward maintaining the status quo, and discussions led solely by the evaluators have been less than influential. In some cases, the evaluator has encouraged staff and managers as well as direct service staff to lobby the decision maker about the value of considering the evaluation information, its reflection on quality, and the need to consider making changes.

Checking Vitals

Social workers need to have the ability to ascertain the type of supports that will be useful in the process, locate those resources, and put the resources in place.

Funding sources inside or outside the organization can often be converted into evaluation supporters.

Staff, supervisors, and managers are also potentially influential in convincing key actors in the organization of the value of using evaluation information to improve services.

Engaging the Users

As previously mentioned, a key to maintaining active relationships with users is the ability to engage the consumers of information in an ongoing fashion. Even the most committed agency staff faces a workload of ongoing duties and emerging crises. So, it is extremely critical to incessantly foster their involvement in the evaluation. This section will forward some of the techniques developed to keep evaluation consumers engaged in the process. Obviously, keeping the users engaged throughout the entire process is critical to their eventual use. Involvement increases the chances of their information needs getting addressed by the evaluation as they are able to integrate their information needs into the design. Continuous involvement contributes to ownership of the study, its data, and respective findings. Finally, involvement can educate the users on the evaluation process, their expectations, and ways to use the information in their practice. The interest of eventual consumers of the information is much like a flame that must continually be protected from the winds of daily distractions so it can burn at a strong continuous rate.

Checking Vitals

Involvement increases the chances of users' information needs getting addressed by the evaluation as they are able to integrate their information needs into the design.

Continuous involvement contributes to ownership of the study, its data, and respective findings.

Involvement can educate the users on the evaluation process, their expectations, and ways to use the information in their practice.

IN THE BEGINNING . . .

The beginning of any evaluation project, just as in a direct service setting, is the perfect time to engage the users in the project and its unlimited potential for impacting services. As stated earlier, the interested parties in the evaluation include the users and key informants knowledgeable about the culture of the organization as well as the assets and barriers to the eventual use of the findings. Additionally, these parties should be given ample opportunity for input into the evaluation design. Their thoughts on the key questions, the type of research design, and the data collection strategy have multiple levels of importance. First of all, they are likely to have a valuable opinion on the technical aspects of the evaluation. In addition, their input at this level is a vital opportunity to begin the ongoing task of persuading them about the value of the evaluation for services. Finally, this is the first chance the evaluator will have to begin developing a positive relationship with the potential users of the evaluation.

KEEPING STAKEHOLDERS INVESTED
THROUGHOUT THE PROCESS

It is imperative to keep evaluation stakeholders actively involved in the process as the evaluation is taking place. The authors have had dismal experience with the following sequence of steps:

1. Engaging consumers of information at the onset and getting them excited about the evaluation project's potential.

2. Proceeding with data collection independently from consumers of evaluation.

3. Completing data collection and analysis.

4. Beginning to discuss findings with evaluation consumers.

At first glance, this sequence of events may seem logical, but remember the earlier discussion about protecting the flame of evaluation interests from the breezes of ongoing agency operations? On a few occasions, when we have followed the aforementioned steps, the consumers seem to have suffered amnesia. The value of the evaluation is a distant memory, and any enthusiasm for the potential has dwindled.

In order to keep evaluation consumers invested in the project during the implementation, keep them engaged in the process by giving them a task in the implementation or by meeting with them routinely to keep them updated. Tasks might include giving them a role in data collection or routinely meeting with the staff engaged in data collection/processing. A natural inclination might be to leave key agency folks out of the evaluation process and involve them in activities that might be closer to key decisions. The commitment to the process must be constantly fostered and reinforced. The likelihood of pulling key actors into the process around key events has some potential efficiency, but it carries a significant risk to the commitment and enthusiasm around information utilization.

An alternative to keeping staff involved in the implementation is to aggressively update them on the progress of the project. The updates on implementation of the evaluation project usually would include an overview of the plan and reports on routine progress. One key aspect is to review the expected plan for the evaluation (i.e., who does what, when, and how often?). Eventual users of the information would review and critique the plan for the implementation, using their critical organizational expertise. For example, is the plan to use clerical staff under the supervision of family workers a feasible method for conducting phone interviews of clients?

The more routine updates would include things like the training of interviewers, the selection of cases for interviewing, the development of human subject protection protocols, stories about the interviewing of survey participants, and so forth. Often, organizational glitches arise that require brainstorming or organizational intervention; information consumers typically have extensive resources to offer in these discussions.

Update discussion can also act as preparatory sessions for the business of utilizing evaluation findings. It is never too early to begin discussing the process of utilizing study findings. It is beneficial to have many of these discussions prior to the reporting of data. This gives the decision makers a chance to think about the various roles in the process of making decisions as well as the variety of results that could occur and their respective possible decision avenues.

Checking Vitals

Strategies for keeping consumers engaged throughout the process:

Give them a task in the implementation.

Aggressively update them on the progress of the project.

Review and critique the implementation plan.

Begin discussing the process of utilizing study findings.

It is useful to give decision makers a chance to practice decision making. One way to do this is to develop decision-making models that anticipate the different findings that may occur (see Figure 9.4). While awaiting the findings, work with decision makers to consider different findings that might occur and the decisions that would be supported by the respective data. The construction of such a model prior to getting the data is helpful, and ignorance about actual findings may create an objectivity and freedom to consider a broad range of options: that is, some of the political ramifications are temporarily held in abeyance, while clear thought is given to possible decision-making scenarios.

| Figure 9.4 | Decision-Making Model |

Percentage of Clients Who Effectively Complete the Program*

70% completion or higher

Promote the program: The staff felt this program dealt with difficult youth who have a chronic history of delinquent behavior. If they achieved this level of performance, they felt the program should be promoted to increase the number of youth who would receive this service.

50–70% completion

Develop improvement plans: If program performance at this level was not acceptable, the staff would consider developing program improvement plans that would enhance program strengths (family treatment) as well as target areas of the program known for poor program processes (aftercare services).

Below 50% completion

Consider major overhaul: If only half of the youth served were succeeding, it would be apparent that major program renovation needed to occur. This initiative would include reviewing the program model for its feasibility and examining staff development related to the expectations of staff and the corresponding training/support.

Below 30% completion

Discontinue program: If only one of three youth in the program were succeeding, the staff felt strongly the program was harmful and should be discontinued.

*This model was developed for a residential treatment program for delinquent youth. The measure was based on the percentage of youth that completed their integrated treatment plan at the end of the program. An effective completion was viewed as a planned release based on the amount of progress toward key treatment goals.

HELPFUL EVALUATION PERSONAS

Clearly, the prospect of helping evaluation consumers use information varies and requires creative customization. Different actors in different contexts need a broad range of supports. Thus far, this chapter has offered strategies for assessing information consumers need for using evaluation, some helpful skill sets for supporting those consumers, and some specific techniques. The last advice is related to some suggestions on different stances an evaluator may assume when providing support. These different roles are driven by the context as well as the philosophy the supporting agent may prefer in his or her role (see Figure 9.5). One of the challenges of this work, and this chapter, is giving evaluators a sense that there is something they can do to help users apply the evaluation findings.

Remember, these approaches are neither exhaustive nor exclusive. As you review them, you will most likely find some overlap, and you may consider some other interpersonal ways of pursuing this work. It is hoped this list will illustrate possible approaches and conceivably inspire some alternatives. Unfortunately, it is not possible to prescribe the exact conditions under which these personas may be most effective. The choice of exactly when, where, and how to use these requires discretion and will hopefully be driven by the assessment as well as personal acumen or level of comfort in various roles.

Many times the consumers of information are fully competent to undergo the tasks and stay the course needed to get the evaluation findings used in program decisions, but they lack confidence. In these cases, a supportive role can be very helpful. As portrayed in Figure 9.5, the main feature of this job description is often hand-holding. Some more concrete examples would include but would by no means be limited to reinforcing the task at hand; providing reminders about the importance of the evaluation or respective supportive tasks; and helping to brainstorm possible solutions to unexpected barriers. The main focus of this role is to provide the evaluation consumers support to do the things they know are right to get the evaluation information included in the conversation.

Figure 9.5	Evaluation Personas

Supportive

Educational

Advocate

Militant

Checking Vitals

Supportive role:

Reinforce the task at hand.

Provide reminders about the importance of the evaluation or respective supportive tasks.

Help to brainstorm possible solutions to unexpected barriers.

Another strategy is to recognize skills that may be missing and attempt to accommodate the future user by providing education in support of the needed competencies. Many evaluators are excellent teachers and feel confident that they can vastly enhance the influence of an evaluation by educating the users. Some of this activity is inherent in the process of explaining the research questions, design, analysis, and possible use in decisions; however, sometimes additional more tangible types of teaching occur. It is common to spend time making sure that the formats that are used to present findings are clearly understood so that basic overviews of graphs and accompanying statistical information is commonplace. The centerpiece of this technique is to inform or educate consumers in areas that seem to be missing and are vital to the use of the evaluation.

Checking Vitals

Educational role:

Explain the research questions, design, analysis, and possible use in decisions.

Make sure that the formats that are used to present findings are clearly understood.

Inform or educate consumers in areas that seem to be missing and are vital to the use of the evaluation.

The first two approaches were primarily supportive and collaborative; the latter two can be employed when it looks like more aggressive encouragement is needed. The first of these is an advocate. The advocate goes beyond the educational and supportive roles by illustrating critical points that are being neglected or overlooked. This role can be effective when there is an emphasis on service consumer needs that may appear to be undervalued. In one case, the evaluation team went to management meetings to advocate for evaluation resources to highlight the importance of investing agency resources in a more thorough follow-up survey with youthful offenders. In another case, the evaluation team made a series of presentations at an executive level management meeting to highlight findings that illustrated the value of family contacts on client outcome and the corresponding need to fully fund the respective service.

Advocate role:

Illustrates critical points that are being neglected or overlooked. Effective when there is an emphasis on service consumer needs that may appear to be undervalued.

The last persona is utilized when the evaluator feels there is a need to apply political pressure to enhance the use of findings. This is used when the more amenable and collaborative channels within the agency do not seem fruitful. Oftentimes this method is used by rallying political power outside an agency. An advocate may want to use the press, outside funders, or interested policymakers. For example, we have gone to interested local legislators in the past to garner support for evaluation work within an agency. It is critical, and probably obvious, to know that the use of this approach could curtail further collaborative work. In one case, an agency used a local judge to get support for an evaluation, and when the findings of the evaluation seemed to be losing steam, one of the authors met with the judge and asked him to encourage the agency to use the findings and report progress on the same routinely. In this case, the agency assumed responsibility for the evaluation, and this author was no longer involved with the agency. This was acceptable as the evaluation was routinely funded, and its usage was reinforced by the routine inquiry of the local judge. The evaluators did not view this as "taking one for the team." Although the evaluation contract was not renewed, the evaluation and its influence in program operations was made a routine and ongoing activity.

Militant role:

Used when the evaluator feels like there is a need to apply political pressure to enhance the use of findings.

Used by rallying political power outside an agency through utilizing the press, outside funders, or interested policymakers.

The use of this approach could curtail further collaborative work.

While these different personas may seem redundant and less than ingenious, it is hoped that reflecting on them will spur innovation when one is faced with various aspects of the evaluation process. Additionally, it is likely that these strategies will be combined at various stages of the evaluation process.

This chapter has addressed an aspect of evaluation that is often neglected in the evaluation literature. Consistent with the remainder of the book, the discussion in this section is based on practice experience. Our experience dictates that if attention and support are not provided to the users of the evaluation findings, it is unlikely that the evaluation will have much influence on program operation. On the other hand, there is no foolproof set of steps to ensure that the information is fully utilized. This chapter is humbly presented as some techniques that we have used with varying degrees of success. Additionally, an assessment of the utilization climate, even a rough one, will usually provide some direction as to which of the techniques and ideas offered in this chapter may be valuable.

REVIEW AND REFLECT

Big Ideas

- It is as important to spend time on supporting the users of the information as it is to implement the evaluation. Obviously, credible evaluation information is vital, but it is unlikely that the findings of the evaluation will be used if time is not spent supporting the users.

- There is no prescribed set of activities that will lead to a higher utilization rate of evaluation, but an assessment of the organization readiness for evaluation use can help to determine possible strategies. Potential users can be a great source of information for the assessment and possible plans to support users.

- There are a variety of different possible strategies that can be considered to support possible users of evaluation information. Many of the skills required to complete the plans are common to social workers and other human service professionals.

Discussion Questions

- Why do the authors think it is so vital to invest resources and time in supporting the users of the evaluation information?

- What are some of the specific ideas proposed for assessing the organization for its readiness to use evaluation information?

- Why do the authors think social workers are well-suited to support the users of evaluation?

- What is the big deal about constantly supporting the potential users of the evaluation process throughout the entire evaluation? What are the concerns and how do the authors suggest you avoid the difficulties?

- What are the different personas suggested by the authors for supporting the users of the evaluation? Do you think one may be more helpful than another?

Activities

- Describe an agency setting that is familiar to you. Consider whether you think the agency would be a good setting for using evaluation information. Why or why not?

- Spell out a plan of support for a local agency. What would you do to support their evaluation utilization efforts and why?

- This chapter is about supporting agencies in the process of using evaluation information. Do you think agencies can be helped with the task of using evaluation information, or is it part of the organizational DNA (something that is inherent and cannot be changed)? Justify your position.

Resources

- Campbell, M., & McClintock, C. (2002). *Shall we dance? Program evaluation meets organizational development in the non-profit sector.* Retrieved from James Irving Foundation: http://www.irvine.org/assets/pdf/pubs/evaluation/Shall_We_Dance.pdf

- Hernandez, G., & Visher, M. G. (n.d.). *Creating a culture of inquiry, changing methods and minds on the use of evaluation in non-profit organizations.* Retrieved from James Irving Foundation: http://www.irvine.org/assets/pdf/pubs/evaluation/Creating_Culture.pdf

- McNamara, C. (Copyright 1997–2008). *Checklist for program evaluation planning.* Retrieved from http://www.managementhelp.org/evaluatn/chklist.htm

- Morley, E., Hatry, H., & Cowan, J. (2002, September). *Making use of outcome information for improving services: Recommendations for nonprofit organizations.* Retrieved from Urban Institute: http://www.urban.org/url.cfm?ID=310572

CHAPTER 10

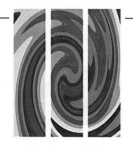

Group Designs and Methods

Treatment   Control

You want the two groups to be fairly comparable.

The purpose of many program evaluations is to make summative statements about the nature of a program and its effectiveness. There are a number of methodological approaches to providing this information. Group designs are a potentially useful methodological approach that permits the evaluation to have some confidence about the impact of the program—that is, that the positive benefits provided to individuals, families, or communities are related to the actual service being provided. This chapter will survey these designs and methods, including specifications, design options, and a range of challenges for the evaluation process.

Design Specifications

When designing an approach to an evaluation, a number of factors could shape the construction of this design. Those factors are going to be determined by one's desire to satisfy two primary questions: Is the evaluation organized in such a manner that one can have confidence in the process for addressing program effectiveness? Can one have confidence in the results of the evaluation? Linked to this confidence is the credibility of the process: Was it thorough? Were all relevant factors or variables identified and taken into consideration? Are the persons who provided information for the evaluation the most relevant informants? Did the evaluation informants include the population that is being served or a representative sample of that population? Were all persons and sources of data identified and described?

This credibility is particularly important in qualitative research and with narrative data. With smaller and sometimes select numbers of people being considered, stating how the data was collected, how the subjects were identified, and a thorough and accurate description of the subjects is very important. Evaluators using qualitative methods are responsible for providing sufficiently descriptive data so that all relevant persons examining the data and evaluative statements can assess the validity of the analyses and the transferability of the findings to other situations (i.e., external validity). The goal is for the observations and interpretations of the evaluation study to be viewed as credible to the participants and to those reading the study results (Franklin & Ballan, 2001).

With quantitative strategies, the key to gaining some power in describing the effectiveness of a program is the ability to compare the persons served with other people who have not been served or received the intervention. This includes engaging a sufficient number of people in the sample for the quantitative analysis. Consequently, the design for the project should seek to gain accurate representations of reality—that is, are the evaluators measuring and observing what they have intended to measure and observe—and does the method for collecting that information allow for some form of comparison to strengthen its ability to answer the questions associated with program effectiveness (Franklin & Ballan, 2001).

Checking Vitals

Two primary questions:

Is the evaluation organized in such a manner that one can have confidence in the process for addressing program effectiveness?

Can one have confidence in the results of the evaluation?

Evaluators using qualitative methods are responsible for providing sufficiently descriptive data so that all relevant persons can assess the validity of the analyses and the transferability of the findings to other situations (i.e., external validity).

With quantitative strategies, the key to gaining some power in describing the effectiveness of a program is the ability to compare the persons served with other people who have not been served or received the intervention.

Crafting the Evaluation Plan

Before beginning the evaluation process there needs to be an evaluation plan that includes the identification of the methods to be used for sample selection, data collection, analysis, and reporting. This process is oftentimes improved by a team approach that engages a diverse group of evaluation professionals to assure expertise, lively consideration, and a discussion of methodological options. While drafting an evaluation plan, it may be helpful to present this tentative model to agency leaders or other key stakeholders to gain their input and to build buy-in. There may also be value in engaging some of the frontline presenters of the intervention or program, along with recipients of services and select persons who will be participants in the evaluation. The purpose of this inclusive approach is to gain the perspective of those involved in the delivery and experience of the program. The evaluation team that crafts an approach in isolation from agency leaders and the persons who deliver and experience the program takes the risk that the evaluation may in some manner miss the goals and objectives of the program and the evaluation, overlook subtle obstacles, miss opportunities, and possibly misunderstand the context in which the program is implemented. In the conduct of a program evaluation, the cooperation if not engagement of the agency and other stakeholders is crucial, and this buy-in and investment will be strengthened by their understanding of the evaluation and by an opportunity to consult and review the evaluation plan.

Example

The faculty team met to sketch out a plan for conducting the evaluation of the department's new program. Eager to evaluate the results of the program and hopefully to generate data that would defend and advance the new program, the agency brought in this external evaluation team early on. The evaluation team drafted a plan and formally presented (in writing and in a verbal presentation) it to the program and agency leadership. Some elements of the proposed plan were dropped or modified based on this conversation. With a revised plan that had been reviewed by the agency leadership, the evaluation team presented an outline of the plan and process to the frontline workers and supervisors who would be interviewed or would assist in gathering data from case files or from clients. This presentation generated a number of questions for clarification but no significant modifications of the plan. The team proceeded to implement the plan with some confidence given the conversations with key stakeholders.

Checking Vitals

Before beginning the evaluation process, there needs to be an evaluation plan that includes the identification of the methods to be used for sample selection, data collection, analysis, and reporting.

While drafting an evaluation plan, it may be helpful to present this tentative model to agency leaders or other key stakeholders to gain their input and to build buy-in.

The evaluation team that crafts an approach in isolation from agency leaders and the persons who deliver and experience the program takes the risk that the evaluation may in some manner miss the goals and objectives of the program and the evaluation, overlook subtle obstacles, miss opportunities, and possibly misunderstand the context in which the program is implemented.

Reviewing the evaluation plan and attempting to gain agency buy-in can have some challenges and drawbacks as well:

1. This process of engagement with stakeholders can be time-consuming, particularly with a large or dispersed agency, with tight schedules in which there may be other priorities for agency leadership; checking back with stakeholders also adds to the time factor.

2. The agency leaders and stakeholders may not understand the purpose or processes associated with a program evaluation. This may require additional time or result in agency-generated suggestions that pose methodological, ethical, and practical difficulties.

3. A preliminary thorough description of the evaluation may begin to shape the responses of the potential evaluation participants as they may be influenced by the discussion of the elements of the evaluation.

4. An agency may expect ongoing collaboration with regard to the process of the evaluation. Modifications of the approach after the evaluation begins may complicate the collection and interpretation of data.

Conversely, the failure to engage stakeholders and the risk of missing subtle factors that may complicate the evaluation can be very time-consuming. The process of educating agency leaders, staff, and community members about an evaluation design and process may present a number of secondary gains for the agency and the evaluator. This tutorial may ease future evaluations in the agency and result in a greater ability to appreciate, assess, and respond to the findings from the evaluation. The presentation to participants and stakeholders may provide an overview and guidelines with specific information sufficient to inform participants and gain their accurate feedback. Modifications and adjustments to an evaluation plan as it is implemented are not unusual, with or without stakeholder input. New opportunities to gain information may present themselves. Steps to increase feasibility and accuracy may arise in the course of the evaluation process. Such modifications pose challenges in interpreting data but can be clearly identified and addressed in the course of the study.

Constructing a Sample

The use of a group design includes specifying the subjects who will be included in the study, as well as the number and type of persons in the study.

In many programs, the number of persons who are enrolled in the pilot program or the target program may be limited in number.

Example

The agency launched a new family conferencing program. Beginning at three different sites, the program staff members worked to recruit referrals from other agencies and from workers within their own agency. The staff made presentations about this new program to multiple agency groups and in the community to inform others, create interest and support for the program, and generate referrals. After 6 months, the program had 11 families at one site, 8 families at the second site, and 15 families at a third site. The evaluation was timed to begin at the end of the first year of service. Given the relatively small numbers, and the effort to recruit these families for this new program, the evaluators included all of the families in data collection.

When an evaluation is being conducted with a pioneering program, new model, or pilot, in particular, there may be some difficulty in recruiting a high number of participants for the service. The evaluator has to decide whether to wait for the program to build up a sufficient client base to allow for a sample to study that would be large enough for analysis or to begin with a small sample or engage the entire population in the study. External expectations or pressures on the agency to launch the evaluation may make it difficult to wait for a desired number of subjects.

Example

Eager to begin to gain some feedback and under some pressure to demonstrate results and report back to stakeholders, the agency wanted to begin the evaluation process. The agency believed that gaining descriptive information and a preliminary assessment of the satisfaction of program participants would begin to reassure the program's external funders. With a total of 34 families between the three sites, the evaluation process began.

Conducting an evaluation with the entire population served due to the small size of that population and the need to begin the evaluation poses a number of challenges for the evaluation.

Example

Although there were 34 families served by the program, as the evaluation began it became apparent that the number of families who could provide complete data would be even smaller. Several families dropped out after less than 3 months of service—not receiving the full intervention and now unavailable for follow-up. In several cases, the worker case records were incomplete and missing information so these records could not provide demographic or program participation information on some families. The number of families who had completed the intervention, who were available for follow-up, and who had complete case record information was fewer than 30 families. In addition, because there was a disproportionate number of families from one site (with almost all of the dropouts and incomplete information at one site), the evaluator was worried that the evaluation would provide skewed information. The evaluation might reflect the results associated with a specific location and the staff members in that location and consequently not have a representative sample. The population studied might not be representative of the persons using the service, let alone the broader population that might be served by this new program.

Addressing Internal Validity

In constructing the evaluation plan, the evaluation team needs to intentionally identify and address threats to internal validity in the study. Internal validity encompasses one's ability to state with confidence that the factors that one plans to measure are in fact the actual factors that are measured. Threats to internal validity are those dynamics and experiences that misshape the information gained such that the credibility of one's measurements and observations are compromised or questioned.

There are a number of classic threats to internal validity (Campbell & Stanley, 1966; Cook & Cambell, 1979; Grinnell, 1997; O'Sullivan & Rassel, 1989; Rubin & Babbie, 2005):

1. *History:* This involves contextual and outside events (other than the independent variable) that coincide with the introduction of the independent variable or occur during data collection that could have affected the participant's experience and the program's outcome. Outside events that could potentially affect the dependent variable should be taken into consideration during the planning process, to the extent that they are known. If discovered during the course of the evaluation, these historical events should be identified and addressed to the extent possible. For example, the increase of sorrow or hopelessness in the sample may be a result of certain local or national events rather than a failure of the depression-reducing intervention. Another example: Asking workers about job satisfaction soon after they have learned that they will be furloughed and have involuntary days off work due to budget constraints.

2. *Maturation and the passage of time:* This involves natural changes (physical growth, mental growth, emotional maturation, and motivation) that take place and affect the behaviors, feelings, thoughts, and responses of participants in a program evaluation. For example, the increasing intelligence or coordination of school-aged children may be less of an outcome from an intervention and more attributable to normal cognitive and physical development.

3. *Testing:* The initial measurement of one's actions or thoughts or a test for a certain quality may influence the person's behavior and consequently affect the outcome of the post-test. The very process of testing may enhance performance on a test. For example, a person may work very hard to improve his or her test score; it is this motivation and test-taking experience that makes the difference, not the program.

4. *Instrumentation:* The survey, questionnaire, observational guide, or other measuring instrument used to collect data may change between the beginning of the study and the study's conclusion. For example, an evaluator may find that several questions that would be helpful to ask should be added to a questionnaire, or questions that are persistently confusing should be reworded, changing the content of the questionnaire that has already been administered to others in the sample.

5. *Statistical regression:* The results that report significant change—improvement or deterioration—may be the result of having measured an extreme behavior or an extreme position. This extreme condition may be unstable, so there is a tendency to move toward the average. This moving toward the mean, rather than the intervention, explains any changes. For example, there may be "nowhere to go but up" as a person is at his or her lowest point of functioning or mood; or there is "nowhere to go but down"

as the person cannot be reasonably expected to maintain or repeat an extraordinarily effective performance.

6. *Selection bias:* The manner in which persons are selected for the study and the type of persons selected affects their reaction to the intervention. For example, choosing new employees in a study on agency climate or conducting exit interviews with persons who have been fired will affect the information and viewpoints gathered in an evaluation intended to give a representative view of the agency.

7. *Experimental mortality and attrition:* The composition and complexion of a sample may change as persons drop out, as intended participants fail to respond, or as subjects relocate during the conduct of the evaluation. The study may turn out to be a de facto survey of program survivors rather than involving a full range of recipients of services.

8. *Ambiguity about the direction of causal influences:* The direction of the impacts and influencing conditions may not be clear or discernible. For example, are people depressed because they are not getting sufficient sleep, or are they not getting sufficient sleep because they are depressed?

9. *Design contamination:* The persons who are participating in a study may behave differently because they know they are being studied. This can result in heightened success or failure for the intervention. This contamination is also called reactive effects—the knowledge that one is participating in a study and experiencing the newness of this scrutiny in a manner that affects the outcome of the study (Grinnell, 1997). For example, workers know that their use of time during the workday is part of the evaluation; therefore, with greater attentiveness to their use of time, they order their days in a manner that will reflect most positively on them.

10. *Diffusion or imitation of treatments:* The study is intending to examine the unique qualities and approach associated with an innovative program. However, many aspects of the approach, philosophy, and techniques associated with the intervention have already influenced the larger setting that might have provided a basis for comparison. For example, comparing a strength-based intervention with traditional practice may not show dramatic results as strength-based language, techniques, and values may have been adopted by or influenced traditional practice.

11. *Interaction effects:* The threats to internal validity noted here (see Table 10.1) may interact with each other—that is, they do not occur in isolation from each other. The differences resulting from changes in groups that are being examined may increase over time due to additional threats to validity and the trajectory initiated by the interaction of threats (Grinnell, 1997).

Table 10.1   Threats to Internal Validity

Internal Validity Dynamics and Threats	Questions to Identify Internal Validity Threats
1. History	1. What are the events that may have occurred during the evaluation process that may have affected the outcome and unintentionally contributed to the results of the study?
2. Maturation	2. Would the situation have changed or improved simply due to the passage of time, and can some of the improvements be attributed to natural changes that would have occurred without the intervention?
3. Statistical regression	3. Were the persons selected for the program and intervention either extremely high or low with regard to the characteristics the intervention was aiming to affect?
4. Selection	4. Were the persons who participated in the program categorically different than other persons not recruited or served by the program?
5. Experimental mortality	5. Did some people who started in the program being evaluated drop out before the program was complete, and did those who remained represent a special group of survivors?
6. Testing	6. Is there something about the process of taking a pre-test or prior tests that affected the persons' approach to the post-test irrespective of the intervention?
7. Instrumentation	7. Did the surveys, questionnaires, interview questions, or other data collection tools change during the course of the evaluation?
8. Design contamination	8. To what extent were the participants aware of their participation in the study, and to what extent did they have an incentive to have the program succeed or fail?
9. Direction of causal influences	9. Are the cause and the effect of participant changes confounded due to the timing of the intervention or ambiguity about participant motivation, experience, and skill?
10. Diffusion of treatments	10. How precise are the program attributes that are being studied, and to what extent might key elements of the program be generally practiced or accepted outside of the program?

(Adapted from O'Sullivan & Rassel, 1989.)

In addition to these classic threats to internal validity, participant behaviors and responses may be shaded by such factors as the likeability of the evaluator, the desire to please the evaluation team, or reactivity to the evaluation team or the sponsors of the evaluation.

In addition to the irrational ways that participants might respond to the evaluation process, researcher bias is a potential threat that shapes the outcome and compromises the accuracy of the evaluation findings. The evaluator may have an interest in the intervention's success or the success of the agency. This may be heightened if the evaluator is an agency employee. Due to this bias or conflict of interest, the evaluator may tend to see what he or she wants to see or expects to see. Unconsciously and without deliberate thought or deceit, the evaluator may manipulate a study so that the actual results agree with the anticipated results. An evaluator may favor an intervention so strongly that the research study is structured to support it by manipulating the design and shaping responses due to suggestive wording of interview or survey questions. The evaluation results may be interpreted and reported most favorably, and contrary information may be excluded, minimized, or reframed. Conversely, the evaluator may be predisposed to see the intervention be less effective or fail (Grinnell, 1997). The evaluator's initial neutrality and objectivity may be tested with familiarity and the development of relationships with agency participants and leaders.

The examination of an evolving evaluation plan with respect to acknowledging and managing internal threats to validity is essential to assure that what is being measured is an accurate reflection of the intervention or program. This management of internal threats to validity includes the use of measurements that have been tested, the use of multiple means to gain measurements (e.g., identifying and describing a phenomenon using three points of examination is called triangulation), the structure of the evaluation process, peer debriefing, having sufficient documentation of one's efforts so as to leave an audit trail, gaining feedback from research participants to test out responses and findings, and gathering extensive descriptions to provide validation of one's findings (Franklin & Ballan, 2001). Central to assuring validity is the selection of a design for the evaluation that collects needed information in a manner that maximizes one's ability to make statements about effectiveness with some degree of confidence and credibility.

Checking Vitals

 Internal validity encompasses one's ability to state with confidence that the factors that one plans to measure are in fact the actual factors that are measured.

Threats to internal validity are those dynamics and experiences that misshape the information gained such that the credibility of one's measurements and observations are compromised or questioned.

In addition to the classic threats to internal validity, participant behaviors and responses may be shaded by such factors as the likeability of the evaluator, the desire to please the evaluation team, or reactivity to the evaluation team or the sponsors of the evaluation.

In addition to the irrational ways that participants might respond to the evaluation process, researcher bias is a potential threat that shapes the outcome and compromises the accuracy of the evaluation findings.

Central to assuring validity is the selection of a design for the evaluation that collects needed information in a manner that maximizes one's ability to make statements about effectiveness with some degree of confidence and credibility.

Types of Group Designs

The evaluation and research literature identified a number of types of group designs for conducting a study (Grinnell, 1997; Rubin & Babbie, 2005). In general, a design involves the following:

1. Defining and describing the intervention or program elements to be evaluated: This is the independent variable. What are the content, boundaries, and components of this independent variable?

2. Establishing the time order of the independent variable: When is the intervention or program element introduced?

3. Manipulating the independent variable: How is the intervention or program element introduced and with what intended effect?

4. Establishing the relationship between the independent and dependent variables: What is the impact of the intervention on the targeted behaviors or the effect on other program goals, and how is this relationship established?

5. Controlling for rival hypotheses: What are the other explanations for the changes that are measured or observed so that there is some degree of confidence that the impact is caused, at least in part, by the intervention?

6. Using at least one control group: How is some method of comparison set up so that the experience with the intervention can be compared and contrasted with similar circumstances in which the intervention has not been introduced?

7. Assigning the persons who are the subjects of the intervention in a random manner: How is the sample designed so that the group that is being studied—that is, that has experienced the intervention—is representative of the larger group of persons served by the agency or eligible for this service (Grinnell, 1997)?

Each of these factors should be considered in an evaluation. These factors are addressed with varying degrees of detail and strength through a series of evaluation and research designs. There are multiple designs and variations on designs. Some of these approaches, designs, and strategies are noted here:

1. *Case Study Approach*. The case study establishes an approach designed to examine a group with some degree of detail and depth. The group in which an intervention has been introduced is the focus of the study that will chronicle the progress and process of the group by describing the changes (or lack of change) after the introduction of the intervention.

The strength of the case study approach is the detail and thoroughness of the exploration and the substantiation of the outcome based on in-depth knowledge of the agency and community context, the multiple and complicated variables that are at play in the intervention experience, and the rich narrative that supports the story and the effectiveness of the intervention.

The limitations of a case study approach include the difficulties associated with the inability to strongly present a comparison group, to compose a sample that has the qualities of randomized selection, and to accurately select and weigh the elements of the narrative.

For an agency, a case study can provide a rich description of the agency's services and its environment. It can provide the foundation for generating a number of hypotheses about the effectiveness of the agency and its interventions. This can provide useful information that can inform agency policies and procedures but may not have the durability and rigor to satisfy requirements for external validation of program effectiveness. It may also be challenging to find the person and the resources to support such an in-depth examination of the topic.

Checking Vitals

 Case study approach:

The group in which an intervention has been introduced is the focus of the study that will chronicle the progress and process of the group by describing the changes (or lack of change) after the introduction of the intervention.

Strengths:

A detailed and thorough exploration and substantiation of the outcome is based on in-depth knowledge of the agency and community context.

Multiple and complicated variables are at play in the intervention experience.

A rich narrative supports the story and the effectiveness of the intervention.

Limitations:

The difficulties associated with the inability to strongly present a comparison group.

The sample may not have the qualities of randomized selection.

The difficulties in accurate selection and weighing of elements of the narrative.

2. *One-Group Post-Test Only Design.* This design involves the implementation of an intervention with a group of people for whom that intervention is designed and then the administration of a simple test (oftentimes literally a test) to ascertain the results of that intervention. This can be described as an A-B design, with A being the pre-intervention status and B representing the post-intervention status.

For example, the state government wanted to know if the statewide joint training for social workers and lawyers had been effective. In addition to their overall satisfaction with the training, social workers and lawyers were asked to what extent their knowledge of either the law or the social services perspective on a legal case had increased due to the training. Individuals in each profession were asked if they would approach their work differently and if they felt better prepared. The results of the post-training survey for hundreds of participants were compiled, and based on aggregated individual responses, the sponsoring agency made a judgment about the effectiveness of the training.

The strengths of a One-Group Post-Test Only Design include its simplicity and practicality. The intervention is intended to increase one's knowledge or skill, to change a behavior, or to accomplish a targeted goal. The intervention is delivered and the results are measured.

The limitations associated with a post-test only design include a range of concerns about the validity of the findings, the validity of the measurement instrument, and consequently, the inability to present the effectiveness of the intervention with a high degree of confidence.

For an agency, One-Group Post-Test Only designs present an opportunity to look for a simple cause-and-effect relationship through an affordable design. The agency has the ability to describe the impact of its training, intervention, or program by presenting the intervention and describing its effect. This can provide useful information for many agency audiences. Consequently, this design has some value to an agency:

> We can evaluate whether change really occurred (with an A-B design) (and this is a good and valuable thing to do) even if we cannot be certain as to what caused these changes. Usually in a successful A-B study, the most generous and legitimate conclusion to make is something such as: "The data are consistent with the hypothesis that Treatment B reduced the problem." (Thyer, 2001b, p. 243)

However, its inability to address a number of validity concerns and the weaknesses inherent in not having a point of comparison underscore the modesty of the results of this design. With an examination at one point in time, typically close to the intervention, an A-B design does not address the sustainability of change effects.

Several variations on this design attempt to address some of the limitations and strengthen confidence in the results gained from this type of design. For example, the Multi-group Post-Test Only design includes the structure of the One-Group Post-Test but administers the intervention and the examination over and over again with other groups. The repeated testing and the compilation of results build a profile that speaks to the effectiveness of the intervention. This introduces some of the elements of comparison—that is, comparing the results of the same test given to different audiences at different times—and assumes that such repetition begins to account for the historical or other threats to validity that are posed when the intervention and test are administered at only one point in time with one audience. A second variation would introduce the use of randomization in the selection of persons to be tested. This randomized One-Group Post-Test Only Design attempts to address the selection factor and adds to one's confidence that the persons being tested represent the persons who have experienced the intervention. In addition, there is less likelihood for a bias to be introduced based on the identity of the persons taking the test (Grinnell, 1997).

Congruent with single-subject designs, other variations on post-test designs have been crafted to strengthen the connection between an intervention and its effects. These include time series designs (e.g., using the logic of single-subject designs), such as a simple interrupted time series design, also called a Longitudinal Case Study Design (Grinnell, 1997), in which there is a one-group post-test that is measured at multiple points in time. This design has the advantage of potentially identifying long-term effects (Grinnell, 1997; Rubin & Babbie, 2005). There are also multiple-time-series designs in which there is a simple, interrupted time series design—that is, an intervention is introduced, then interrupted, and again introduced with accompanying measurements at each change in the process. These designs can be strengthened with a non-equivalent comparison group. Oftentimes, given the simplicity of the approach due to limited expertise, time, and resources, it may be difficult to have an equivalent comparison group. However, a nonequivalent group has the potential to strengthen the evaluation versus no comparison group at all.

Checking Vitals

One-Group Post-Test Only Design:

This design involves the implementation of an intervention with a group of people for whom that intervention is designed, and then the administration of a simple test or other measurement to ascertain the results of that intervention.

This can be described as an A-B design, with A being the pre-intervention status and B representing the post-intervention status.

Strengths:

Design is simple and practical.

Intervention is intended to increase one's knowledge or skill, to change a behavior, or to accomplish a targeted goal.

Intervention is delivered, and the results are measured.

> Limitations:
>
> There are concerns about the validity of the findings, the validity of the measurement instrument, and consequently, the inability to present the effectiveness of the intervention with a high degree of confidence.

3. *One-Group Pre-Test and Post-Test Design.* In this design, a target group is asked to take a test, or their state of knowledge or behavior or proficiency is in some way measured. This measurement of certain variables takes place before an intervention is introduced that is intended to affect those variables. After the completion of the pre-test—that is, after learning the condition of the persons before they are exposed to the intervention—a post-test is provided that is intended to measure the change or improvement that presumably was caused by the intervention.

The strengths of a pre-test and post-test design include the ability to show a comparison between one's state before an intervention and then after an intervention. This progress (assuming there is improvement) is more likely to be attributable, at least in part, to the intervention than any progress that does not have the anchor and baseline provided by the pre-test. To the extent that the pre-test and post-test are administered to randomly selected participants and administered over and over again, this confidence in the impact of an intervention would grow.

The limitations of this design, similar to a Post-Test Only Design, are related to various threats to internal validity—particularly historical considerations, maturation, testing, and instrumentation factors.

For the agency, the use of a pre-test requires additional planning and anticipation, sufficient knowledge of the details and intended impact of the intervention, and the ability to construct a pre-test and post-test that accurately measure one's pre-intervention state and one's post-intervention progress. While producing more satisfactory conclusions than a post-test alone, this becomes more time-consuming and introduces the complexity associated with crafting valid and useful tests to be administered at two points in time.

One of the complicating factors with regard to validity and the use of a pre-test and post-test design is when an evaluation begins sometime after the program or intervention has begun. The agency may have belatedly decided that there is a need for an evaluation at a later point in the implementation of the intervention. This later implementation may result from a delay due to insufficient resources at the launching of the intervention, lack of time and energy at the time of the design and implementation of the intervention, a later request for an evaluation from a key stakeholder, or simple oversight. Once the intervention is introduced, particularly if the program is fully enrolled, it is very difficult to conduct a pre-test that would lead to valid conclusions. The evaluator can attempt to locate information in case records or other existing documents to capture a description of the pre-intervention state. It is also possible to pose a series of questions to program participants in which they are asked to reflect back to the time before the intervention and indicate their level of knowledge, skill, or behavior before the intervention and then to rate their knowledge, skill, and behavior after experiencing the intervention or program participation. This self-report attempts to re-create a pre-test and to gain a perspective that assists in assessing progress and change that can be attributed to the intervention. It is subject to distortions based on memory loss, inaccurately re-creating one's pre-intervention state in either pessimistic or optimistic terms, or being influenced by history, maturation, or other factors when engaged in this historical re-creation. However, these perceptions of change may have more value than forgoing any measure of progress due to the late introduction of the evaluation.

Checking Vitals

One-Group Pre-Test and Post-Test Design:

In this design, a target group is asked to take a test, or their state of knowledge or behavior or proficiency is in some way measured. After the completion of the pre-test—that is, after learning the condition of the persons before being exposed to the intervention—a post-test is provided that is intended to measure the change or improvement that presumably was caused by the intervention.

Strengths:

It has the ability to show a comparison between one's state before an intervention and then after an intervention.

This progress, assuming improvement, is more likely to be attributable, at least in part, to the intervention than any progress that does not have the anchor and baseline provided by the pre-test.

Limitations:

Threats to internal validity.

Historical considerations.

Maturation.

Testing and instrumentation.

4. *Post-Test Only Design With Nonequivalent Groups.* The post-test only aspect of this design means that the impact of the intervention delivered to the clients served by the program is measured after the intervention has been delivered (there is no pre-test). In addition, the experience and success of other clients also served by the agency, who have not received the intervention, is also measured. So to determine effectiveness, the functioning of the clients who received the intervention is compared with that of another group of agency clients who have not received the intervention. Presumably, if the group who had the intervention shows a difference (hopefully in the direction intended by the program), that difference or improvement is attributed to the intervention because the group of clients who did not receive the intervention did not show evidence of such improvement.

The strengths of this design include the simplicity of the post-test only design combined with a simple, accessible method for comparison—that is, an available group who has not experienced the intervention. If this available group is composed of persons served by the agency or in the agency's community, the non-equivalency may not be so dramatic. Significant differences in groups will make the comparison irrelevant and ineffective.

The use of a comparison group begins to address the limitations associated with history and maturation. However, concerns about the ability to compare nonequivalent groups and the lack of randomization mean that strong questions about internal validity persist.

For the agency, the use of a post-test design continues to be a method that is relatively simple and easily implemented. The measure of success and the outcomes of the intervention across multiple clients may be part of routine statistics and program characteristics that are already measured by the agency. With higher confidence in the outcome, due to some element of comparison with persons who have not received the intervention, this evaluation may produce information that is sufficient to assure agency leaders with regard to the direction and results of their program and program priorities. The validity threats may still pose complications for convincing external stakeholders of program success.

Checking Vitals

Post-Test Only Design With Nonequivalent Groups:

The post-test only aspect of this design means that the impact of the intervention delivered to the clients served by the program is measured after the intervention has been delivered (there is no pre-test).

The experience and success of other clients also served by the agency, who have not received the intervention, is also measured.

Strengths:

Simplicity of the post-test only design combined with a simple, accessible method for comparison—that is, an available group who has not experienced the intervention.

Limitations:

Concerns about the ability to compare nonequivalent groups and the lack of randomization mean that strong questions about internal validity persist.

5. *Experimental Design.* This design includes strategies intended to address multiple threats to internal validity. For example, the persons to be studied are randomly assigned to two groups. One group is administered the intervention and the other group is not administered the intervention. The condition and status of both groups—that is, the experimental group who received the intervention and the control group who did not receive the intervention—are measured. The results of the intervention are compared between the control and experimental groups with the assumption that the significance of the difference between these groups is attributable to the intervention.

The strengths of this design include the ability to control for threats to internal validity through randomization and the construction of two comparison groups. By controlling for most threats to validity, there is a higher degree of confidence in the results of the evaluation and the effectiveness of the intervention based on this design. The value of a randomized group design is that it provides a potentially powerful means to make statements about effectiveness and satisfy the program's sponsoring agency and funders. Consequently, an experimental design is the preferred method for assessing program effects. As the principal means of determining whether or not people benefit from service, it is used to substantiate best practices and is often viewed as the "gold standard" for evaluation.

The limitations to this design include a range of practical concerns including the cost and effort required to create the conditions to conduct such an experiment and the ethical concerns associated with withholding treatment from a portion of the population. The specific challenges include the following:

1. The structure of the research design may interfere or be perceived as interfering with the delivery of the service.

2. Implementation requires extensive supervision from start to finish—for example, group assignment, data collection, and maintenance. This is very expensive and time-consuming.

3. There may be ethical considerations, as a group of clients may be seen as being deprived of services.

4. There may be an insufficient number of clients to compose an experimental and a control group.

For an agency, this degree of confidence is desirable and may be required to satisfy the most demanding of external stakeholders. However, the limitations pose strong obstacles, and the expense and time and expertise required combined with concerns about withholding service may produce a barrier to employing experimental designs in the evaluative process.

Consequently, although experimental design is the highest level of rigor, it faces formidable practical and ethical complications and obstacles.

Checking Vitals

Experimental Design:

The persons to be studied are randomly assigned to two groups.

One group is administered the intervention and the other group is not administered the intervention.

(Continued)

(Continued)

The condition and status of both groups—that is, the experimental group who received the intervention and the control group who did not receive the intervention—are measured.

Strengths:

It allows the ability to control for threats to internal validity through randomization and the construction of two comparison groups.

It presents a higher degree of confidence in the results of the evaluation and the effectiveness of the intervention based on this design.

The value of a randomized group design is that it provides a potentially powerful means to make statements about effectiveness and satisfy the program's sponsoring agency and funders.

Limitations:

The cost and effort required to create the conditions to conduct such an experiment.

The ethical concerns associated with withholding treatment from a portion of the population.

One of the alternatives to an experimental design is the use of matched comparison groups. This supports the use of a comparison but may not present the dilemmas posed by an experimental design. The use of a comparison group is more compatible with ongoing service delivery. It offers some degree of rigor as it attempts to answer the question as to the effect of experiencing the benefits of the intervention or program, or not. It provides a stronger statement than no group comparisons.

Two examples of comparison groups follow.

Example 1: An agency introduced a new family support program to five counties. In its relatively early days of implementation, there were some struggles in getting a sufficient number of referrals as either other agencies did not know about the new program or other agency workers preferred their established referral patterns. Consequently, the new programs in the five counties were reluctant to use an experimental design as the agency wanted to serve all persons referred to its program. Due to the risk of family violence, delaying the delivery of the intervention to some families was also viewed as impractical and potentially dangerous. However, the agency also wanted to be able to describe the effectiveness of its program through comparison to persons who had not received these services. The agency identified comparison counties for this purpose. The "control" counties to be used to compare to the "intervention" counties were matched based on (1) population; (2) persons per square mile; (3) the percentage of individuals below the poverty level; (4) the percentage of the county population below the age of 18; (5) racial demographics (percentage of African Americans, Hispanics, and Native Americans); (6) the number of persons receiving food stamps; and (7) the number of families receiving public assistance. The agency also selected the comparison counties based on geographic proximity to the intervention counties with an attempt to match counties based on the seven identified variables and preferring proximity.

Example 2: A study on the use of mediation in child welfare cases was primarily descriptive in nature—that is, it described the implementation process, including the factors that facilitated the development of the pilot programs as well as the obstacles encountered, and it also described the elements of the mediation intervention. This description of mediation included examining the degree of success in reaching an agreement, the time that it took to gain a resolution, a description of the types of dispositions, and the rate of compliance with agreements by participants. There was also a description of the stages of the mediation conference and the satisfaction of various categories of participants (mediators, parent, attorney, and child welfare worker). To strengthen the evaluation by using some form of comparison (so that inferences about the effectiveness of mediation versus not using mediation could be made), there was a comparison of child welfare cases referred to the court that were mediated and those that were not mediated in the same county. There was also a comparison between the present outcomes—that is, staying in one's home, removing a child and placing the child in foster care, recommending adoption—with the outcomes and descriptive statistics for the county prior to the implementation of the mediation project.

The use of comparison groups, instead of an experimental design, raises a central question: Is it possible to identify a reasonable and suitable comparison group such that the evaluator can demonstrate that on the basis of a number of variables the group receiving the intervention or participating in the program being evaluated is sufficiently similar to the group not receiving the intervention? It can be difficult to make the case for comparability. Matching a sample from an urban population with another urban population may address the type of living environment in general terms, but there may be a number of uncontrolled and unidentified factors that have an impact on the behavior and status of subjects. Assuming that one urban neighborhood is similar to all other urban neighborhoods defies the diverse reality of most urban areas. This matching can be strengthened by identifying a range of indicators and seeking some level of comparability between communities. However, there may be some circumstances where it is difficult to employ a comparison. For example, one study attempted to match based on county: however, the largest county had a population in the millions, and there was no reasonable comparison county. The smallest county had less than 20,000 inhabitants, and again a comparison county was difficult to locate.

The concern about sample size and sufficient numbers of cases for comparison can be addressed by simply using the number of persons served that is available to the agency. For example, in a study of an agency program, 39 cases were selected to look at the impact of mediation on parental compliance with case plans—with 22 cases assigned to the experimental group and 17 to the comparison group. Parents received a 17-statement questionnaire to describe their experience with the child protective service (CPS) system and measure compliance with plans. The finding: There was no difference in compliance patterns or rates between persons who had experienced mediation and those who had not been in mediation. However, mediation did result in self-reported commitment to the plan, a decrease in parental alienation toward Child Protective Services and a self-reported reduction in a sense of coerciveness (Mayer, 1989).

Checking Vitals

Use of comparison groups:

May not present the dilemmas posed by an experimental design.

Is more compatible with ongoing service delivery.

Offers some degree of rigor as it attempts to answer the question as to the effect of experiencing the benefits of the intervention or program, or not.

Provides a stronger statement than no group comparisons, but groups might be challenging to identify.

Addressing External Validity

External validity is concerned with the ability to state with some degree of confidence that the results obtained in one program with one population would also be demonstrated in similar locations implementing the same program: "External validity is the degree to which the results of a research study are generalizable to a larger population or to settings outside the research situation or setting" (Grinnell, 1997, p. 276). This transferability of findings depends on the degree of similarity between one sample and its setting and other comparison settings. In qualitative studies, researchers may try to form a working hypothesis that may be transferred from one context to another depending on the degree of match between the contexts. However, regardless of approach or design, the number of contingencies, differences in agency and community settings and persons served, and other contextual and historical constraints limit generalizability (Franklin & Ballan, 2001). The primary purpose of a group design for many agencies is to support a credible statement with regard to program success. The ability to generalize those findings to other agencies or locations is not their primary concern, as contributing to knowledge is a less pressing motive than satisfying one's mission, funding bodies, and stakeholders.

Checking Vitals

External validity:

It has concerns with the ability to state with some degree of confidence that the results obtained in one program with one population would also be demonstrated in similar locations implementing the same program.

Transferability of findings depends on the degree of similarity between one sample and its setting and other comparison settings.

The ability to generalize those findings to other agencies or locations is not their primary concern, as contributing to knowledge is a less pressing motive than satisfying one's mission, funding bodies, and stakeholders.

CHALLENGES FOR AGENCIES

This chapter has identified the opportunities and the challenges for agencies. There are powerful reasons why an agency would want to address and present the effectiveness of its programs. Consequently, designing an evaluation that can credibly identify the program's successes and impact has great utility for an organization.

The design of a helpful evaluation requires a number of intentional steps to be planned and performed by an evaluation team and informed by agency leaders and program participants to assure accuracy and the ability to implement the evaluation plan. The design elements have the central purpose of presenting the effectiveness of the program; consequently threats to that confidence and credibility need to be identified and neutralized. However, addressing these threats to internal validity pose a number of tasks for the evaluation and requirements for the agency. Some threats can be identified and explicitly monitored—such as researcher bias. Most will require a commitment of time, energy, and resources from the agency to invest in an evaluation team to plan for the study in a systematic and thoughtful manner. This team will need to design a methodology and process that controls for internal validity threats.

In times of crisis and limited resources, when an agency's attention and assets are directed toward the provision of core and essential services, the time that it takes to commission, participate in, and engage in an evaluation process may be difficult to commandeer. The resources required for a purposive and random sample and an extensive design may be beyond the capability of the agency. The need for quick results and practical guidance may shape the choice of design and process. The evaluation team will be expected to understand the environmental context and the nature of the stressors for the agency and yet maximize their efforts to explicitly involve the agency in the evaluation design, select a usable and available sample, manage threats to validity and maximize the credibility of the study, and adapt design options to the realities of the environment and the needs of the study. Acknowledging limitations, the value in describing program effectiveness and participant experiences associated with the intervention motivate the research team to construct a "good enough" evaluation plan and process. Ultimately, an evaluation does not need to be exhaustive or perfect to have value. An evaluation design that is developed carefully will provide agency leaders and other decision makers more information than would have been available without an evaluation (Community Research Associates, 1989).

REFLECT AND REVIEW

Big Ideas

- Focus on the design of the evaluation and involve key stakeholders in the construction of the evaluation plan.

- Heighten the credibility of the study by identifying potential weaknesses in the evaluation through attentiveness to internal validity.

- Select and craft a group design that buttresses the credibility of the study, maximizes the level of confidence in the findings and effectiveness of the intervention or program, and balances these decisions with the reality of agency resources and stressors.

Discussion Questions

- Four levels of evaluation in relation to training programs were identified by Professor Donald Kirkpatrick (1998). The four levels included (1) Level 1—evaluating satisfaction. Were the trainees satisfied with training and was the training content viewed as helpful and useful to the trainee? (2) Level 2—evaluating learning. Have the trainees gained the knowledge or skills that were taught? (3) Level 3—evaluating behavior. Have the trainees put their new skills or knowledge to use in the real world? and (4) Level 4—evaluating results. Is there a lasting effect on the work environment? How do these levels fit with the group designs used in evaluation research?

- To what extent is it possible for an evaluator to build positive relationships in the course of the evaluation and still maintain sufficient objectivity to conduct all aspects of the evaluation?

- While the outcomes of a program are important in determining what works, there are times when the process engaged in during the implementation of the program is also of interest. What process elements might be of special interest to an agency?

Activities

- Identify an evaluation study in the social work literature and examine how explicitly the study addresses the topic of internal validity. Are threats to validity identified? How credibly are they addressed in the study? Are there additional threats that you recognize?

- Design a brief pre-test and post-test for acquiring some type of knowledge. What factors do you need to consider in constructing this test? How difficult is the pre-test? Are essential elements of knowledge the focus of the exam? Is the pre-test so simple that it will be difficult to show successful acquisition of knowledge? Is the pre-test so difficult and focused on remote information that it assures success based on its design rather than gaining the most critical knowledge or skills?

• If you were presenting an experimental design methodology to a board of directors at an agency, what practical and ethical objections would you expect and how would you respond to the board's concerns?

Resources

• National Center for Mental Health Promotion and Youth Violence Prevention. (n.d.). *Evaluation: Designs and approaches.* [Evaluation brief.] Retrieved from www.promoteprevent.org/Publications/center-briefs/evaluation_brief_designs_approaches.pdf

• Substance Abuse and Mental Health Services Administration. (n.d.). *Evaluation for the unevaluated.* [A step-by-step guide to conducting an evaluation.] Retrieved from http://pathwayscourses.samhsa.gov/eval101/eval101_intro_pg1.htm

CHAPTER 11

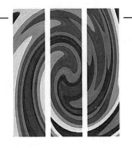

Evaluation Design

Qualitative Designs
and Applications

Some service struggles can't be resolved by
referencing occupancy reports.

*I would appreciate it if you wouldn't take notes. The last person
that took notes when I was talking was the cop I confessed to and
I caught a life sentence. I can't deal with you takin' notes.*

—*(imprisoned research participant during interview).*

This quote came from an interview with an adult inmate in a state correctional facility. One of the authors was conducting life history interviews with residents of the facility about their childhood in the juvenile justice system. This author initiated the interviews with those former residents of a juvenile treatment facility who eventually were placed in adult prison. The study was designed to investigate factors that may have contributed to adult incarceration.

As the interview progressed, the inmate became more and more aggravated. Recording equipment was not allowed in this particular correctional facility, so the interviewer was attempting to capture the interview with frantic note-taking. At first, the inmate seemed to express mild annoyance. As his irritation became apparent, the interviewer asked if there was a problem. The inmate's explanation is above (Kapp, 1997).

The above scenario demonstrates the complex nature of some evaluation questions. Under the guise of asking this individual about his experience as a youth in the juvenile justice system, unforeseen complications developed. While taking notes would seem to be a fairly benign and safe activity, it was clearly unacceptable to this individual. This chapter is devoted to qualitative evaluation strategies that might offer additional flexibility to address exceedingly complex and ambiguous questions. Qualitative methods can offer a more exploratory evaluation approach. Often in agency practice there are prickly questions about services that require going beyond previously collected administrative data or preexisting questionnaires. This chapter will provide a brief overview with some examples. For a more complete treatment, there are some detailed texts, cited in this chapter and listed in the references section at the end of the book.

BENEFITS OF A QUALITATIVE APPROACH

Qualitative methods of research are often viewed as a close relative of the clinical methods that drive social work practice. Although qualitative research should not be considered to be a less rigorous alternative (Royse, Thyer, Padgett, & Logan, 2005), the method may be more intuitive to a social worker than trying to interpret statistical data or tables/charts of numbers. The in-depth interview process prevalent in qualitative research is very familiar to a social worker. Additionally, the excerpts from qualitative interviews that might be presented in the qualitative evaluation reports are easy for practitioners to grasp. We will discuss this in more detail at the end of the chapter.

Not unlike the consumer satisfaction tools described in Chapter 12, qualitative approaches can allow consumers to tell their stories. This occurs when evaluators can ask unstructured questions about the service experience and its relative impact. The responses to these questions allow service recipients to use their own words to describe the experience. Oftentimes, the stories provided by consumers produce powerful and pertinent testimonials about the service delivery by articulating service issues in an explicit manner. Additionally, the viewpoint of a consumer will often raise unique and previously unconsidered service concerns or benefits. The use of a qualitative approach and its inherent ability to provide the consumer with a voice in the evaluation process is fully supported by professional social work ethics (National Association of Social Workers, 1999).

As with the example in the beginning of this chapter, qualitative evaluations may afford a variety of different approaches for evaluation questions identified by agency staff and/or consumers. While it may be possible to identify the prospective question, the best way to collect data about such questions may not be evident. If you were the director of a walk-in counseling center and there were some questions about referrals, you might wonder, Why do people use our services? What brings them to us? Is it proximity, reputation, specific staff, and so forth? The staff in the agency would be able to develop a list of possible reasons, but you may want to find out if there are explanations that were not considered previously, or you might want to know what the consumers of your services think without the benefit of suggestions offered in a preconceived questionnaire.

When students are initially exposed to qualitative evaluations, they sometimes find it difficult to distinguish between this approach and any other approach to evaluation. Research texts will employ words like "inductive" or "emergent" designs to describe this approach. A single qualitative design may include asking consumers, interviewing practitioners, reviewing records, and observing interactions between consumers and staff or managers and direct service workers. Table 11.1 lists some possible qualitative topics and respective data sources that may be engaged to address the "question." The various data sources enumerated in this figure should remind you of the resources a social worker might tap in the context of their routine practice. When considering this material, note that this design will rely on a wide range of data sources, and the sources take a variety of different shapes and sizes. Throughout the book, we talk about the process of program evaluation as having many facets and unexpected twists and turns determined by the question, data source, and political context. Qualitative designs embrace this ambiguity and attempt to include multiple sources to develop an improved understanding of the situation, question, service challenge, and so forth. In some cases, evaluation projects may identify new ideas that were not initially considered in the design. This type of evaluation may allow the evaluators to pursue the new twist raised in the course of collecting the data.

Table 11.1	Qualitative Questions and Possible Data Sources

Issue in Question	Possible Data Sources
Presenting circumstances of a new client	Review the case file; interview the client; ask the family members about why they think the client needs service; interview the referring agent and peripheral parties (case worker, teacher, judge, parole officer, foster parent, personal friends, etc.) about why they think the client needs services.
Client experience during the initial contact	Interview the client; ask an objective, unrecognizable observer to watch new clients in the waiting room; watch intake assessments; interview intake workers; interview support staff; interview direct service staff who do not do intake work.
Challenges of aftercare services from a residential program	Review numerical reports about youth placements in the community; interview the following staff: direct service staff in the facility, aftercare staff, supervisors, and managers; ask recently released youth to provide a tour of their community and describe the challenges they face; meet and interview community members about their ideas of the resources and barriers related to sustaining community placement.

EXAMINING QUALITATIVE DESIGNS

The fundamentals of this type of research have very deep roots in anthropology, feminist theory, and other social science theories. Many social science disciplines ground this type of inquiry in a particular world view (Denzin & Lincoln, 1994; Drisko, 1997). In academic papers and doctoral dissertations, the values of the various theoretical paradigms receive extensive attention. However, in agency-based evaluation, the techniques afforded by qualitative methods are extremely useful, and the explication of their theoretical origins is typically unnecessary. Patton (2002) suggested that not all questions require theoretical grounding. He suggested a more pragmatic use of these approaches with less emphasis on their genesis, especially when dealing with questions about the impact of a service on its recipients (p. 135).

Students often encounter some ambiguity when first exposed to qualitative methods. Lofland (1971) describes qualitative research as having four distinct characteristics: (1) a closeness between the setting and the researcher; (2) a focus on what is occurring and what is said about it; (3) a highly detailed description; and (4) the presentation of thorough quotes from study participants. In an attempt to highlight the distinctive attributes of this approach, this section will describe some of the features of this type of design and then provide some examples.

Checking Vitals

Agency-based evaluation questions may present unknown complexities warranting the unstructured nature of qualitative methods.

Qualitative methods offer service consumers a clear voice in the evaluation process.

Evaluators need to employ methods from various disciplines in a manner that honors the information needs of the agency.

DATA SOURCES

As illustrated in Table 11.1, there are a broad range of sources that are utilized to collect useful information. This section will describe some of the more prominent tools that are commonly used and tend to personify this approach.

Open-Ended Interviews

A common trait of qualitative research is an open-ended interview. This type of interview is quite different than the standardized instruments used to measure depression, self-esteem, family functioning, and so forth. The purpose of those scales is to apply the instrument and collect the same information from a group of individuals for comparison. These data would be used to inform questions like these: Who is doing well? Who is not? How can we help those who are not doing so well?

The questions in a qualitative interview are very close to the same across the various interviewees, but the effort focuses on providing for very different types of responses. If you asked a youth in an intake assessment about his or her background, the structured questionnaire would have the standard questions about a variety of areas: family, school, peers, drugs, legal issues, and so forth. In a qualitative interview (Table 11.2), the interviewer might just ask a general question such as this: "Think about events that occurred before you got here today; what are some of the things you think may have caused your problems?" Obviously, these two approaches would have very different responses. In the first interview, the youth would respond to structured items. The qualitative interview would allow the youth to identify the most prominent issues. It would also permit the youth to describe the concerns from his or her perspective. It may be of value to hear from the youth which issues are at the forefront of his or her mind. The issues listed by the youth without prompting could be compared with the agency's treatment repertoire. In other words, how do the agency's treatment specialties compare with what the youth sees as the most prominent issue?

Table 11.2	Open-Ended Intake Questionnaire

From your point of view, what are the primary reasons you were placed in this facility?

(With each issue, ask the following follow-up questions.)

1. How long have you been dealing with (each specific issue)?

2. How does this issue seem to impact your daily life?

3. What factors seem to influence this issue?

4. What might help you to improve this part of your life?

Observations

Observation can be a powerful method for learning about a service context. Often, observation (described as participant observation in many qualitative traditions) can offer insights that would not be yielded in an interview (Graue & Walsh, 1998; Greig & Taylor, 1999; Patton, 2002; Ward, 1997). An interview assumes a level of verbal skills that is not always possible with children in services settings with special needs. Things may be discovered through observation that were not considered when developing a questionnaire.

Also, watching someone interact in any type of social situation may be very different than what the same person might report in an interview. The interview is dependent on a fit between the interviewer's question and the respondent's view of the situation. Levels of verbal and cognitive ability influence this interaction. Additionally, when a person is embedded in a social situation, it is often hard to be aware of the entire situation. As a parent, you learn more about your children's social skills by watching them interact in various social situations than by asking them about the situation. A more concrete example may help to clarify this point.

In a study of special needs children in a services setting, Cocks (2008) uses observation to gain an understanding of peer interaction in a particular service setting. Asking children in this situation to describe their notions of peer influence would not have yielded the level of understanding gained by watching them. In this example, the researcher became knowledgeable about the rules in the setting, it routines, the role of staff, the various relationships between various youth, and more. Cocks found that the understanding of peer interaction did not advantage youth with higher verbal skills.

Some child welfare programs offer services to parents to prepare and support them for their child's return to the home. One example is an anger management program where a facilitator works with parents to make them aware of issues related to controlling their temper and its respective impact on parenting. Additionally, techniques for controlling their temper are introduced and often used in simulated circumstances. While it would be valuable to interview the parents and facilitator about the program, observing the class would provide a unique outlook on the service.

The observation could occur by sitting in the class or videotaping the class and watching it later. It would be crucial in this case to follow human subject protocols addressed in Chapter 4 (on ethics) to get consent for this observation. The observer could then watch the class with a series of questions in mind. Additionally, the observations may raise new considerations. Table 11.3 lists some possible questions. In our experience, this

Table 11.3	Guiding Questions for Observing an Anger Management Group

1. How do the parents respond to the facilitator? Are they open to the facilitator's direction? Do they seem resistant?

2. Does there seem to be a balance between discussion and lecture, or is there more emphasis on one or another?

3. Are there experiential activities included in the class? How do the parents respond to these activities?

4. Do the parents appear to grasp the material?

5. How does the facilitator attempt to engage the parents in the session?

6. What is the level of discussion?

7. How much do the parents interact with each other? How does the facilitator seem to support this interaction?

8. What other things were observed from watching the class?

type of observation has generated very useful details about the consumer's commitment to getting his or her children back; the level of interaction between the facilitator and the service consumer; and the role of support across the various consumers.

Focus Group Interviews

Focus group interviews permit data collection to occur through a group process. This technique combines the efficiency of a group interview, which offers the views of multiple persons, with a structure that provides for group opinions, minority views, and the opportunity to investigate anticipated and unanticipated discussion points (Krueger & Casey, 2000; Morgan & Scannell, 1997; Stewart & Shamdasani, 1990). An evaluation team is able to collect unique information about a program using an open discussion guide in this group format. Magill (1993) provides a clear example of using this technique to talk with low-income clients about an energy program.

Under a large budget cut, one agency conducted focus groups with staff groupings to determine if the agency was providing a clear message about its approach to the shortfall. After presentations throughout the agency, a focus group interview was conducted at each locale to get an assessment of the clarity of the message, the response to the message, and any unanticipated consequences. Table 11.4 illustrates the types of questions that were asked in the interviews.

The questions were fairly straightforward. Also, the executive team disciplined itself to focus on the most important concerns. The anonymous interviews were conducted by a consultant who had experience with focus groups but did not know the staff. It was hoped that staff would feel comfortable sharing their opinions with a professional who did not know them and would not be able to link their comments to specific programs or administrators. The focus

Table 11.4   Staff Response to Budget Cutbacks Presentation

1. How is the agency planning to address the budget situation?
2. Do you have any questions about the agency's response?
3. What is your reaction to this message?
4. How do you think agency personnel are responding to this news?

group results showed that the staff truly appreciated the executive director's efforts to describe the situation and the accompanying response as well as an opportunity to ask questions. Additionally, the focus groups also pointed out that the presentation was focused on an agency level which was hard for staff to grasp. So, when the presentation enumerated the hundreds of thousands of dollars cut from specific program budgets, it was often hard for individual staff members to equate those numbers with the small raise they would not receive or seemingly small cuts to their specific part of the agency. Specific administrators were able to follow up in staff meetings and address some of this confusion.

Managing a focus group interview is an art that requires a variety of skills. It is critical to make sure all members feel they have been heard and it is safe for them to express their opinions. A successful discussion includes input from all the members. A good interview will include many divergent opinions as well as new ideas that are generated as a result of the exchange.

Table 11.5 lists some probes to use in a focus groups interview. The trick to maintaining a smoothly flowing interview is to make sure all opinions are heard while not discouraging dissenting or minority views and keeping the discussion moving. Challenges include the focus group member who monopolizes the discussion, the shy participant, making sure that all opinions are heard and honored, and so forth.

Table 11.5	Generic Focus Groups Probes and Prompts

The goal of the facilitator is to conduct an interview that engages as many group members as possible while staying on the topic. The input of multiple members will often create a rich exchange of ideas. The exchange may lead to the open expression of many opinions, and sometimes new ideas will be generated by the group. Here are some common challenges, and some ideas for addressing them.

1. To reinforce that a person's opinion has been heard, paraphrase that person's opinion and ask if you have it right. This technique should be used as often as possible as it lets the group members know that you are listening.

2. To seek other opinions, ask the group if they agree with this person (Ralph) or disagree; for example, "Ralph has made his position very clear. Does everyone agree or does anyone feel differently?" Review the positions of those who have spoken and ask if the remaining members agree or disagree—specifically ask individual members who have not spoken their point of view.

(Continued)

Table 11.5   (Continued)

3. Review the positions of the entire group: Ralph felt this way, Susan felt this way, and so forth. After the review, ask the group if that captures all of the positions. If there is a particularly quiet member, you can simply ask that member where he or she stands: "I would really like to know what you think about this, Mary Ellen."

4. After hearing the ideas of your fellow group members, ask if anyone has a different idea; or does this discussion introduce any new ideas not yet covered?

5. When a specific member will not stop talking, say, "We have heard your opinion, Ralph. I need to know if others feel the same way or if they have a different opinion."

6. To move on from a heated argument, you might say, "Ralph has taken this position (state the position) and Susan feels (state her position). Then, do I have your positions right?" (Ask each to say yes or no). These are complicated issues; we would not expect everyone to agree. In fact, this type of disagreement is to be expected. The interviewer can either ask the others to weigh in on this topic or move to another topic: "I think that is enough time on that topic; I wanted to ask about (name topic)."

Participant Recruitment

A vital task in the focus group process is the recruitment of members. Market research firms that do significant numbers of focus groups usually have a person who specializes in recruitment. When possible, it is optimal to have a person devoted to this task: a person who is knowledgeable about the interview topic and able to present it to potential participants in a nonthreatening manner. A good recruiter focuses on the importance of the subject, the potential member's vital knowledge of the topic, and the interesting nature of the upcoming opportunity.

Members should be provided with an incentive to participate in the focus group. Cash is always a good incentive; but if funding for incentives falls short, approach local merchants to secure some type of gift certificate. Incentives are crucial to recruiting because they give potential participants the message that their time is valuable and their investment is being recognized by a concrete reward.

Field Notes

An additional qualitative tool comes from ethnographic studies that originated in anthropology. Anthropologists have traditionally engaged in intense forms of field research where they relocate to a specific community that is the focus of their research. The focus of their research is to develop an understanding of the lifestyle and culture of the members of that community. During a lengthy period of fieldwork, researchers use a variety of techniques to collect data, including interviews, observation, and field notes. The field notes, which function as a type of journal of the data collection process, are critical. Researchers engaged in this type of fieldwork invest immense amounts of time in their field notes. It is in the field notes where they capture the vital details of interactions, their impressions, and reactions to a broad array of critical events (Bernard, 2002; Emerson, Fretz, & Shaw, 1995).

Critical events in ethnography are recorded in field notes. Celebrated anthropologist Clifford Geertz (1971) described the story of a cockfight in Bali using his field notes. This event is infamous for describing the process of becoming accepted into a community. As qualitative methods have been translated to evaluative projects, field notes have become very important.

One of the authors earlier in his career observed a tour of a residential treatment program with a consultant known for his prowess in a particular model of group therapy. Under the guise of observing the consultant (referred to as James) in action, the author expected to watch group and treatment meetings. Instead, the experience was very different. Following a 3-day weekend, the consultant conducted an assessment of the different program sites on the grounds in preparation for his meeting with treatment teams that evening. The first visit was to the maintenance barn where he quizzed the maintenance staff about any repairs made over the weekend. There he learned that a couple of sites required some furniture repair; so James jotted a note in his pocket planner. Next, we headed off to the cafeteria to speak to its manager to find out if any programs either missed a meal or had to have sandwiches (peanut butter and jelly) delivered to the program.

James's example is clearly a case of a very astute and sophisticated fieldnote practitioner. After years of experience, he had learned that he could get extremely valuable information from these types of ancillary sources. He would seek out and collect all kinds of information from these sources and make explicit field notes that would include what he learned, his thoughts about the findings, the questions raised by his new findings, and possible ways to further investigate the various issues raised. This is a unique case of someone gathering valuable information, making sense of it, and creating field notes to capture its importance. His field notes provided an excellent assessment of the various groups' activity over the previous 3-day weekend. The field notes provided vital information that he was able to utilize in his follow-up meetings with the group therapists.

Checking Vitals

Qualitative methods afford data sources that provide great detail and depth about service delivery.

Open-ended interviews provide greater detail than a more structured questionnaire and allow the study participant to decide the most critical information.

Observations allow the evaluator to watch crucial events with an interest in specific aspects or an interest in the unexpected (waiting to see what happens).

Focus groups provide a focused discussion of service-related topics. Multiple opinions can be forwarded and group interactions can shed light on evaluation questions. Focus groups require some specialized skills around managing group discussion.

Field notes can provide a rich source of data about interviews, reactions, observations, feelings, impressions, and other phenomena that are encountered by evaluators in an agency or service setting.

MORE ASPECTS OF QUALITATIVE DESIGN

Again, this chapter is intended to provide an overview of this approach. There are many great texts on qualitative research that should provide a more detailed presentation and primer in specific cases. This section will hit on some additional distinctive characteristics of this method, specifically sampling and data collection.

Sample Selection

Selecting cases to study can be a delicate task. In some cases, you may use techniques that focus on developing a representative sample. Unique attributes of your study population may require alternative methods. If you are confident that you have access to a population that varies by critical factors of interest, like race or gender, it would be appropriate to use some type of probability sampling technique. (A probability sampling technique is used when the intent is to draw a sample that represents the overall population.) A systematic or a random sample may work in this situation (Rubin & Babbie, 2005).

Systematic Sample

You may want to review case files to determine the degree to which initial assessments are following the agency's protocols. This information could be useful for training new and more seasoned staff.

For example, if you had 350 case files in your agency, you might want to look at 50 of them to evaluate the initial assessment documentation. Start by dividing the total number of files by the desired sample size: 350 divided by 50 = 7. Start counting with the first case file; when you get to the 7th file, remove that file. Then count to the 14th file, remove it, and so on. You are selecting every 7th file until you have pulled 50 files. Next, read the initial assessment documentation for each case. While this little evaluation plan is not sophisticated, it provides valuable information that could be used to design the initial assessment training. The findings would inform some critical questions, such as the following: Are the agency protocols being followed? To what degree? What are some key areas that seem to be lacking? The information provided would not only answer some of these questions; it would also be helpful when considering the design of a training session.

Many other qualitative designs would not use a probability type of sample. Patton (2002) points out that most probability samples are designed to generalize from a small group to the overall population. Unlike the previous example, the rationale for many qualitative studies is to gain in-depth understanding. For qualitative studies with this focus, Patton suggests a more purposeful selection of cases (pp. 46–47). Three different sampling techniques will be described here: convenience, purposive, and snowball.

Convenience Sampling

A convenience sample, as it sounds, is a group of individuals who are selected because they meet the criteria of interest and are available (Berg, 2004, p. 34). Many times program evaluation efforts that focus on education will draw on the students in a professor's classroom or in the class of a teacher who may be completing research for a graduate requirement. If a program evaluation project required information about community attitude, a convenience sample could be selected by soliciting participation from people in an open environment. In one example, the staff at a local homeless shelter was concerned about the negative publicity they had received because a specific resident's behavior was described as creating a public nuisance by county commissioners. To further explore the prevalence of this impression, the facility trained a crew of volunteers to conduct short surveys in the downtown area on a Sunday afternoon during prime foot-traffic hours. The members of the community were overwhelmingly aware of the specific incident, but claimed that it did not have any impact on their impressions about the city. In this instance, a convenience sample was a valuable strategy.

Purposive Sampling

The intention of many qualitative studies is to gain detailed knowledge about a specific group of individuals. When selecting a purposive sample, the evaluators know the specific characteristics of interest, and sample participants are chosen because they meet those criteria (Berg, 2004; Patton, 2002). One of the authors has conducted research with youth who are receiving services from both the juvenile justice and mental health systems. While it may be feasible to draw a random sample of clients from either of these systems, it is a waste of resources to talk with youth who may potentially not meet either criterion. We worked closely with the mental health centers in five locations to draw our sample for this study. Specifically, we met with the administration and eventually the case managers of each center and asked them to help us select our sample. We described our interest in the youth and their families who were receiving services from both mental health and juvenile justice systems. The case managers knew exactly which children met this profile. We asked the case managers to describe the study to these families to see if they would be willing to participate. After the families signed the informed consent documents, the case managers forwarded their names on to us.

Snowball Sampling

As with the previous examples, qualitative evaluation projects often seek thorough information from service consumers who are not easily accessible by routine mechanisms. While it may be clear who the intended study participants are, it is unclear how to contact or find them. A snowball sample requires a chain of events that result in the identification of the sample. Key informants who are knowledgeable about the specific group of interest assist the evaluator in finding the possible participants. The key informant may be knowledgeable about the specific group or may be a member. The key informants identify possible participants and ask them if they would be interested in the specific project and, if so, ask them to contact the evaluation team (Berg, 2004; Patton, 2002).

If a child welfare agency wanted to learn more about the barriers faced by gay/lesbian potential adoptive parents, it would be difficult to find a roster of these couples who are serious about this possibility. However, it would be possible to seek some possible study participants by asking the agency staff to identify some known gay/lesbian couples who have shown interest historically. First, the agency personnel could ask the possible participants if they would be interested in this evaluation project. If so, the agency could ask them to meet with the evaluation team, and an interview could be conducted. At the end of the interview, the couple could be asked if they know other couples with something to say about this topic. Through repetition of this cycle, some very critical information can be developed about an often overlooked population of potentially viable adoptive parents. It is critical, when using this method of sample selection that potential subjects are allowed to remain anonymous and only divulge their identity to the evaluation team after they have decided to participate. Their privacy is protected by giving them the option of contacting the evaluation team only after they agree to participate. Until then, the evaluation team has no knowledge of their existence.

This sampling method has been used to locate and interview high-risk and low-profile individuals, such as sex workers in London (Scambler, 2007) and HIV-positive individuals in rural areas (Rounds, 1988).

Checking Vitals

Qualitative evaluations present unique challenges for selecting subjects for various data collection efforts.

Systematic samples can be used to select participants when the desire is to represent an overall population.

In many situations, qualitative evaluations require access to individuals with very unique characteristics and specialized sampling techniques. These studies are intended to provide an in-depth examination of exceptional circumstances.

These techniques require the ability to judiciously pick individuals who fit a topic of interest.

Convenience samples allow the selection of available participants who meet the criteria of interest.

Purposive samples permit the evaluator to handpick specific subjects.

Snowball samples utilize initial participants to help identify additional candidates for involvement in the evaluation.

DATA COLLECTION

Whether the data is generated through focus groups, observation, field notes, or interviews, it must be captured in a manner that is conducive to some type of analysis. The analysis provides meaning for the data (Patton, 2002). Before the analysis can occur, the data needs to be put into the appropriate format. Interviews can be taped and eventually transcribed. Observations and field notes can be transferred to written documents. The various types of data need to be transferred to some type of written document that can be utilized for data analysis. A written document allows for various levels of review ranging from simple readings to breaking it down with exhaustive analysis. Transcripts provide a written record of the rich, detailed stories from consumers, providers, funders, constituents, and detractors.

While the conversion of these vital bits of information can be tedious, this task calls for meticulous attention to detail. In some cases, someone on the evaluation team may create the transcripts. Most university communities, given the demand from doctoral dissertations, have professional transcriptionists who are skilled at creating accurate documents. In any case, the need to pay close attention to this task is clear. If careful attention is not paid to this task, it can inadvertently sabotage an entire effort.

Early precautions can also have a momentous impact on the quality of the eventual interview transcripts. Small digital recorders can create very clear recordings that you can download to a computer for transcription. Additionally, software is being developed, if it has not been already, to literally transcribe digital files. But these amazing tools depend on an intelligible initial recording. When preparing to interview either individuals or groups, plan as if you are creating a production. Just as you would pilot test a questionnaire, give the sound arrangements a serious trial run. Execute some dummy recordings with individuals situated as the interviewees would be; then, record them talking and listen to the trial recordings. Sometimes simple changes like closing windows, eliminating other background noises, and adjusting the recorders can really help the quality of the recording.

Transcribers also need to be apprised of the purpose of the project and the profound importance of transcribing the recording as close as possible to a verbatim recount. We have tried a variety of approaches to help with transcriptions in focus groups. For example, the interviewer should precede every question with a person's name: "John, have you ever received a mail survey from the state?" This will help the transcriber keep track of who is talking. These precautionary efforts can make a big difference; therefore it is critical for the evaluators to decide what level of detail is needed and to produce the recordings with that in mind (for more tips on transcription, see Patton, 2002, pp. 380–384). Some specific examples that illustrate the successful use of transcripts include examining women adopted as children (Howard, 2001);

therapeutic change (Brandell, 1989); and commitment among same-sex couples (Rostoscky, Riggle, Dudley, & Wright, 2006).

This chapter focuses on the use of program evaluation in an agency setting to improve services. Qualitative evaluation methods present special challenges while holding immense promise. As stated earlier, the roots of many qualitative methods are grounded in theoretical viewpoints that are connected to prescriptive ways of knowing. Each of these paradigms is accompanied by a deep-rooted commitment to following a method in a disciplined manner. As Patton (2002) eloquently states, the various methods can stand on their own and be employed accordingly to address specific evaluation questions. While the evaluator considers the wealth of tools in the qualitative inventory, the focus is on the needs of the evaluation focus and not an allegiance to a specific theoretical tradition.

An additional difficulty is the selection, application, and successful implementation of these various tools within the confines of an agency setting where information needs to be instructive and timely. While an anthropologist spends months and sometimes years in a specific locale to examine cultural practices, an evaluator does not have the advantage of this type of time commitment. However, the same tools can be functional in an agency setting. Additionally, these tools often require some modification that might compromise the methodological muster offered by a specific theoretical orientation. The evaluator has to pick and choose the right tool, which usually requires some tailoring toward the evaluation question and the agency context. Finally, this needs to be completed in time to inform agency practice.

For example, a qualitative interview completed with two points of view (a youth and a parent/guardian) can provide a veritable wealth of data that can be exceedingly enlightening. However, if an evaluator is not careful, this same plan can result in an exorbitant amount of data that may not be fully analyzed in time to meet the agency-imposed deadlines. In one case, an evaluation of a day treatment program included a wealth of data generated by exhaustive interviews with the youth, the parents, the treatment staff, and the referring worker. Instead of completing a comprehensive analysis of each interview, the interviewers reviewed the transcripts and created critical notes about information that related to the implementation of the program model. Those notes were analyzed and the findings were generated from that slice of the data. The agency and the accompanying funding agency were wedded to the specific model, so the evaluation efforts focused in that arena. It was determined that the new model was competing with a payment scheme that was more rewarding for the agency financially.

Future implementation had to be clearly tied to existing funding schemes for it to get a fair chance at implementation.

Other rich elements that came from these data remain for possible analysis in the future, such as some interesting findings about the interaction between clinical supervisors, staff, and youth. However, that was not the focus of the evaluation, and pursuing that topic in the analysis would have precluded hitting the agency reporting deadline. While some of these shortcuts may mortify purists, the evaluator has to make pragmatic decisions that suit the context.

Evaluators who use qualitative techniques need to understand the technique, the agency setting, and the specific research questions. Caudle (2004) describes a number of ways qualitative evaluations can be designed to collect data that is manageable and suitable to providing useful findings that can influence program decision making. While a qualitative evaluation project can produce a wealth of rich data, the focus of the project needs to remain on answering the evaluation question in a timely manner.

Checking Vitals

Qualitative data from various sources (focus groups, open-ended interviews, or field notes) needs to be organized in written transcripts that can be used for analysis.

The setting for data collection needs to be tested to make sure that recordings capture the information in a clear and accurate manner.

In qualitative projects, evaluators need to manage both the value of unforeseen findings and the need to answer original evaluation questions in a timely manner.

EXAMPLES OF APPLYING QUALITATIVE METHODS

The three examples described below offer possible insight into different aspects of qualitative techniques in an agency setting. The first project reviews case files to answer questions about a service population. A second example describes a strategy for interviewing children, and the third illustrates a common data analysis technique.

Event Maps

Qualitative interviews with children or adults are sometimes difficult. An effective interview requires an open and detailed conversation about life circumstances that are usually difficult to recount. The situations may be connected with negative memories and are often complicated. A variety of social science disciplines have used life histories to get detailed accounts from study participants (Clausen, 1998; Denzin, 1989; Hyde, 2005; Takkinen & Suutama, 2004). When interviewing children and young adults, it has been useful to organize the discussion around critical events and use that structure to organize the interview. This interview process requires the interviewer and the interviewee to create event maps.

These interviews require a general outline and strategy, as opposed to a list of specific questions. The first step is to decide the key events that will provide the focus and structure for the interview. The events can be out-of-home placements, specific service encounters, emergency room visits, community-based services, or any occurrence that seems key to the service being evaluated. In the first example, young adult offenders were interviewed about their experiences in the juvenile justice system (the events were the various placements). Each placement was listed (see Figure 11.1). After the placements were listed in chronological order, the interviewer went back to the beginning and asked each young man to comment on how he came to be placed in that setting and what he thought about it.

In another case, we interviewed young offenders with a history of mental health services about their experience with the mental health and juvenile justice systems. We asked the youth to list their various service encounters with mental health services (the events); and then to comment on each of the services, specifically the role of the local juvenile corrections department in their service experience.

The progression of events presented in Figure 11.1 is typical of the interviews completed in that study (Kapp, 1997). It was easy for these young men to create these maps. Each young man watched the interviewer draw the map and consulted on the location of each event as well as the overall structure. This series of events created a clear structure for the interviews. A natural flow was created during each interview as the interviewer would point to a specific event and ask the young man to comment on the service. At the end of the discussion, each young man was asked to comment on the overall system, to list its strengths and drawbacks, and to offer suggestions for improvement.

Figure 11.1   Event Map Interview

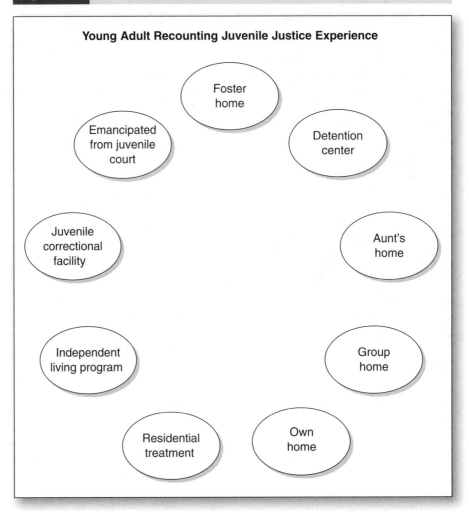

This interview approach has been useful as it facilitates an active discussion with young individuals about their experiences. The youth are active participants and are allowed to take some control of the discussion by verifying the correctness of the event order, describing the events as well as the overall context. Once the overall map is created, the participants appear comfortable as they are aware of the plan for the interview. This technique has proven to facilitate some meaningful discussion with study participants while making them active participants in the discussion.

A Field Study of Files

Chapter 8 (Program Description: Evaluation Designs Using Available Information) addresses the use of a variety of data sources for answering evaluation questions. The following example also illustrates the use of case files, a valuable data source, using a qualitative approach. The administrative and direct service staff at a residential facility for delinquent children were curious about the discrepant findings from multiple sources of data around the prevalence of sexual abuse events in their clientele's history. The information sheet completed at intake reported that about one-third of the clients had been involved in some type of sexual abuse incident as either a perpetrator or a victim. Conversely, group therapists and the child-care staff that dealt with the daily living needs of the youth had a very different impression. In various group sessions that occurred throughout the facility, it appeared that the majority of clients had been involved in some type of sexual abuse incident. The program staff and clinical supervisors consulted with the evaluation department, resulting in a small-scale study using the case files.

A small sample of case files was selected for a qualitative study. Each reviewer combed through a file to determine if there was any evidence that a youth was involved in any type of sexual abuse as a perpetrator or a victim. The case file typically included the process notes documenting client and staff encounters like group meetings, individual sessions, or spontaneous exchanges; treatment plans that addressed specific goals and interventions related to group treatment, family therapy, education, and daily living; and a collection of biopsychosocial and other reports. All documents included in the case file were open for consideration by the reviewer. Any mention of sexual abuse as a perpetrator or victim that was reported in the file was captured and recorded. When the small sample of files (30 of the 125 youth in the program) was closely scrutinized, it turned out that about two-thirds of the children had some involvement as a perpetrator or a victim (Kapp & Grasso, 1993).

As it turned out, the youth completed the intake form almost immediately after their arrival at the facility. Thus, when they were asked a question about sexual abuse involvement, the youth would not divulge their involvement unless there was a court order documenting the adjudication for an offense. Although the intake staff at the facility was highly skilled, they were not able to solidify the type of relationship that would permit a youth to disclose such an incident in the short time span of the initial interview. In retrospect, the information system report that a youth was involved in sexual abuse (collected at intake) turned out to be an extremely conservative measure. The qualitative review of the files documented a more inclusive and accurate appraisal. To address this, the facility developed a specialized program to address sexual abuse with the entire population. The program included specialized assessment tools and a comprehensive training and supervision component directed at the treatment of sexual abuse among delinquent offenders.

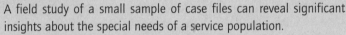

Checking Vitals

A field study of a small sample of case files can reveal significant insights about the special needs of a service population.

Event maps are an effective technique for interviewing youth and young adults:

Participant and interviewer co-construct the framework.

Structure provides familiar context for discussion.

Discussion can focus at many levels.

Coding and Analyzing Qualitative Data

One of the most ambivalent tasks in the qualitative evaluation process is the coding and analysis of the data. By definition, it is laborious. The task is geared to reduce a wealth of rich data to a relevant, manageable set of key quotes and insights. This notion seems to conflict with a data collection process designed to give participants a free forum for expressing their voice. At the same time, the coding and analysis is very exciting because it reinforces impressions developed during the interview process. Additionally, new unintended findings typically emerge through the analysis. This section is intended to give readers a taste for the process. There are excellent resources that provide a more complete treatment (Miles & Huberman, 1994; Patton, 2002; Uehara et al., 1997; to mention just a few).

In this example, interviews were completed with a youth, a family member, and professionals from a mental health provider and juvenile justice. The study was designed to assess the level of collaboration across the two service systems for this group of youth (Kapp, Robbins, & Choi, 2008). Interviews were completed, transcribed, and transferred to a qualitative data analysis software package (see Patton, 2002). The examples in the next section will illustrate some of the salient steps in the process.

Coding Qualitative Evaluation Data

Coding requires the evaluators to review the transcripts and to essentially label specific sections of the text in a manner that informs the evaluation questions. The coding process is driven by two separate techniques. One is guided by topics that are generated from the original evaluation questions. An additional set of codes emerge when the data is being reviewed. These two sources have often been called the *etic* and *emic*, respectively (Morris, Leung, Ames, & Lickel, 1999). Table 11.6 shows a portion of an interview with a youth describing his notions of success. The youth's impressions in this section were coded in three different ways. One of the codes came from the evaluation questions, while the other two were inspired solely by the youth's words.

The example also illustrates that one section can have multiple meanings and be coded multiple times. The coding process is an ongoing enterprise. Initially, the evaluation questions are used to generate an initial set of codes, but this list of codes continues to grow as new relevant ideas are stimulated by reviewing the transcripts.

Table 11.6   Coding Youth Comments About Success

Youth: Uh, [case manager] thought that he can help me, because I was really not the nicest person when I moved here. We had just gotten away from Ruben, my step dad, the one who used to hit us. And so [case manager] was kind of trying to help me keep my emotions under wrap. And I think he did a really good job with helping with that.
    I do not think I would have been able to do it without him there.

Codes for this section:

What is the benefit of the mental health service (from evaluation questions)?

How did the mental health service help (from the youth's comments)?

Keeping the Evaluation Questions Front and Center

Coding data for a qualitative evaluation project requires discipline. It is vital to maintain the focus on the evaluation questions. As stated earlier, unforeseen codes typically surface during the process. While new codes are usually interesting and compelling, the evaluator must make sure the codes are relevant to the evaluation question. While evaluators may desire to pursue every new perspective in a qualitative evaluation, timelines and resources usually do not allow such a luxury. One of the virtues of a qualitative evaluation is the freedom to pursue an open structure when examining a service-related issue. The evaluator must balance this luxury with the challenge of accommodating information needs in a timely fashion. Additionally, the evaluation is usually driven by specific questions, and addressing those questions remains primary.

When developing codes, the evaluator must constantly remain aware of the agency context. Once the evaluator develops a master list of codes (often called a codebook), it is helpful to organize those codes according to the most critical evaluation questions. The priority of the original evaluation questions can help to determine which codes receive the most attention in the analysis. The link between the codes and the evaluation questions is vital to maintaining the focus in an evaluation. For example, interesting issues were raised in this study about specific assessment tools during juvenile justice and mental health intakes in various locales. Some preliminary analysis was completed, but the primary questions did not focus on this topic. The data on the assessment tools was not a vital aspect of the study of collaboration; however, it remains available for us to evaluate in greater detail, if this topic becomes a higher priority. Table 11.7 shows the codes organized under a specific evaluation question.

In Table 11.7, the first evaluation question is, "How does the mental health assessment work?" There are many pieces related to this important question. The questions listed in *1a* through *1h* are topics that fall under the broad question. Each of these questions is linked to a code or a set of codes in the right-hand column. For example, consider Question 1c: Who made the referral? Each referral source has a separate code (court, school, etc.). The referral source is a critical part of the assessment process. Each of the multiple sources of referral gets a separate code. When preparing to analyze the data related to this critical question, the evaluators can decide which aspects are the most important and invest resources to analyze those specific codes.

Table 11.7	Qualitative Data Analyses Codes Organized by Evaluation Question

Question	Code
1. How does the mental health assessment work**?**	
1a. How and from what contexts are youth's MH needs identified?	MH id-JJIntake MH id-Other JJ MH id-School MH id-Home MH id-Other
1b. What assessment tool was used?	JIAQ POSIT MAYSI-2 Pre-Sent Interview Other [create code] No Asmt Tool
1c. Who made the MH referral?	Court Ordered Other JJ referred School referred Soc Wrkr referred Comm referred Home referred Unknown referral
1d. Describe the process of initiating and obtaining services. (MH referral *process*)	Dscp-initiatingMH
1e. Was collateral assessment information collected? From whom?	CollInfo-MH CollInfo-JJ CollInfo-School CollInfo-Parent CollInfo-Other
1f. Was the youth involved in giving assessment information?	YthAsmtInfo
1g. Was the family involved in giving assessment information?	FamilyAsmtInfo
1h. Did the process of obtaining services work? (pros and cons)	ProObtnMHSrvc ConObtnMHSrvc

Triangulation

Triangulation is a technique that organizes multiple sources of information around a similar question (Patton, 2002). The compilation of several pieces of information provides a more complete understanding. It is also presented as a technique for verifying the accuracy of the information. In this example, a variety of perspectives are used to consider the notion of success for a specific youth. In Table 11.8, success for a specific youth is discussed by four individuals (the youth, his parent, his mental health case manager, and his juvenile justice worker).

Table 11.8	Four Takes on Success for Nathan

Nathan: Freedom. Freedom, that's the main thing. That's what anybody here wants. Anybody in jail. Few people have it worse at home. You know, some people say, I'd rather be here than at home. Those are the people you really feel sorry for.

Control. Life itself. Mind.

Just take responsibility for what I did and stay out of trouble. Probation guidelines . . . because they can't do anything to me if I don't mess up.

Nathan's mother: Successful? (chuckles) Well . . . let's see. Successful . . . well, for one thing, if he can just get home and stay out of trouble, like not leaving the house and stuff, follow the detention center's rules and get himself through this. I mean he's gonna be 18 in November. Get himself through this and everything and quit putting his mother through so much stress—I think that would be a great success to me. So if he can just get through that.

His therapist: My diagnosis for success for him would have been to follow through with some of the recommendations I gave. I know I recommended intensive therapy with case management services and the whole nine yards—community based kind of things for him. And I don't think that's what happened.

His probation officer: For Youth to go home and to be taken out of juvenile court custody.

The example in Table 11.8 shows different points of view on what it means for Nathan to be successful. This example illustrates that each party has unique views of the meaning of success. When considering collaboration across these parties, it is crucial to understand that the end goals are not exactly the same and the differences have implications for the various ways of supporting this youth along with potential barriers for working together. The integration of these viewpoints clearly provides for a more comprehensive understanding.

Checking Vitals

Data coding is a foundation of qualitative data analysis.

Codes may be based on predetermined evaluation questions or emerge from the data.

Organizing codes around evaluation questions can help to maintain the evaluation focus.

Triangulation combines multiple sources of data to develop a more complete understanding.

Qualitative evaluation methods may be an attractive alternative when the examination of a service issue warrants a more exploratory and less structured inquiry. This chapter has examined many different aspects of qualitative design and provided examples of various applications. Evaluators employing qualitative methods are constantly confronted with the tension of maintaining the evaluation focus on the original evaluation questions. The promise of unanticipated and original findings that are common to this method must be managed in a manner that honors the agency's need for relevant and timely information.

REVIEW AND REFLECT

Big Ideas

• Qualitative evaluation methods are useful when the question is more abstract and an exploratory approach is warranted.

• Qualitative methods may offer consumers a chance to express themselves in a manner that offers them more control over their opinions.

• Qualitative evaluation methods require a special talent to create a balance between the rigors offered by the technique and its respective discipline with the information needs of the agency.

Discussion Questions

• What are some of the benefits of using a qualitative evaluation method? List some specific circumstances when it might be useful.

• What is unique about the type of data that would be generated by open-ended interviews, observations, and focus group interviews?

• What is distinctive about qualitative sampling methods, and how are they suited to this type of research?

• What features of the study of the case files were unfamiliar to you?

• What is triangulation, how does it work, and what do you see as its major strengths?

Activities

• Think of an agency-based question that may require a qualitative approach and develop a plan to draw a sample.

• Choose one of the examples listed in this chapter, then identify the unique needs of the evaluation question that led to the choice of a qualitative method, and then comment on whether the approach that was taken adequately addressed those needs.

• A variety of examples were presented in this chapter. Pick one that you think is a good example, and one that you think is flawed. Describe why you chose the good example and why you chose the bad example.

Resources

• National Science Foundation. (1997). *Chapter 4: Analyzing qualitative data*. Retrieved from http://www.nsf.gov/pubs/1997/nsf97153/chap_4.htm

• USAID Center for Development Information and Evaluation. (1996). *Performance monitoring and evaluation tips: Conducting focus group interviews*. Retrieved from http://pdf.dec.org/pdf_docs/PNABY233.pdf

• USAID Center for Development Information and Evaluation. (1996). *Performance monitoring and evaluation tips: Using direct observation techniques*. Retrieved from http://pdf.dec.org/pdf_docs/PNABY208.pdf

CHAPTER 12

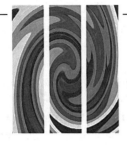

Consumer Satisfaction

How happy do you think the Johnsons are with
my services?

Much of our energy in this book has been focused on collecting credible
information about the delivery of services and the respective impact of
those services on the recipient children, families, and communities. A key piece
of any evaluation is the opinions of those receiving the service. They have a

unique insight about the timeliness of the services, the performance of the staff, the quality of their relationships with them, and many other key aspects of services. The value of client voices in planning and evaluation has been promoted for decades (Maluccio, 1979).

Social work places high value on the dignity and worth of the individual receiving the services (NASW, 1999). An excellent way to apply this critical principle is to acknowledge the valuable information consumers possess by asking them to reflect on the quality of services from their point of view. Gilman and Huebner (2004) argue that a full assessment is not complete without the inclusion of client satisfaction data. Additionally, if that data is collected, efforts should be made to put direct services staff, administrators, and executives in a position to use that information to influence the design and operation of services, but more on this specific aspect later.

A certain amount of controversy about consumer satisfaction exists in some services settings. Many consumers, often the recipients of involuntary services, are assumed to be dissatisfied with their circumstances, leading some providers to question the value of their feedback. The argument goes like this: Parents with children in foster care, for example, are going to be reticent, if not hostile, about the service experience. Their children were withdrawn from their home, most likely against their will, and it is predictable that they will feel contempt for any services surrounding this experience. The line of reasoning suggests that a person struggling with housing, or a youth on probation or a resident in a nursing home, as well as other less than voluntary clients, are assumed to be too embittered to provide constructive feedback about their services.

In this argument, the measurement of consumer satisfaction *with services* often gets treated as a proxy for contentment with an individual's situation. The focus of consumer satisfaction is not solely focused on perceptions related to individual circumstances but on the delivery of services to address their struggles in that situation. In the case of a child undergoing chemotherapy for throat cancer, consumer satisfaction is not focused on how the child feels about having cancer. The point of this data collection is to find out how the child feels about the services he or she is receiving, the treatment he or she is getting from various medical and social work staff, and if services are meeting the child's needs. Service providers can learn important things about the services and get ideas about how to make things better. It is a social worker's charge to engage involuntary clients in a manner that focuses on the proposed treatment plan and its respective goals, such as finding housing, getting their children back in the home, and so forth. Consumer satisfaction data is an excellent way to assess the level of that type of engagement, as well as other critical elements of service delivery, and to explore methods of improving it.

Social workers have an obligation to provide consumers with the highest quality of service (NASW, 1999). Service consumers usually have few other service alternatives. In many cases, service recipients are picking up some part of the tab for services, and as paying consumers, they deserve their money's worth (Bear & Sauer, 1990). In summary, service recipients in even the most dire circumstances deserve the opportunity and are well-equipped to provide constructive feedback. In many cases, they are paying for some part or all of the service. They have intimate knowledge of the service experience, and this information should be fully exploited for its unique and instrumental value for assessing and improving the service. The innumerable possibilities for using this information fit nicely with social work's ethical commitment to provide the best possible service.

EMPIRICAL ARGUMENT

The recent growth in consumer satisfaction measurement has led to a burgeoning body of research that supports its value in an agency setting. Consumer satisfaction is related to positive outcome. Additionally, high satisfaction scores are a basic expectation of policymakers (McMurtry & Hudson, 2000) and administrators (Ingram & Chung, 1997). Research has identified a positive relationship between satisfaction and functional outcomes (Berg, 1992; Cook & Kilmer, 2004; Kuperschmidt & Coie, 1990; Manteuffel & Stephens, 2002) as well as clinical outcomes (Manteuffel & Stephens, 2002). Others have promoted satisfaction as offering a refreshing perspective compared with pathology-based measures of success (Gilman & Huebner, 2004), such as a diagnosis or breaking the law or one's living situation. As a critical component of the service experience, consumer satisfaction should be measured and integrated into discussions focused on service delivery.

Oftentimes, the relationship between consumer satisfaction and other program components is useful to supervision, staff development, and program management. Positive changes in satisfaction have been linked to changes in critical aspects of treatment (Diener, Suh, Lucas, & Smith, 1999; Lewinson, Redner, & Seeley, 1991). The role of case managers and their service impact on children's ability has been emphasized in service satisfaction studies (Measelle, Weinstein, & Martinez, 1998). For managers, consumer feedback may be a useful way to discuss service delivery with staff as it relates to effectiveness. How do happy consumers act, how does that impact services, and what can our service do to promote their happiness?

Children's satisfaction has been reported to be related to the relationship between a significant adult and a nurse or doctor (Hennessy, 1999). Some studies showed little or no agreement between parents/caregivers and children/adolescents on satisfaction, including the levels of satisfaction with staff and their treatment, and with lower levels of satisfaction in child/adolescent clients than parents (Barber et al., 2006). In addition, satisfaction data has been collected to identify services to specific at-risk target populations (Lord & Pockett, 1998), assess program innovations (Fischer & Valley, 2000), identify critical staff characteristics (Sturg et al., 2003) and services challenges such as attrition (Primm et al., 2000), and determine the value of specific program components (Locke & McCollum, 1999). For managers and supervisors, this kind of information can fuel critical conversations related to the delivery of services to multiple family members, the attraction of specific populations, and program adjustments. For us as managers, supervisors, and service providers, how does the way we do business impact our consumers?

You may be getting the idea that we support the use of consumer satisfaction as a critical part of evaluation. It provides a key outlet for consumers to get their voices heard in the assessment of services, which is consistent with the ethics of social work. Additionally, it can be a vital tool for practitioners to learn about many aspects of their approach to service. Table 12.1 is a short list of some of the settings where we have seen consumer satisfaction measures used effectively.

Table 12.1   Settings Effectively Using Consumer Feedback

Cancer treatment groups

Health care

Services for people with developmental disabilities

Services for the elderly

Marriage preparation courses

Mental health services for children and adults

Victims of interpersonal violence

METHODOLOGICAL CONSIDERATIONS: THE CONTEXT OF DATA COLLECTION

As with all data collection, the context for gathering information warrants some attention; untended, it can really devastate the quality of the information. Earlier in this chapter, we mentioned the seriousness of the challenges faced by most individuals receiving many of the services (voluntary or involuntary). It is often useful to tie the collection of data with the delivery of services, but, in some cases, that can create unanticipated complications.

Some service recipients may have considerable consequences on the line when they are receiving services. The outcome of said consequences typically is influenced by the opinions of their social workers and other service providers. Service consumers need safe environments to submit their views when satisfaction data is collected without having to think about any recourse for expressing their opinion.

In one case, a new initiative included the collection of consumer satisfaction data from family preservation recipients. To address the immediacy of the request, the agency had the family preservation workers collect data from each family on their caseload. The agency was happily surprised when the survey results portrayed their client families as very satisfied to be receiving these services, in a variety of different ways. One of the authors of this book assisted in the analysis of this data. After finding no questions under a 98% satisfaction level, some inquires were made into the process for collecting the data.

It turns out that each family preservation worker asked his or her client families to complete a questionnaire about satisfaction with services and then give it back to the worker. To be clear, a family preservation worker intervenes with families where a child is at risk of being removed from the home. This program includes concentrated clinical and concrete services for the family while the child stays in the home. At the end of the short service plan, family preservation workers offer their professional opinions on what should happen with the child. Should the child remain at home? What services should the family receive? So, when the worker handed the forms to family members and asked them to rate their performance, the consumers knew that the worker had significant influence on the future of their families; specifically, when recommendations were made at the end of service about the possible placement of their children out of the home. This is not to say that workers with less-than-positive scores would consider recommending anything that was not in the best interest of the child based on the result of their consumer feedback, but it does raise a question about the value of the data. When we discussed this with the staff of the agency, it seemed plausible that a family member might inflate his or her score for a worker just to be on the safe side. Obviously, while there are some benefits to piggybacking data collection on the service enterprise, it is also important to be cautious about the impact of the context on the results.

STUDYING CONTEXT OF SATISFACTION DATA COLLECTION

This experience informed a subsequent project to develop a system for getting feedback from parents with children in foster care. In this project, one of the authors was given the opportunity to conduct a focus group with some of these parents to talk with them about the development of useful strategies for collecting this data. The parents were very interested in these discussions and had some critical insights about some viable ways to proceed.

The parents were very helpful and willing to explain the role of consumer satisfaction within their lives and offer some helpful suggestions about the structure of consumer satisfaction measures. Here is an example of a concrete suggestion:

Well, if I'm going to fill out a form and take a lot of time out of my day, because I think that one of the ways a form could be more, um, meaningful, is that if you had, if you broke it down into categories, like maybe, um, transportation being one, and many questions under that, because our experience has been that the private agency has no transportation available for these kids.

The parents offered other valuable suggestions. They commended the idea that someone would call them up and ask how they were doing. The mail surveys they had received, seemed cold and cruel in the context of the intensity of their experiences. The written surveys seemed to minimize their typical circumstances: for example, their children had been removed from the home; in court, they were told they had to accomplish a number of things to get their own kids back; they struggled to complete and pay for those services in the context of their own daily circumstances with poverty, other children, child support payments, and so forth. They preferred a telephone survey method and felt that if the data was going to be collected, the state agency should make serious efforts to use it for improvement (Kapp & Propp, 2002).

In another case, an agency was providing support services to adults with emotional and mental difficulties. In this agency, the clients had a positive and comfortable relationship with the staff member who answered the phone and performed clerical/support tasks in the waiting room where they waited prior to each appointment. Each month, this staff person would ask them to complete a confidential form that addressed their satisfaction with services. The survey was presented in a nonthreatening manner by an agency staff person with whom the clientele was very comfortable. The data was collected in a timely manner, and the client satisfaction survey respondents felt confident that their responses would have no impact on the delivery of their individual services. The collection of client satisfaction data, like most other program evaluation data, is very sensitive and needs to be collected in a context where the service recipients feel comfortable submitting their honest opinions with no fear of recourse.

FINDING THE RIGHT SURVEY INSTRUMENT

At the end of this chapter is a list of survey instruments. The authors of these instruments have been gracious enough to allow us to display their work as examples of the types of tools that are available. Each of them spent time and energy developing the instrument and testing its psychometric properties. The task of instrument development is a significant undertaking and should be avoided, whenever possible, especially when viable options are currently available. These examples do not constitute an exhaustive list of available instruments; however, this is a list that the authors have discovered in their travels.

When choosing a consumer satisfaction instrument, consider some of the following factors:

- *How well does the instrument fit the service setting?*

Some instruments are somewhat general and some are specific. Will a general instrument work? Are there specific aspects of your service that would benefit from the insight afforded by consumer feedback? If you feel your needs are very specific, do your best to match the items to your needs with specific areas assessed by the various instruments. Some of the examples are for foster care or for mental health or other settings. However, the collection at the end of the chapter is not exhaustive. The number of instruments has grown significantly in the last few years. So, investing a little bit of time searching for a suitable instrument is a reasonable idea. You might be able to find good things using your favorite search engine on the Web or tapping scholarly databases that might include social service citations.

- *Does the instrument provide an overall assessment or is it more topic specific?*

Some instruments give an overall score for client satisfaction. Others will break the concept of satisfaction into more precise categories. For example, an instrument may provide more specific feedback on the worker's performance versus the agency's performance. When shopping for an instrument, consider if your needs would be met by having a general score that describes consumer satisfaction or if you have more specific parts of the program you would like to assess.

- *Does the language fit my population?*

Most authors do their best to avoid technical jargon or social work professional speak, but your review will help to ensure that there are not terms or words that will make no sense to your consumers. Although the instruments are written in English, many have been translated into additional languages. Contact the authors to see if a specific instrument has been translated.

- *Use the complete instrument.*

As mentioned earlier, each instrument is the result of much testing and revision, which is supported with concise psychometric testing. While it may seem fairly benign to substitute a word or possibly add or subtract an item, these kinds of changes threaten the reliability and validity of the instrument. One agency used a family assessment scale to solicit specific feedback, and the instrument had an item that rhymed. The clinicians wanted to change this item as it seemed to be a distraction. In another case, each item on an instrument included a "not applicable" response. Workers viewed this as confusing to families, and it required constant explanation. On the surface, these suggestions seem innocent. However, seemingly small changes related to wording or possibly adjusting the scale, in effect, negate the hours of work invested in making the instrument conceptually and psychometrically sound.

- *Consult with the authors.*

If you are planning or considering the use of a specific instrument, contact the authors. Even though the authors were generous enough to approve the inclusion of their instrument in this book, each of the instruments has copyright considerations. You must discuss your intended uses with each author. Furthermore, the individual authors may have suggestions about the application of the particular instrument for your purposes. As authors of client satisfaction instruments, we have discussed its application with many possible users. Believe us when we say that we know the good, the bad, and the ugly about our instruments, and we are happy to share those insights. In some cases, the authors may be willing to disclose new developments. This might include revised versions of the instruments, training materials or training sessions, and in some cases, software that is available for data entry and feedback by and for either an interviewer or a consumer. We can attest that despite our busy schedules, it is interesting and usually enjoyable to speak with other professionals who share our commitment to consumer feedback.

TECHNICAL CONSIDERATIONS FOR DATA COLLECTION

There are several different data collection options to consider. One option is to have a paper-and-pencil type survey that the consumer completes and gives to someone to enter into a database for storage, processing, and reporting. Another option is to have a telephone interviewer contact the consumer to complete the interview. In one case, we had telephone interviewers enter the information into a database while on the phone with the consumer. In another case, a database was configured in a computer where the consumer could sit down and complete the interview. Another possibility uses Web-based survey tools where the survey can be completed from any computer that has access to the Internet.

Some of the details of the various strategies are outlined in Table 12.2. Face-to-face interviewers can offer high-quality data if the interviewers are trained and competent. One caveat is that the interviewers may be associated with the agency, possibly inflating the responses. In our experience, we have found consumers to be very responsive to telephone interviews. However, this approach involves some specialized technical support to train and manage the interviewers, the phone equipment, and the supportive database applications. While consumers enjoy telling their stories using this approach, it is a struggle to maintain accurate phone numbers with a population that is fairly mobile. Additionally, some consumers do not have access to phones.

Computer applications can often allow the service recipient anonymity by providing feedback without the aid of an interviewer. One approach is to develop a stand-alone database application that allows consumers to complete the survey independently at a designated computer at the agency. While this option removes the threat of skewed responses that may occur with an interviewer, it takes specialized skills to create a database application that can be self-administered by a consumer. Another option is the use of a Web-based survey that the consumer would complete online. There are many possible online

Table 12.2	Consumer Satisfaction Survey Data Collection Techniques

Technique	Requirements	Considerations
Paper-pencil survey with interviewer	Trained interviewers	Interviewers need to be secured, trained, and managed. Competent interviewers can draw in-depth information from consumers; face-to-face interview may inflate responses, especially if interviewer is viewed as having a relationship with service provider.
Telephone interview	Trained interviewers; phone equipment; database application to manage data entry and storage	Specialized technical support is required to develop and manage phone and database applications. Data collection and entry is single task; respondents appreciate effort to pursue their opinions. Completed at consumers' convenience. Keeping phone number current is a challenge with consumers who are often on the move. Many consumers may not have access to phones.
Consumer completion from individual computer	Database application offering ease of use, data entry, storage, and reporting capability	Consumers are able to provide feedback anonymously and autonomously. Requires advanced technical support to develop.
Web-based survey	Access to Web-based survey tool	Provides anonymity. Development does not require limited technical expertise to develop and report. Data analysis options are often provided. Consumers need access to Internet.

survey tools. These applications typically do not require sophisticated computer skills or a facility with a particular database application. However, the consumers need some type of Internet access, which can be provided by public alternatives, such as the local library or Internet cafes or the agency.

In each of these cases, it is necessary to consider the ultimate purpose of the survey. As parents of children in foster care reminded us, if the agency is going to the trouble to collect the data, they need to make a commitment to use it to make things better (Kapp & Propp, 2002). Somehow the data needs to be transferred from its original form as a data collection tool to some type of format that can be used to influence service delivery. The phone survey with data entry into a database, the stand-alone computer, and the Web-based survey organize the data into a format that can be manipulated for reporting purposes. The face-to-face method requires a data entry step to put the information into a form that can be manipulated. Usually database software or a spreadsheet program will suffice for basic reporting, but more sophisticated analysis can be conducted by transferring this data to a statistical package.

REPORTING CONSUMER SATISFACTION DATA

While more sophisticated analysis can provide useful insights, we strongly recommend that social service professionals plan the kinds of decisions and considerations that may be influenced by satisfaction data and develop simple, straightforward reports that address those possible uses.

Data Reporting Options

Two different examples were created with fictitious data to illustrate the kinds of discussions that can be fueled by this type of data. Both examples use a satisfaction instrument for parents with children in foster care. In this case, plugging our own instrument, satisfaction of parents with children in foster care, is driven more by familiarity than pure self-promotion (Kapp & Vela, 2004). The first example (see Table 12.3) is organized around the caseload of a caseworker. This report is designed to examine the work of a single practitioner and facilitate discussion around the respective worker's performance. The second example looks at the program level with a focus that might stimulate conversations between a group of practitioners, such as the administrators, supervisors, and direct service staff with that program.

Single Worker Report

Consider the types of conversations that Table 12.3 might stimulate between a clinical supervisor and a worker about his or her caseload and the

Table 12.3 Caseworker Report of Consumer Satisfaction Scores

Client Name & (Race)	Respect	Clear Expectations	Working w/Me	Preps Me Court/Mtgs	Stands Up for Me in Mtgs	Respects My Values/ Beliefs	Would Refer to Others	Overall Satisfied
Nicholson (Caucasian)	1	2	1	3	2	1	2	1
Lopez (Latino)	3	2	3	1	1	3	3	2
Penn (Caucasian)	1	2	2	3	2	1	2	2
Wahlburg (Caucasian)	1	3	1	3	2	1	3	1
Chapelle (African American)	3	1	3	1	1	3	2	3
Shaw (African American)	1	2	3	1	1	2	2	2
Purim (Latino)	3	2	3	1	1	3	3	2
Mickelson (Caucasian)	1	2	2	3	2	1	2	2
DiCaprio (Caucasian)	1	3	1	3	2	1	3	1
Woods (African American)	3	1	3	1	1	3	2	3
Averages	1.8	2	2.4	2.0	2.5	1.9	2.4	1.9

1 = Agree, 2 = Undecided, 3 = Disagree

corresponding skill development needed to accomplish this type of work. Obviously, these data are not intended to describe any type of unquestionable truth about a practitioner's work with his or her clients. The intent is to use these numbers to raise questions that can be explored within a broader context created by the knowledge shared by these two professionals interested in improving service to clients. It is hoped that a commitment to improving practice along with an ongoing constructive relationship will facilitate a focus on service delivery. This type of relationship will help to diminish defensiveness and other barriers that might impede such a conversation.

There are a number of ways to view this data and suggest possible topics for discussion (remember, in Table 12.3, a "1" represents agreement with the statement and a "3" disagreement). Starting with the most basic approach, simply look at the overall averages at the bottom of the table. In this example, the worker seems to do better with issues related to overall respect, the respect of values, and overall satisfaction. At the same time, scores are lower around working with the parent, standing up for parents in meetings, and referring others to this worker. The supervisor and worker could focus discussion on what might be possible reasons that the first set of scores seem to be higher and why the latter may be low.

Another level of discussion (still based on Table 12.3) can be pursued by checking to see if there are different scores by subgroup. In this case, it looks like Caucasian parents report higher scores on the item related to working together (working with me) but report lower scores on the preparation for meetings. So, parents of color feel like they are better prepared for meetings than Caucasian parents. Again, these numbers can be used to cultivate discussions on what might be behind these numbers. Does the worker think the subgroups are being treated differently? The supervisor could ask the worker to describe what he or she does to prepare clients for meetings. As stated, the point of these reports is to stimulate a variety of conversations about practice.

Here is a list of possible suggestions for discussions of consumer satisfaction data in this type of context:

1. Keep the reports confidential between the supervisor and the worker.

2. Both parties should examine the information privately prior to meeting.

3. Ask the worker to identify specific trends.

4. Discuss possible explanations of the trends.

5. Investigate supervisor identified trends.

6. Discuss strategies:

Collect more data from clients by asking them specific questions about an area of practice: How could I do a better job of preparing you for meetings?

Develop plans for improving scores.

Implement plans.

Identify a time to determine if scores seem to be improving.

This discussion illustrates a possible format for the use of data to foster discussion between an individual worker and a supervisor, with an eye toward possible strategies for improving practice.

Multiple Program Report

Table 12.4 is developed around a different level of discussion, at the programmatic level. For example, program managers could meet with a middle-level manager, presumably their supervisor, about these consumer satisfaction scores. Table 12.4 reports average scores for parents discharged from services the previous quarter. Again, it is helpful to give the individual managers this data prior to any discussions. Program managers could review this data by looking at their own program's high and low scores. In this example, Davidson's parents seem to have their highest score on parents feeling respect and their lowest score on preparing clients for meetings and court.

Furthermore, managers could compare their program scores against overall averages along the bottom of the report. Mason would see that their scores are below the average on respect and respecting beliefs, while scoring above average on standing up for clients in meetings. Another version of comparing scores against other program scores would be to look at the program with respect to others. Duke would see that they are the highest on respect, respect for beliefs, working with me, and overall, but they are lowest on expectations, court/meeting preparation, and parents referring others to them. Each of these strategies is a way for a manager to give these numbers some meaning and begin to talk about their program's strengths and growth areas.

Before the discussion of this data, the middle-level manager could ask program managers to assess their own strengths and areas for improvement, as well as looking for programs that are doing well in areas where they are not.

| Table 12.4 | | Average Consumer Satisfaction Scores by Program (Clients Discharged Last Quarter) | | | | | | | |

Program Name	Respect	Clear Expectations	Working w/Me	Preps Me Court/ Mtgs	Stands Up for Me in Mtgs	Respects My Values/ Beliefs	Would Refer to Others	Overall Satisfied
Davidson N = 14	1.5	2.2	1.2	3	1.2	1.1	2.2	1.3
Kansas N = 16	3	2	3	1	1	3	3	2
Memphis N = 19	1	2	2	3	2	1	2	2
Duke N = 12	1	3	1	3	2	1	3	1
Mason N = 17	3	1	3	1	1	3	2	3
Averages	1.8	2	2.4	2.2	1.6	1.8	2.4	1.8

1 = Agree, 2 = Undecided, 3 = Disagree

The middle-level manager could begin the discussion by asking managers to talk about their struggles and successes with service delivery and how these numbers support or contradict those impressions. In addition, programs could consult with each other. Specifically, Davidson and Duke could talk about the things they think are critical to their high scores on working with their parents. Another approach would be for all the managers to confer on their scores related to the not-so-high scores on getting parents to refer others to them. What are some of the struggles here? What could be done better? Do any of the managers have any examples of success that could provide some insight? As a group, the managers could reflect on what is going well and what needs some attention, and then develop some plans for improvement. These meetings could occur periodically to help managers hold each other accountable, provide fresh energy to these discussions, and focus on service effectiveness.

Consumer satisfaction is a critical aspect of service delivery. Any assessment of a program's performance is incomplete without this type of data. This chapter has introduced some considerations around the collection of this data, specifically choosing an instrument, and some technical and contextual factors of data collections. It is critical for practitioners to think about the types of decisions that they would like to influence with these data. As illustrated, specific information needs can be addressed through the development of tailored reports. Those reports can make the data come alive by serving as springboards for discussions of service delivery and methods of assessing as well as improving effectiveness.

Appendix

EXAMPLES OF CONSUMER SATISFACTION INSTRUMENTS

1: CLIENT EXPERIENCES QUESTIONNAIRE (CEQ)

Authors:	James R. Greenley & Jan Steven Greenburg
Description:	The Client Experiences Questionnaire (CEQ) is a 42-item measure consisting of two instruments, which are intended to analyze client satisfaction with services, in addition to client satisfaction with life. There are three subscales: (1) satisfaction with humanness and staff (SHS: items A2, A4, A6, A8, A9, and A13); (2) satisfaction with perceived technical competence of staff (SPTCS: items A1, A3, A5, A7, A11, and A12); and (3) appropriateness of services (AES: items B1 and B5). The subscales of SHS and SPTCS can be added together in order to get the satisfaction with services score (SS). The third part of the CEQ measures client satisfaction with life in the domains of living situation, finances, leisure time/activities, family and social relations, past and current health, and access to health care. Since the third subscale measures quality of life, if desired, it can be scored separately from the other two scales. To get an overall score of the CEQ, sum all of the numbers in each subscale together and then divide by the number of answered responses. For section A, responses can range from 1 to 7, with 1 being the highest in satisfaction and 7 being the lowest. Part B responses range anywhere from 1 to 5, and the third section, regarding quality of life, can run from 1 to 7.
Psychometric Data:	Concerning reliability, the CEQ has been shown to have an internal consistency coefficient of .96 with the first two subscales and .88 with the third subscale. The

quality of life instrument has been shown to have an internal consistency ranging from .80 to .91. In reference to validity, the CEQ has been supported by factor analysis. The total quality of life scores correlated strongly with patient functioning levels. Criterion-related validity is supported by the fact that clients who reported high satisfaction also confirmed higher scores of life satisfaction.

Reference: Greenley, J. R., & Greenberg, J. S. (2000). Client experiences questionnaire (CEQ). In K. Corcoran & J. Fischer (Eds.), *Measures for clinical practice* (Vol. 2, pp. 163–168). New York: The Free Press.

Note: Used by permission.

CEQ

For each question, write the number of the answer that best corresponds to how you feel in the space to the left of the item.

A. Below are some questions about your satisfaction with the services you receive.

1 = Extremely satisfied
2 = Very satisfied
3 = Somewhat satisfied
4 = Not certain
5 = Somewhat dissatisfied
6 = Very dissatisfied
7 = Extremely dissatisfied

_____ 1. The general quality of services you receive in this program?
_____ 2. The courtesy and friendliness of the staff?
_____ 3. The thoroughness of the staff in gathering all important information about your problem?
_____ 4. The staff's warmth and personal interest in you?
_____ 5. The degree to which the staff thoroughly explains what you are suspected to do?
_____ 6. The amount of respect shown to you by the staff?
_____ 7. The technical competence of the staff?
_____ 8. The consideration shown for your feelings?
_____ 9. The amount of concern the staff expresses about your problems?
_____ 10. The degree to which the staff seems to be familiar with your kind of problem?
_____ 11. How well the staff checks up on the problems you have had before?
_____ 12. The comprehensiveness or completeness of services which were provided to you?
_____ 13. Attempts by staff to explain how things are done so you won't worry?

B. Below are some questions about the program you are in.

1 = Yes, definitely
2 = Yes, somewhat
3 = Neither, yes nor no
4 = No, somewhat
5 = No, definitely

_____ 1. Do you like being in this program?
_____ 2. Do you feel excellent progress has been made on your problem since you entered this program?
_____ 3. Are you getting the kind of help here that you need?
_____ 4. Is the help you are receiving in this program appropriate for your problem?
_____ 5. Has the condition that led to your being in this program improved a great deal?

C. Below are some additional questions about how satisfied you are with some aspects of your life.

1 = Terrible
2 = Unhappy
3 = Mostly dissatisfied
4 = Equally satisfied/dissatisfied
5 = Mostly satisfied
6 = Pleased
7 = Delighted

Concerning your living arrangements, how do you feel about:

_____ 1. The living arrangements where you live?
_____ 2. The rules there?
_____ 3. The privacy you have there?
_____ 4. The amount of freedom you have there?
_____ 5. The prospect of staying on where you currently live for a long period of time?

Here are some questions about money. How do you feel about:

_____ 6. The amount of money you get?
_____ 7. How comfortable and well-off you are financially?
_____ 8. How much money you have to spend for fun?

Here are some questions about how you spend your spare time. How do you feel about:

_____ 9. The way you spend your spare time?
_____ 10. The chance you have to enjoy pleasant and beautiful things?
_____ 11. The amount of relaxation in your life?
_____ 12. The pleasure you get from the TV or radio?

Here are some questions about your family. How do you feel about:

_____ 13. Your family in general?
_____ 14. The way you and your family act toward each other?
_____ 15. The way things are in general between you and your family?

Here are some questions about your social life. How do you feel about:

_____ 16. The things you do with other people?
_____ 17. The amount of time you spend with other people?
_____ 18. The people you see socially?
_____ 19. The chance you have to know people with whom you feel really comfortable?
_____ 20. The amount of friendship in your life?

Here are some questions about your health. How do you feel about:

_____ 21. Your health in general?
_____ 22. Your physical condition?
_____ 23. The medical care available to you if you need it?
_____ 24. How often you see a doctor?

2: CLIENT SATISFACTION: CASE MANAGEMENT (CSAT-CM)

Author:	Chang-Ming Hsieh
Description:	The Client Satisfaction: Case Management (CSAT-CM) is intended to be an instrument that conceptualizes client satisfaction as the client analyzes his or her own sense of services. It also requests for the client to identify their least and favorite thing about services. The first subscale in the CSAT-CM acknowledges satisfaction with different services with five different questions. Answers for these questions can vary from a response of 1 to 7, with 1 indicating completely dissatisfied while a ranking of 7 specifies completely satisfied with services. The second set of questions in the CSAT-CM pays attention on the importance of services. This part of the instrument tries to recognize people perceptions on how important some aspect of services may be greater than another. Scores vary from 1 to 5, whereas 1 means not at all important and 5 meaning extremely important. A third subscale is intended for a trained interviewer to ask participants to rank in order 1 through 5 the five items of importance in the second subscale. Percentages are tallied on each subscale to compute the scores for each.
Psychometric Data:	The CSAT-CM has construct validity with a correlation between the CSQ at .70. Concerning reliability, the CSAT-CM test-retest reliability has been as high as .81.
Reference:	Hsieh, Chang-Ming. (2006). Using client satisfaction to improve case management services for elderly. *Research on Social Work Practice, 16,* 605–612.
Note:	Used by permission.

(CSAT-CM)

APPENDIX A: SATISFACTION ITEMS

The following questions ask how satisfied you are with different services provided by the Central West Case Management. Please use a number from 1 to 7 to indicate your satisfaction where 7 means *completely satisfied* and 1 means *completely dissatisfied*. If you are neither completely satisfied nor completely dissatisfied, you would put yourself somewhere from 2 to 6; for example, 4 means neutral, or just as satisfied as dissatisfied.

S1. How satisfied are you with your case manager's assessment of your needs? ____

S2. How satisfied are you with the plan of care your case manager developed? ____

S3. How satisfied are you with your case manager's knowledge regarding the services that are available? ____

S4. How satisfied are you with your case manager's ability to get services for you? ____

S5. How satisfied are you with the availability of your case manager? ____

Important Items

Some people may feel some areas of the case management services are more important than others. What areas of case management services do you consider extremely important or not at all important to you? Please use a number to indicate the importance of services from 1 through 5, where 5 means *extremely important* and 1 means *not at all important*.

11. Case manager's assessment of your needs ____

12. Your plan of care ____

13. Case manager's knowledge regarding available services ____

14. Case manager's ability to get services for you ____

15. Availability of your case manager ____

APPENDIX B: CONSTRUCTING
THE IMPORTANCE OF THE HIERARCHY

Directions to interviewer:

Based on responses to the importance items, please rank the five areas of case management services from 1 (*the most important*) to 5 (*the least important*) below. For items with the same importance ratings, ask the respondents to rank order to their importance. Use the same ranking number for any areas the respondent believes are equally important.

_____Case manager's assessment of your needs

_____Your plan of care

_____Your case manager's knowledge regarding available services

_____Case manager's ability to get services to you

_____Availability of your case manager

3: CLIENT SATISFACTION INVENTORY

Author:	Steven L. McMurtry
Description:	The Client Satisfaction Inventory (CSI) is a 25 item instrument that is suitable for measuring client's feelings regarding services. Client responses can range from a score of 1 to 7, with 1 indicating a response of "none of the time" and 7 representing a response of "all of the time." Respondents do have an option of placing an X on each item, referring to "does not apply." The full version CSI has 20 items worded positively and 5 items worded negatively. This is done to control the amount of answering bias that tends to accompany survey questionnaires. The total score for the scale should range from an amount of 0 to 100. To compute this score, all reverse coded items should be calculated first. To finalize scores, plug in amounts and generate this equation: $S = (\text{Sum }(Y)) - N)(100)/[(N)(6)]$. (S corresponds to the item score, and N is the items answered sufficiently by the respondent.)
Psychometric Data:	Internal consistency for the full scale CSI has demonstrated correlation by having coefficients as high as .93. The CSI also has shown strong inter-item correlations. Moreover, the CSI has a minimal total of standard amount of error of measurement (SEM) at 3.16. Keep in mind, strong scales generally contain high coefficients with a small amount of SEM. With questionnaires using 100 point scales, a SEM score lower than 5 illustrate satisfactorily strong correlations. In regards to validity, the CSI has demonstrated good content validity as item correlation score of .57 was calculated. Furthermore, each item correlation was found to be statistically significant at the .01 level. On the topic of construct validity, because of the high levels of correlation between items, a good amount of construct is present by the means of convergence. As for discriminatory construct, the CSI has shown to have minimal relationships with scales measuring other factors besides service satisfaction.

References:

McMurtry, S. L. (1994). *Client Satisfaction Inventory (CSI)*. Tallahassee, FL: Walmyr Publications.

McMurtry, S. L., & Hudson, W. W. (2000). The client satisfaction inventory: Results of an initial validation study. *Research on Social Work, 10*, 644–663.

Note:

Used by permission.

CLIENT SATISFACTION INVENTORY (CSI)

This questionnaire is designed to measure the way you feel about the services you have received. It is not a test, so there are no right or wrong answers. Answer each item as carefully and as accurately as you can by placing a number beside each one as follows.

1 = None of the time
2 = Very rarely
3 = A little of the time
4 = Some of the time
5 = A good part of the time
6 = Most of the time
7 = All of the time
X = Does not apply

1. _____ The services I get here are a big help to me.
2. _____ People here really seem to care about me.
3. _____ I would come back here if I need help again.
4. _____ I feel that no one here really listens to me.
5. _____ People here treat me like a person, not like a number.
6. _____ I have learned a lot here about how to deal with my problems.
7. _____ People here want to do things their way, instead of helping me find my way.
8. _____ I would recommend this place to people I care about.
9. _____ People here really know what they are doing.
10. _____ I get the kind of help here that I really need.
11. _____ People here accept me for who I am.
12. _____ I feel much better now than when I first came here
13. _____ I thought no one could help me until I came here.
14. _____ The help I get here is really worth what it costs.
15. _____ People here put my needs ahead of their needs.
16. _____ People here put me down when I disagree with them.
17. _____ The biggest help I get here is learning how to help myself.
18. _____ People here are just trying to get rid of me.
19. _____ People who know me say this place has made a positive change in me.
20. _____ People here have shown me how to get help from other places
21. _____ People here seem to understand how I feel.
22. _____ People here are only concerned about getting paid.
23. _____ I feel I can really talk to people here.
24. _____ The help I get here is better than 1 expected.
25. _____ I look forward to the sessions I have with people here.

4, 7, 16, 18, 22.

4: CLIENT SATISFACTION INVENTORY (CSI-SF)

Author:	Steven L. McMurtry
Description:	The short form CSI is an altered version of the full scale CSI. It is a 9 item subscale of the full CSI, it analyzes items 2, 3, 8, 9, 10, 11, 21, 23, and 24. Since all of the items in the CSI-SF are positive in terms of scoring, no reverse coding is necessary. To get the total sum, use the equation $S = (Sum (Y))-N)(100)/[(N)(6)]$, ($S$ represents the total score; Y, in this case, corresponds to the item score, and N is the total items answered correctly by the respondent. Just like the full version, scores should vary from 0 to 100.
Psychometric Data:	The CSI-SF has established internal consistency as high as .89. Inter-item reliability is also prevalent. The total of standard amount of error for the measurement with the CSI-SF is at 4.11. Again, just like the full version, a SEM score lower than 5 indicates good correlations for a scale that adopts a scoring base of 0 to 100. On the topic of construct validity, because of the high levels of correlation between items, a strong amount of construct validity is present by the means of convergence. As for discriminatory construct, the CSI has shown a small amount of relationship scales measuring other factors besides service satisfaction.
References:	McMurtry, S. L. (1994). *Client satisfaction inventory (CSI)*. Tallahassee, FL: Walmyr Publications.
	McMurtry, S. L., & Hudson, W. W. (2000). The client satisfaction inventory: Results of an initial validation study. *Research on Social Work, 10*, 644–663.
Note:	Used by permission.

CLIENT STATISFACTION INVENTORY (CSI-SF)

The questions below are designed to measure the way you feel about the services you have received. This is not a test, so there are no right or wrong answers. Answer each item as carefully and as accurately as you can by circling the appropriate number on the right	None of the time	Very rarely	A little of the time	Some of the time	A good deal of the time	Most of the time	All of the time
1. People here really seem to care about me.............................	1	2	3	4	5	6	7
2. I would come back here if I need help again..........................	1	2	3	4	5	6	7
3. I would recommend this place to people I care about..........	1	2	3	4	5	6	7
4. People here really know what they are doing........................	1	2	3	4	5	6	7
5. I get me kind of help here that I really need........................	1	2	3	4	5	6	7
6. People here accept me for who I am......................................	1	2	3	4	5	6	7
7. People here seem to understand how I feel.........................	1	2	3	4	5	6	7
8. I feel I can really talk to people here...................................	1	2	3	4	5	6	7
9. The help I get here is better that I expected........................	1	2	3	4	5	6	7

5: CLIENT SATISFACTION QUESTIONNAIRE (CSQ-8)

Authors:	C. Clifford Attkisson & Daniel L. Larsen
Description:	The Client Satisfaction Questionnaire, abbreviated as CSQ, is a self-administered survey that was originally adopted for use with adult consumers in mental health and human services. However, the CSQ can be used to measure a wide range of health and human services. The administration of the scale usually takes between 1.5 and 8 minutes. An overall score is the result of adding all of the item responses together. Scores can range from 8 to 32. Higher scores indicate a greater degree of satisfaction.
Psychometric Data:	The CSQ-8 has been shown to have strong internal consistency by an alpha coefficient of .83 to .93. The highest values were drawn from the two largest samples. In regard to validity, the CSQ-8 has been shown to be moderately correlated with the Brief Psychiatric Rating Scale. The CSQ-8 has also been shown to be effectively correlated with symptom reduction, evidenced by the results of the Client Check List.
References:	Larsen, D. L., Attkisson, C. C., Hargreaves, W. A., & Nguyen, T. D. (1979). Assessment of client/patient satisfaction: Development of a general scale. *Evaluation and Program Planning, 2,* 197–207.
	Attkisson, C. C., & Greenfield, K. G. (2004). The UCSF client satisfaction scales: The Client Satisfaction Questionnaire–8. The use of psychological testing for treatment planning and outcomes assessment. *Evaluation and Program Planning, 3,* 799–811.
	Attkisson, C. C., & Zwick, R. (1982). The Client Satisfaction Questionnaire: Psychometric properties and correlations with service utilization and psychotherapy outcome. *Evaluation and Program Planning, 6,* 299–314.
Note:	The CSQ Scales are used worldwide and are translated into 20 languages. Additional information can be obtained from the CSQ Scales web site: www.csqscales.com

| **CLIENT SATISFACTION QUESTIONNAIRE** |
| **CSQ-8** |

Please help us improve our program by answering some questions about the services you have received. We are interested in your honest opinions, whether they are positive or negative. *Please answer all of the questions.* We also welcome your comments and suggestions. Thank you very much. We appreciate your help.

CIRCLE YOUR ANSWERS

1. How would you rate the quality of service you received?

4 *Excellent*	3 *Good*	2 *Fair*	1 *Poor*

2. Did you get the kind of service you wanted?

1 *No, definitely not*	2 *No, not really*	3 *Yes, generally*	4. *Yes, definitely*

3. To what extent has our program met your needs?

4 *Almost all of my needs have been met*	3 *Most of my needs have been met*	2 *Only a few of my needs have been met*	1 *None of my needs have been met*

4. If a friend were in need of similar help, would you recommend our program to him or her?

1 *No, definitely not*	2 *No, I don't think so*	3 *Yes, I think so*	4 *Yes, definitely*

5. How satisfied are you with the amount of help you received?

1 *Quite dissatisfied*	2 *Indifferent or mildly dissatisfied*	3 *Mostly satisfied*	4 *Very satisfied*

6. Have the services you received helped you deal more effectively with your problems?

4 *Yes, they helped a great deal*	3 *Yes, they helped somewhat*	2 *No, they really did't help*	1 *No, they seemed to make things worse*

7. In an overall, general sense, how satisfied are you with the service you received?

4 *Very satisfied*	3 *Mostly satisfied*	2 *Indifferent or mildly dissatisfied*	1 *Quite dissatisfied*

8. If you were to seek help again, would you come back to our program?

1 *No, definitely not*	2 *I don't think so*	3 *Yes, I think so*	4. *Yes, definitely*

6: FAMILY EMPOWERMENT SCALE

Authors:	P. Koren, N. Dechillo, & B. Friesen
Description:	The Family Empowerment Scale is intended to ask parents three different groups of questions: (1) about your family, (2) about your child's services, and (3) your community. The second section is designed to evaluate the parents' overall satisfaction with the services the child received. The scale is designed by a 34 Likert itemizing. Item scores can range from 1 to 4. To get an overall score, add each subscale's items together and then divide by the number of questions in each. Next, proceed to add all scores of the subscales together and then divide by the number of answered questions.
Psychometric Data:	The subscale pertaining to satisfaction with services has proven to have an internal consistency as high as .87. Test-retest reliability has shown good results as high as an alpha coefficient of .77. There are no known validity results solely dedicated to the section concerning satisfaction with services.
Reference:	Koren, P. E., Dechillo, N., & Friesen, B. J. (1992). *Family empowerment scale.* Portland, OR: Portland State University, Research and Training Center, Regional Institute for Human Services.
Note:	Used by permission.

FAMILY EMPOWERMENT SCALE

These questions ask about several areas of your life—your family, your child's services, and your community. The questions include many different activities that parents may or may not do. For questions that do not apply to you, please answer "Never". Also, we know that other people may be involved in caring for and making decisions about your child, but please answer the questions by thinking of your own situation. Feel free to write any additional comments at the end.

ABOUT YOUR FAMILY...	NEVER	SELDOM	SOME-TIMES	OFTEN	VERY OFTEN
1. When problems arise with my child, I handle them pretty well.	1	2	3	4	5
2. I feel confident in my ability to help my child grow and develop.	1	2	3	4	5
3. I know what to do when problems arise with my child.	1	2	3	4	5
4. I feel my family life is under control.	1	2	3	4	5
5. I am able to get information to help me better understand my child.	1	2	3	4	5
6. I believe I can solve problems with my child when they happen.	1	2	3	4	5
7. When I need help with problems in my family, I am able to ask for help from others.	1	2	3	4	5
8. I make efforts to learn new ways to help my child grow and develop.	1	2	3	4	5
9. When dealing with my child, I focus on the good things as well as the problems.	1	2	3	4	5
10. When faced with a problem involving my child, I decide what to do and then do it.	1	2	3	4	5
11. I have a good understanding of my child's disorder.	1	2	3	4	5
12. I feel I am a good parent.	1	2	3	4	5
ABOUT YOUR CHILD'S SERVICES...	NEVER	SELDOM	SOME-TIMES	OFTEN	VERY OFTEN
13. I feel that I have a right to approve all services my child receives.	1	2	3	4	5
14. I know the steps to take when I am concerned my child is receiving poor services.	1	2	3	4	5
15. I make sure that professionals understand my opinions about what services my child needs.	1	2	3	4	5
16. I am able to make good decisions about what services my child needs.	1	2	3	4	5
17. I am able to work with agencies and professionals to decide what services my child needs.	1	2	3	4	5

18. I make sure I stay in regular contact with professionals who are providing services to my child.	1	2	3	4	5
19. My opinion is just as important as professionals' opinions in deciding what services my child needs.	1	2	3	4	5
20. I tell professionals what I think about services being provided to my child.	1	2	3	4	5
21. I know what services my child needs.	1	2	3	4	5
22. When necessary, I take the initiative in looking for services for my child and family.	1	2	3	4	5
23. I have a good understanding of the service system that my child is involved in.	1	2	3	4	5
24. Professionals should ask me what services I want for my child.	1	2	3	4	5

ABOUT YOUR INVOLVEMENT IN THE COMMUNITY...	NEVER	SELDOM	SOME-TIMES	OFTEN	VERY OFTEN
25. I feel I can have a part in improving services for children in my community.	1	2	3	4	5
26. I get in touch with my legislators when important bills or issues concerning children are pending.	1	2	3	4	5
27. I understand how the service system for children is organized.	1	2	3	4	5
28. I have ideas about the ideal service system for children.	1	2	3	4	5
29. I help other families get the services they need.	1	2	3	4	5
30. I believe that other parents and I can have an influence on services for children.	1	2	3	4	5
31. I tell people in agencies and government how services for children can be improved.	1	2	3	4	5
32. I know how to get agency administrators or legislators to listen to me.	1	2	3	4	5
33. I know what the rights of parents and children are under the special education laws.	1	2	3	4	5
34. I feel that my knowledge and experience as a parent can be used to improve services for children and families.	1	2	3	4	5

COMMENTS_____

_____

7: REID-GUNDLACH SOCIAL SERVICE SATISFACTION SCALE (R-GSSSS)

Authors:	N. P. Reid & P. J. Gundlach
Description:	The R-GSSSS measures consumer satisfaction with human and social services. It is a 34-item instrument that calculates consumer satisfaction with services as well as it gathers reactions from consumers in regards to social services. The following three subscales are part of consumer's reactions: (1) relevance, (client's perception of his or her problem); (2) impact, (evaluation how services reduce the client's problem(s); (3) gratification, (measuring the extent to which services enhanced client self-worth). Items 1 to 11 are part of the relevance subscale, items 12 through 21 are part of the impact subscale while items 22 through 32 make up the foundation of the gratification subscale. Respondent answers can vary from 1 to 5, higher scores relating to stronger satisfaction.
	To score subscales in the instrument, add the total number of item scores by the total number of items in the scale.
Psychometric Data:	For reliability, the sums of all scores in the scale have shown strong internal consistency at alpha coefficients as high as .95. The three subscales totals have ranged anywhere from .82 to .86. A number of authors have proposed that each subscale could be used as a separate entity for measure. As for validity, the scale has good face validity. Although validity is not represented in other ways, research suggests that oppressed individuals have reported cumulatively lower degrees of satisfaction levels.
Reference:	Reid, N. P., & Gundlach, P. J. (2000). Reid-Gundlach social service satisfaction scale (R-GSSSS). In K. Corcoran & J. Fischer (Eds.), *Measures for clinical practice* (Vol. 2, pp. 635–638). New York: The Free Press.
Note:	Used by permission.

R-GSSS

Using the scale from one to five described below, please indicate on the line at the left of each item the number that comes closest to how you feel.

1 = Strongly agree
2 = Agree
3 = Undecided
4 = Disagree
5 = Strongly disagree

___ 1. The social worker took my problems very seriously.
___ 2. If I had been the social worker I would have dealt with my problems in just the same way.
___ 3. The worker I had could never understand anyone like me.
___ 4. Overall the agency has been very helpful to me.
___ 5. If a friend of mine had similar problems I would tell them to go to the agency.
___ 6. The social worker asks a lot of embarrassing questions.
___ 7. I can always count on the worker to help if I'm in trouble.
___ 8. The social agency will help me as much as they can.
___ 9. I don't think the agency has the power to really help me.
___ 10. The social worker tries hard but usually isn't too helpful.
___ 11. The problem the agency tried to help me with is one of the most important in my life.
___ 12. Things have gotten better since I've been going to the agency.
___ 13. Since I've been using the agency my life is more messed up than ever.
___ 14. The agency is always available when I need it.
___ 15. I got from the agency exactly what I wanted.
___ 16. The social worker loves to talk but won't really do anything for me.
___ 17. Sometimes I just tell the social worker what I think she wants to hear.
___ 18. The social worker is usually in a hurry when I see her.
___ 19. No one should have any trouble getting some help from this agency.
___ 20. The worker sometimes says things I don't understand.
___ 21. The social workers are always explaining things carefully.
___ 22. I never looked forward to my visits to the social agency.
___ 23. I hope I'll never have to go back to the agency for help.
___ 24. Every time I talk to my worker I feel relieved.
___ 25. I can tell the social worker the truth without worrying.
___ 26. I usually feel nervous when I talk to my worker.
___ 27. The social worker is always looking for lies in what I tell her.
___ 28. It takes a lot of courage to go the agency.
___ 29. When I enter the agency I feel very small and insignificant.
___ 30. The agency is very demanding.
___ 31. The social worker will sometimes lie to me.
___ 32. Generally the social worker is an honest person.
___ 33. I have the feeling that the worker talks to other people about me.
___ 34. I always feel well treated when I leave the social agency.

8: THE PARENTS WITH CHILDREN
IN FOSTER CARE SATISFACTION SCALE

Authors:	Gardenia Harris, John Poertner, & Sean Joe
Description:	This is a 24-item scale that was developed to evaluate parents' satisfaction with services for children in out-of-home placement. Of the 24 items, scoring ranges from 1 to 5, with 1 representing a response of "never" and 5 representing a response of "frequently." There is an option of 6, which gives respondents an opportunity of answering "not applicable." There is no evidence of a total score for this scale; relatively a mean score was calculated for each item.
Psychometric Data:	Good inter-item reliability is evident. Internal consistency is also prevalent seeing that it has reached an alpha coefficient as high as .97. In regards to validity, the scale was compared to a general satisfaction scale designed to measure mental health services. There was a positive correlation between the two scales at .60. These results were found to be statistically significant at the .01 level.
Reference:	Harris, G., Poertner, J., & Joe, S. (2000). The parents with children in foster care satisfaction scale. *Administration in Social Work, 24,* 15–27.
Note:	Used by permission.

Factor Loadings for Satisfaction Scale Items:
PCFCSS—Parents of Children in Foster Care Satisfaction Survey

My caseworker encourages me to discuss when things were better in my family.	.873
When my caseworker makes a mistake, she admits it and tries to correct the situation.	.873
My caseworker speaks up for me with other professionals involved in my case.	.870
My caseworker understands how hard it is to get your children taken away.	.850
My caseworker informs me about the help that is available to complete my case plan.	.843
My caseworker's expectations of me are reasonable.	.835
My caseworker tells me what she plans to say in court about my family and me-both the negative and the positive.	.834
My caseworker listens to my side of the story.	.833
My caseworker cares about my kids.	.825
When my caseworker says she will do something she does it.	.824
My caseworker devotes enough time to my case.	.818
My caseworker tells me who I can contact for help when she is gone for more than a day or two.	.816
My right to make decisions about my children has been respected during the time they have been in foster care.	.810
My caseworker gets me necessary services in a timely manner.	.793
My caseworker returns my calls.	.787
My caseworker has experience dealing with the kinds of problems my family and I are experiencing.	.779
I am involved in decisions made about my case.	.779
My caseworker is clear about what she expects of me.	.775
Meetings with my caseworker occur at least once a month.	.769
My caseworker respects my right to privacy.	.768
My caseworker helps me talk to my child often.	.767
My caseworker explains to me what will happen in court.	.766
My caseworker respects my social/cultural background.	.765
My caseworker calms my fears about what the agency can do to my children and me.	.754

9: PARENT SATISFACTION WITH FOSTER CARE SERVICES SCALE

Authors: Stephen A. Kapp & Rebecca H. Vela

Description: The PSFCSS is a 45-item instrument in which the majority of the questions ask about participants' satisfaction with services. The initial five questions ask participants to answer questions about the child's relationship with the respondent and general information about the child. The following 34 items ask respondents to reflect on their level of satisfaction with services. There are also four open-ended questions, which allow for consumers to give feedback. To end with, there are six questions at the conclusion of the questionnaire that gather information from participants regarding the survey itself, plus some demographical information. A total of 27 items are measurable for satisfaction with services. Scoring for the 27 items can range from 1 to 3, with 1 representing *agree*, 2 as *unsure*, and 3 as *disagree*.

Psychometric Data: Several researchers scrutinized the PSFCSS and found the scale to have favorably strong construct and face validity. Of the 27 core items, all were examined and can be considered sensitive. The PSFCSS has had internal consistency as high as .94.

Reference: Kapp, S. A., & Vela, H. R. (2004). The parent satisfaction with foster care services scale. *Child Welfare, 83,* 263–287.

CLIENT SATISFACTION TELEPHONE SURVEY

General Information:

1. How are you related to the child in care? (*circle*)
   - mother
   - father
   - guardian
   - grandparent
   - other relative
   - adoptive parent

[*If multiple children in foster care, ask #2–#5 for each child*]

2. I'm going to ask you about your child's health. Does your child have special needs or disabilities, such as (*check all that apply*)
   - MRDD (mental retardation/developmentally delayed) _____
   - learning disabled _____
   - physically disabled _____
   - SED (seriously emotionally disturbed) _____
   - BD (behavior disorder) _____

3. Which of the following is your child's permanency goal? (*circle*)
   - family reintegration/reunification
   - adoption
   - guardianship
   - independent living

4. How many months was/has your child been in out-of-home placement?

5. Is your child in an out-of-home placement at this time? (*circle*)

   yes   no

If yes, what kind of placement? (*circle*)

   - foster home
   - group home/residential facility
   - psychiatric hospital
   - kinship/relative placement

Circle the participant's responses: 1 = agree; 2 = unsure; 3 = disagree

To begin with, I'm going to read you some statements about your contract provider worker (Kaw Valley, KCSL, United Methodist Youthville, St. Francis Academy, The Farm) that you may agree with, or not agree with, or be unsure about.

[Contract Provider Worker Competency:]

1. My worker treats/treated me with respect.

    1   2   3

2. My worker is/was clear with me about what he/she expects/expected from me and my family.

    1   2   3

3. My worker is working/worked with me to get my child/children back.

    1   2   3

4. My worker helps/helped prepare me for meetings and court hearings.

    1   2   3

5. In meetings with other professionals, my worker stands up/stood up for me and my child/children.

    1   2   3

6. My worker respects my values and beliefs.

    1   2   3

7. If I could, I would refer other families who need help to this worker.

    1   2   3

8. Overall, I am satisfied with my worker.

    1   2   3

Now, I would like to read you some statements about the contract provider agency (Kaw Valley, KCSL, UM Youthville, SFA, The Farm). Again, I'd like you to respond as to whether you agree or disagree with the statement or whether you are unsure about it.

[Contract Provider Agency Quality:]

9. The (agency) has/had realistic expectations of me.

    1   2   3

10. Overall, I am satisfied with the services I have received from the agency.

    1   2   3

11. If I could, I would refer other families who need help to this agency.

    1   2   3

12. Is there anything else that you would like to tell us about the agency or your worker?

    Now, I would like to read you some more general statements about your experiences with the contract provider agency and worker.

    [Empowerment:]

13. My worker asked for my opinion about the problem my family and I were having.

    1   2   3

14. My worker asked for my opinion about the services my family and I needed.

    1   2   3

15. My worker has included me in decision making.

    1   2   3

16. The agency or my worker has told me my rights.

    1   2   3

17. I was told who to call if I felt that my rights had been ignored.

    1   2   3

18. Is there anything else that you would like to tell us about what aspects you may have liked or disliked about the agency or the worker?

    We're about half-way through with the survey.

    Now, I would like to read you some statements about your SRS worker.

    [Satisfaction with SRS worker:]

19. My SRS social worker treats/treated me with respect.

    1   2   3

20. My SRS social worker does/did a good job of explaining what was required of me.

    1   2   3

21. My SRS worker respects my values and beliefs.

    1   2   3

22. Overall, I am satisfied with my SRS worker.

    1   2   3

23. Is there anything else that you would like to tell us about your SRS worker?

The next statement(s) refer to the planning process with your family.

[Outcomes:] [For clients w/ a perm. goal of <u>adoption</u> or <u>guardianship</u>, or whose parental rights were terminated, go directly to #27.]

24. The services and resources provided will help/helped me get my child/ren back.

    1   2   3

25. The case goals will prevent/will help prevent future out-of-home placement of my child/ren.

    1   2   3

26. (Name of agency) has helped my family do better.

    1   2   3

[Stop here and go to the next section on cultural competency.]

27. As difficult as it was for me, the case goals achieved a situation for my child/ren that I could accept.

    1   2   3

The next statements may or may not refer to you. They concern the worker's sensitivity to cultural and ethnic differences and diversity.

[Cultural Competency:]

28. My worker was respectful of my family's cultural/ethnic background.

    1   2   3

29. I felt comfortable talking with my worker about what my culture and race have to do with my situation.

    1   2   3

30. My worker spoke the language most appropriate for me and my family.

    1   2   3

31. My worker is/was of a different cultural or ethnic background than me.

     1   2   3

32. My worker and I were able to work well together.

     1   2   3

And now for the last set of statements in the survey:

33. Overall, I am satisfied with the services I received/am receiving.

     1   2   3

34. We are almost finished. Is there anything else you would like to tell us that we did not think to ask?
And now we would like to know just a few things about yourself.

35. Please tell me your age: _____

36. Now I need to know your racial or ethnic background:

_____

37. Is this your first experience with SRS Children & Family Services in Kansas or other states?

     Yes   No

The last three statements concern this survey, and then we'll be done. Again, please respond "agree" "disagree" or "unsure."
38. I had trouble understanding the statements in this survey.

     1   2   3

39. The survey had too many questions.

     1   2   3

40. I would recommend to others in my situation that they complete this survey.

     1   2   3

Well, we're through. I want to thank you for your time and your cooperation.

University of Kansas, School of Social Welfare Revised 12/2000

10: PATIENT SATISFACTION SURVEY (VSQ-9)

Author:	Unknown
Description:	The VSQ-9 is a nine-item visit-specific instrument that is used to measure consumer satisfaction with services. To score the VSQ-9, the responses from each consumer should be altered to a scale in which scores range anywhere from 0 to 100, with 100 being equivalent to "excellent" and 0 being equivalent to "poor." Following the score transformation, all of the nine VSQ-9 items should then be averaged collectively to produce a VSQ-9 score for each consumer.
Psychometric Data:	Unable to locate data on reliability or validity measures for this instrument.
Reference:	*Patient satisfaction survey (VSQ-9)*. Retrieved February 22, 2007, from RAND Publications, Santa Monica, CA: http://www.rand.org/health/surveys_tools/vsq9/vsq9.pdf
Note:	Used by permission. The authorization of the use of this survey is in no way an endorsement of the commercial product being tested or the program evaluation.

Patient Satisfaction Survey

Thinking about your visit with the physician/health care professional you saw, how would you rate the following:

	Poor	Fair	Good	Very Good	Excellent
1. How long you waited to get an appointment	○	○	○	○	○
2. Convenience of the location of the office	○	○	○	○	○
3. Getting through to the office by phone	○	○	○	○	○
4. Length of time waiting at the office	○	○	○	○	○
5. Time spent with the physician/health care professional you saw	○	○	○	○	○
6. Explanation of what was done for you	○	○	○	○	○
7. Technical skills (thoroughness, carefulness, competence) of the physician/health care professional you saw	○	○	○	○	○
8. The personal manner (courtesy, respect, sensitivity, friendliness) of the person you saw	○	○	○	○	○
9. The visit overall	○	○	○	○	○

11: THE PATIENT SATISFACTION
QUESTIONNAIRE SHORT FORM (PSQ-18)

Authors:	Grant N. Marshall & Ron D. Hays
Description:	The PSQ-18 is a devised short form version of the Patient Satisfaction Questionnaire. The item scale taps into evaluating satisfaction with various medical care services. Each item score can range from 1 to 5, with 1 specifying a response of "strongly agree" and 5 specifying a response of "strongly disagree." The PSQ is scored by seven different subscales. Items 3 and 17 measure general satisfaction; items 2, 4, 6 and 14 measure technical quality; items 10 and 11 measure interpersonal manner; items 1 and 13 measure communication; items 5 and 7 measure financial aspects; items 12 and 15 measure accessibility; and items 8, 9, 16 and 18 measure convenience. All item scores are worded to reflect high scores as strong satisfaction and low scores as dissatisfaction. To score each subscale, simply calculate all scores together then divide by the number of adequately answered questions.
Psychometric Data:	The majority of the subscales have an internal consistency above .70. Many of the items in each subscale of the PSQ-18 were to a large extent correlated with other similar scales.
Reference:	Marshall, G. N., & Hays, R. D. (1994). *The patient satisfaction questionnaire short form (PSQ-18)*. Santa Monica, CA: RAND Publications.
Note:	Used by permission. The authorization of the use of this survey is in no way an endorsement of the commercial product being tested or the program evaluation.

SHORT-FORM PATIENT SATISFACTION QUESTIONNAIRE (PSQ-18)

These next questions are about how you feel about the medical care you receive.

On the following pages are some things people say about medical care. Please read each one carefully, keeping in mind the medical care you are receiving now. (If you have not received care recently, think about what you would <u>expect</u> if you needed care today.) We are interested in your feelings, <u>good</u> and <u>bad</u>, about the medical care you have received.

How strongly do you AGREE or DISAGREE with <u>each</u> of the following statements?

(Circle One Number on Each Line)

	Strongly <u>Agree</u>	<u>Agree</u>	<u>Uncertain</u>	<u>Disagree</u>	Strongly <u>Disagree</u>
1. Doctors are good about explaining the reason for medical tests	1	2	3	4	5
2. I think my doctor's office has everything needed to provide complete medical care	1	2	3	4	5
3. The medical care I have been receiving is just about perfect	1	2	3	4	5
4. Sometimes doctors make me wonder if their diagnosis is correct	1	2	3	4	5
5. I feel confident that I can get the medical care I need without being set back financially	1	2	3	4	5
6. When I go for medical care, they are careful to check everything when treating and examining me	1	2	3	4	5
7. I have to pay for more of my medical care than I can afford	1	2	3	4	5
8. I have easy access to the medical specialists I need	1	2	3	4	5

How strongly do you AGREE or DISAGREE with <u>each</u> of the following statements?

(Circle One Number on Each Line)

	Strongly Agree	Agree	Uncertain	Disagree	Strongly Disagree
9. Where I get medical care, people have to wait too long for emergency treatment	1	2	3	4	5
10. Doctors act too businesslike and impersonal toward me	1	2	3	4	5
11. My doctors treat me in a very friendly and courteous manner ...	1	2	3	4	5
12. Those who provide my medical care sometimes hurry too much when they treat me	1	2	3	4	5
13. Doctors sometimes Ignore what I tell them	1	2	3	4	5
14. I have some doubts about the ability of the doctors who treat me	1	2	3	4	5
15. Doctors ususally spend plenty of time with me	1	2	3	4	5
16. I find it hard to get an appointment for medical care right away	1	2	3	4	5
17. I am dissatisfied with some things about the medical care I receive	1	2	3	4	5
18. I am able to get medical care whenever I need it	1	2	3	4	5

12: SERVICE SATISFACTION SCALE 30 (SSS-30)

Author:	Thomas K. Greenfield
Description:	The SSS-30 is a multidimensional instrument that is intended to measure various types of services in physical and mental health and addiction settings. There are 30 items in the instrument, along with items asking for some demographic information and three open-ended questions for feedback on the instrument itself. Each item is scored on a 5-point Delighted–Terrible scaling. Within the 30 items, there are a number of subscales: manner and skill (9 items), perceived outcomes (8 items), office procedures (5 items), accessibility (4 items), and waiting (2 items).
Psychometric Data:	The subscales in the SSS-30 have shown excellent internal reliability, with Cronbach's reliability coefficients of .88 for the manner and skill subscale, .83 for perceived outcomes, .74 for office procedures, and .67 for accessibility. As a whole, the internal reliability for the SSS-30 has been as high as .96. In a particular study comparing the correlation between the CSQ-8 and SSS-30 it was found that a correlation of .70 existed. It is evident for this reason that the SSS-30 has respectable construct validity.
References:	Greenfield, T. K., & Attkisson, C. C. (2004). The UCSF client satisfaction scales: II. The service satisfaction scale–30.
	Maruish, M. E. (2004). *The use of psychological testing for treatment planning and outcomes assessment: Vol. 3. Instruments for adults* (3rd ed., pp. 799–811). Hillsdale, NJ: Lawrence Erlbaum.
	Faulkner & Gray's 1998 Behavioral outcomes & guidelines sourcebook (pp. 475–477). New York: Faulkner's & Gray's Healthcare Information Center.
	Faulkner & Gray's 2000 Behavioral outcomes & guidelines sourcebook (pp. 617–619). New York: Faulkner's & Gray's Healthcare Information Center.
Note:	Used by permission. Copyright (©) held by Tom Greenfield (tgreenfield@arg.org). Use is on a fee-for-use basis except in authorized collaborations with the author.
Contact Information:	Thomas K. Greenfield, Ph.D., Senior Scientist & Center Director, Alcohol Research Group, Public Health Institute, 6475 Christie Ave., Suite 400, Emeryville, CA 94608. tgreenfield@arg.org. Phone (510) 597-3440. Voice Mail (510) 597-3454. FAX: (510) 985-6459.

Faulkner & Gray's 1998 Behavioral Outcomes & Guidelines Sourcebook pp 475-477; the same, 2000 edition, pp 617-619. NY: Faulkner & Gray's Healthcare Information Center, 11 Perm Plaza, New York NY 10001.

SERVICES EVALUATION (SSS-30 Practitioner Version*)

CONFIDENTIAL

SUBSCALE KEY

☑   Please read the following statements carefully. Indicate the answer that best describes your feeling about each aspect of the services you have received. We are interested in your *overall experience* based on all visits or contacts you have had *during the last year*. By "practitioner" we mean the one or more doctors, psychologists, counselors, clinicians, etc., who have worked with you.

What is your overall feeling about the . . .

M   1.   Kinds of services offered

G	G	G	G	G
DELIGHTED	MOSTLY SATISFIED	MIXED	MOSTLY DISSATISFIED	TERRIBLE**

M   2.   Opportunity to choose which practitioner you see

G	G	G	G	G
TERRIBLE	MOSTLY DISSATISFIED	FIXED	MOSTLY SATISFIED	DELIGHTED**

O   3.   Effect of services in helping you deal with your problems
P   4.   Office personnel (receptionists, clerks) on the telephone or in person
P   5.   Office procedures (scheduling, forms, tests, etc.)
M   6.   Professional knowledge and competence of the main practitioner(s)
A   7.   Location and accessibility of the services (distance, parking, public transportation, etc.)
        8.   Appearance and physical layout of the facility (e.g., waiting area)
M   9.   Ability of your (practitioners) to listen to and understand your problems
M   10.   Personal manner of the main practitioner(s) seen
W   11.   Waiting time between asking to be seen and the appointment (date and time) given
W   12.   Waiting time when you come to be seen or keep an appointment made
A   13.   Availability of appointment times that fit your schedule
        14.   Cost of services to me
O   15.   Effect of services in maintaining well-being and preventing relapse
M   16.   Confidentiality and respect for your rights as an individual
O   17.   Amount of help you have received
O   18.   Availability of information on how to get the most out of the services
O   19.   Prescription (or nonprescription) of medications
M   20.   Explanations of specific procedures and approaches used
O   21.   Effect of services in helping relieve symptoms or reduce problems
A   22.   Response to crises or urgent needs during office hours
A   23.   Arrangements made for after hours emergencies or urgent help
M   24.   Thoroughness of the main practitioner(s) you have seen
O, P   25.   Appropriate use of referrals to other practitioners or services when needed
P   26.   Collaboration between service providers (if more than one)
        27.   Publicity or information about programs and services offered
P   28.   Handling and accuracy of your records (as best you can tell)
O   29.   Contribution of services to achievement of your life goals
M   30.   In an overall general sense, how satisfied are you with the service you have received?
        31.   (If applicable) Support of the group as a whole, helpfulness and caring of its members

It is important to know something about our clients as a whole, so we request some demographic information. Only grouped data will be used, and you will never be identified. However, if you prefer not to answer any or all questions, you may freely do so.

32. About how many miles (one way) from the facility do you live?
     G   G   G   G   G   G
          5 or Less   6-10   11-15   16-20   20-25   26 or more

33. Approximately how many *weeks* have you been involved with this program?
     G   G   G   G   G   G
     Less than 1   1-2   3-4   5-6   7-12   more than 12

34. Including today's, approximately how many sessions have you had in this program?
     G   G   G   G   G   G   G   G   G   G
     0   1   2   3   4   5   6-10   11-20   21-30   31-50   51 +

35. Your Sex: MALE   G   FEMALE G

36. Your Age: G   G   G   G   G   G   G
                 UNDER 20   21-25   26-35   36-45   46-55   56-65   66-75   76-85   86+

37. Yearly Family Income:
        Under $10,000   G $10,000 - $20,000   G
        $20,001 - $40,000   G $40,001 - $60,000   G
        $60,001 - $80,000   G $80,000 - $100,000   G
                                             $100,000 or more   G

38. Your Education:
        Grade 8 or less   G   Some high school   G
        High school grad.   G   Some college   G
        College grad.   G   Some post grad.   G
        Masters   G   Ph.D., M.D., etc.   G

39. Ethnic Background:
        Caucasian/White   G   Asian/Pacific American   G
        Native American/Indian   G   Hispanic/Latino   G
        African American/Black   G   Other (Specify)   G
        Prefer not to answer   G   _____

40. In general these days, how do you feel about your life as a whole?
     G   G   G   G   G   G   G
     TERRIBLE   UNHAPPY   MOSTLY   MIXED   MOSTLY   PLEASED   DELIGHTED
                          DISSATISFIED   SATISFIED

41. In general these days, how do you feel about your health?
     G   G   G   G   G   G   G
     TERRIBLE   UNHAPPY   MOSTLY   MIXED   MOSTLY   PLEASED   DELIGHTED
                          DISSATISFIED   SATISFIED

THANK YOU VERY MUCH FOR YOUR HELP WITH THIS SURVEY. WE WOULD APPRECIATE ANY ADDITIONAL COMMENTS ABOUT THIS SERVICE YOU WOULD CARE TO ADD. YOU MAY WRITE THEM BELOW

42. The thing I have liked best about my experience here is:

43. What I liked least was:

Copyright (c) held by Tom Greenfield (tgreenfield@arg.org).

SUBSCALE KEY (and summary of Cronbach's reliability coefficients)

M = Manner and Skill (9-items; average α = .88)
O = Perceived Outcome (8-items; average α = .83)
P = Procedures (5-items; average α = .74)
A = Accessibility (4-items; average α = .67)
W = Waiting (2 items, may optionally be combined with Access)

*Counselor version substitutes counselor in Instructions and items 2, 6, 9, 10 & 24. **Example Item scale. Note that individual item scale anchors alternate direction throughtout the instrument; scoring reverses every other item, allowing validity check for rote responding.

(C) 1986,1987,1989, 1990, 1995, 2000 T. K. Greenfield, C. C. Attkisson, and G. C. Pascoe

13: SESSION EVALUATION QUESTIONNAIRE (SEQ)

Author:	William B. Stiles
Description:	The SEQ simultaneously critiques human services and psychotherapy sessions by evaluating the session in terms of value, and in terms of level of comfortableness. The SEQ has 21 items in a 7-point bipolar adjective format. The 21 items are split up into two sections. The first section's focal point is to evaluate the session while the second set assesses participants' post mood. Each participant is directed to circle the most fitting answer for each item. In each of the two separate scales, adjectives are placed on the far right and left of the item scales. Answers can be answered as indicated by a score from 1 to 7. However, note that the second set of items are reversed coded. To score each index, a mean score is easier for interpretation for the reason that it lies on the same line of each item. In this way, scores for each item can be seen on the same 7-point line as in each item index, making comparisons easier. Possible ranges can consist of anywhere from 1.00 to 7.00. The SEQ can be implemented into many areas of service satisfaction. It is best used when both the patient and therapist questions as a way to better determine feelings about the session.
Psychometric Data:	The SEQ in terms of reliability has shown a high degree of internal consistency ranging from .90 for depth and .93 for smoothness. Since the SEQ can vary session to session, test-retest reliability is difficult to calculate. The adjectives used in the item indexes have shown to be consistent in distinguishing a relationship between client and therapist on session satisfaction.
Reference:	Stiles, W. B. (2002). *Session evaluation questionnaire: Structure and use.* Retrieved January 23, 2007, from Department of Psychology, Miami University, Oxford, OH: http://www.users.muohio.edu/stileswb/session_evaluation_questionnaire.htm
Note:	Used by permission.

SESSION EVALUATION QUESTIONNAIRE (FORM 5)

ID# _____   Date: _____

Please circle the appropriate number to show how you feel about this session.

This session was:

bad	1	2	3	4	5	6	7	good
difficult	1	2	3	4	5	6	7	easy
valuable	1	2	3	4	5	6	7	worthless
shallow	1	2	3	4	5	6	7	deep
relaxed	1	2	3	4	5	6	7	tense
unpleasant	1	2	3	4	5	6	7	pleasant
full	1	2	3	4	5	6	7	empty
weak	1	2	3	4	5	6	7	powerful
special	1	2	3	4	5	6	7	ordinary
rough	1	2	3	4	5	6	7	smooth
comfortable	1	2	3	4	5	6	7	uncomfortable

Right now I feel:

happy	1	2	3	4	5	6	7	sad
angry	1	2	3	4	5	6	7	pleased
moving	1	2	3	4	5	6	7	still
uncertain	1	2	3	4	5	6	7	definite
calm	1	2	3	4	5	6	7	excited
confident	1	2	3	4	5	6	7	afraid
friendly	1	2	3	4	5	6	7	unfriendly
slow	1	2	3	4	5	6	7	fast
energetic	1	2	3	4	5	6	7	peaceful
quiet	1	2	3	4	5	6	7	aroused

14: WORKING ALLIANCE INVENTORY (WAI)

Author:	Adam O. Horvath
Description:	The WAI is a 36-item instrument that measures three different areas of the working relationship between client and professional. The three areas of measures are tasks, goals, and bonds. The WAI aims to measure treatment of these three aspects by seeing where do the feelings of the client and worker stand. There are two scales for the WAI, one for the client and one for the clinician. For the client scale, answers can vary in response by a marking between 1 and 7. One represents "not at all" and seven represents "very true." To score the WAI, simply sum all of the individual responses together and then divide by the number of questions answered. There is a short form version of the WAI available, and it analyzes items 2, 4, 8, 12, 21, 23, 24, 26, 27, 32 and 35.
Psychometric Data:	In accordance with reliability, the WAI has good internal consistency. This is prevalent giving that the WAI subscales have had alpha coefficients at the level of .98. Same type of internal consistency was discovered with the WAI short version. Concerning validity, discriminate and convergent validity have been tested. Both areas have shown excellent results. The WAI also has favorably good concurrent validity as all three of the subscales had immense relationships between items in relation to the working partnership.
Reference:	Horvath, A. O. (2000). Working alliance inventory (WAI). In K. Corcoran & J. Fischer (Eds.), *Measures for clinical practice* (Vol. 2, pp. 888–891). New York: The Free Press.
Note:	Used by permission. Horvath, A. O. (1994). Empirical validation of Bordin's pantheoretical model of the alliance: The working alliance inventory perspective. In A. O. Horvath & L. S. Greenberg (Eds.), *The working alliance: Theory, research and practice.* New York: Wiley.

WAI

Below are six questions taken from the short form Working Alliance Inventory.

The questions ask about your relationship with your therapist. Using the following scale, rate the degree to which you agree with each statement, and record your answer in the space to the left of the item.

1 = Not at all true

2 = A little true

3 = Slightly true

4 = Somewhat true

5 = Moderately true

6 = Considerably true

7 = Very true

_____ 1.   _____ and I agree about the things I will need to do in therapy to help improve my situation.

_____ 2.   _____ does not understand what I am trying to accomplish in therapy.

_____ 3.   I am confident in _____'s ability to help me.

_____ 4.   _____ and I are working toward mutually agreed upon goals.

_____ 5.   _____ and I have different ideas on what my problems are.

_____ 6.   I feel _____ cares about me even when I do things that he/she does not approve of.

15: SESSION RATING SCALE (SRS)

Authors:	Scott D. Miller & Barry L. Duncan
Description:	The Session Rating Scale is an alliance tool that is intended to be used in conjunction with the Outcome Rating Scale. Note: alliance instruments are different than satisfaction instruments. Alliance instruments are related to outcome and satisfaction instruments are not.

The SRS is a 4-item measure to be completed by client that measures the relationship and alliance between worker and client in each session. By evaluating each session, it is easier to predict change. The scale assesses: quality of the relational bond, agreement and disagreements between the alliance, value of methods used, and the overall quality of approach. The expected time to complete this scale is less than a minute.

Psychometric Data:	Reliability: the SRS when compared to the Revised Helping Alliance Questionnaire (HAQ-II) had a coefficient alpha at .88 versus .90. For test retest reliability, the SRS had after six administrations a level of .74 compared to a .69 for the HAQ-II. Other studies concerning the reliability of the SRS have shown coefficient alpha levels up to .96.

Validity: there is evidence of concurrent validity. Comparing the HAQ-II with the SRS, there was a .48 average correlation between the two scales. Also, there is some evidence of construct validity. There is a correlation between the administration of the SRS at the second session of therapy and the Outcome of Treatment Scale.

References:	Miller, S. D., & Duncan, B. L. (2004). *The outcome and session rating scales*. Chicago: Institute for the Study of Therapeutic Change.

Miller, S. D., Duncan, B. L., Brown, J., Sparks, J. A., & Claud, D. A. (2003). The outcome rating scale: A preliminary study of the reliability, validity, and feasibility of a brief visual analog measure. *Journal of Brief Therapy, 2,* 91–100.

Note:	Used by permission.

Outcome Rating Scale (ORS)

Name _____Age(Yrs): ____Sex: M/F
Session # _ Date:_____
Who is filling out this form? Please check one: Self ___ Other _____
If other, what is your relationship to this person?_____

Looking back over the last week, including today, help us understand how you have been feeling by rating how well you have been doing in the following areas of your life, where marks to the left represent low levels and marks to the right indicate high levels. *If you are filling out this form for another person, please fill out according to how you think he or she is doing.*

Individually
(Personal well-being)

I----Examination Copy Only----I

Interpersonally
(Family, close relationships)

I----Examination Copy Only----I

Socially
(Work, school, friendships)

I----Examination Copy Only----I

Overall
(General sense of well-being)

I----Examination Copy Only----I

Institute for the Study of Therapeutic Change

www.talkingcure.com

© 2000, Scott D. Miller and Barry L. Duncan

Session Rating Scale (SRS V.3.0)

```
Name _____ Age (Yrs): _____
ID# _____ Sex: M/F
Session # _____ Date: _____
```

Please rate today's session by placing a mark on the line nearest to the description that best fits your experience.

Relationship

I did not feel heard, understood, and respected.

I----Examination Copy Only----I

I felt heard, understood, and respected.

Goals and Topics

We did *not* work on or talk about what I wanted to work on and talk about.

I----Examination Copy Only----I

We worked on and talked about what I wanted to work on and talk about.

Approach or Method

The therapist's approach is not a good fit for me.

I----Examination Copy Only----I

The therapist's approach is a good fit for me.

Overall

There was something missing in the session today.

I----Examination Copy Only----I

Overall, today's session was right for me.

Institute for the Study of Therapeutic Change

www.talkingcure.com

© 2002, Scott D. Miller, Barry L. Duncan, &
Lynn Johnson

CHAPTER 13

Dissemination

Spreading the News

Possible uses of an evaluation report.

Once the evaluation has been completed, the information needs to be shared in a manner that will most likely complement its eventual use. This can be tricky as tension often exists between accurately portraying complicated evaluation methodologies and presenting a captivating report that maintains the attention of the users and encourages its use. Throughout the book, we have discussed the importance of engaging the intended users of the information and the number of ways that it should drive the evaluation process. This is especially true in the presentation of the evaluation findings.

The strategy for presenting evaluation findings should be heavily swayed by the needs of the users and their intended uses. There are many possibilities for "getting the word out" about the evaluation.

In this chapter, many of those options will be described along with some other considerations that may influence the possible choices. Although evaluation projects often include a final report at the end of the project, the strategy for documenting the results and sharing the findings still warrants additional consideration. While a report may be needed, the organization and presentation style of the report deserves some attention. In other cases, a report may be needed, but it may be valuable to supplement the report with additional mechanisms. This chapter will focus attention on some useful ideas for producing a report, as well as some other techniques for sharing crucial evaluation information. The additional methods may either support the report or stand on their own depending on what the situation may require.

The various options can be tailored to meet the needs of a specific user group or a certain type of action that would facilitate a program improvement. The discussion of options will be preceded by some ideas for framing the findings and some thoughts about writing style. As with many of the chapters in this book, we will suggest some ideas and ways to think about this piece of evaluation practice and will also identify other more comprehensive tools that can serve as future resources.

Checking Vitals

Reporting the findings is a critical step in the evaluation process. The end product of the evaluation needs to be heavily influenced by the users of the information.

FRAMING THE EVALUATION FINDINGS

When thinking about packaging evaluation findings, one important distinction is to frame the information in a manner that is consistent with the point of view of the eventual user. There may be times when a report is mandated and the findings may need to be reported in a generalized manner, but often agencies have a clear focus as to the specific pieces of the evaluation results. At times, you may actually package things to fit the unique purposes of a specific group of staff. When the focus is on specific groups of users, then language, timing, the level of aggregation, and formatting can be positioned accordingly.

A Compatible Framework and Language

As discussed in Chapter 7 (Program Definition: Using Program Logic Models to Develop a Common Vision), the staff working with the same program may have very different views of the program based on a perspective informed by their location in the organization (Kapp & Grasso, 1993). Although managers and direct service staff are equally devoted to the same program, their ideas about its intended operation may differ. When presenting evaluation data, these differences may be important. Figure 13.1 illustrates the various views. Obviously, all staff in an agency are interested in the overall success rate, and executive directors are also committed to the clinical gains by individuals clients, but when the occupants of these positions are confronted with different aspects of the program, they tend to have a framework that drives their worldview. Consequently, if information is being presented to direct services practitioners, the language should be framed in terms of positive clinical or therapeutic changes for individuals. For example, in one project, the findings supported a positive link between family therapy and the adjustment of youth in the community. Our intent was to impress upon family therapists the value of their contact with families in the facility and in the community. The evaluation report supplemented a program listing of individual youth family contacts and their status in the community at 12 months; statistical charts that reinforced this relationship were avoided.

Figure 13.1   Framework/Language Based on Position

Position	Framework	Language
Direct service	Therapeutic models, treatment intervention	Clinical gain or therapeutic change with a single consumer.
Manager, supervisor	Single program performance	Therapeutic change across a single program; average length of stay, percentage of clients successfully completing the program.
Upper management, executive director	Agency-wide performance	Percentage of successful discharges across the agency.

Chapter 8 (Program Description: Evaluation Designs Using Available Information) describes evaluation projects that rely on information that resides in the agencies' client files or information systems. While this data has great potential, it may be fruitful to present this information in a language that makes some sense to the eventual user and to abandon jargon that may have been germane for its initial purpose. An example of this would be to describe client contacts collected in accounting information systems as "billable hours." A direct service practitioner would be more accepting of terms such as "client contacts" or "hours of therapeutic contact."

Aggregate to Meet the User's Needs

The level of aggregation is also very closely related to the placement of a person in the organization (Poertner & Rapp, 2007). Agency workers easily identify with data that is organized around their organizational viewpoint. This is comparable to the framework and language issue just stated. A direct service staff would prefer to see information about specific clients or at least a breakdown that is compatible with a single case, while a manager would prefer to see the information organized around the program(s) under their direction. Likewise, an executive director would more closely identify with data that is summarized at the agency level.

In the example described above, two strategies were used to reinforce the importance of individual family contacts to youth success in the community. An overall report displayed statistical results for the upper management and funders of the services, but individual workers were shown the information organized around their individual clients. Not only did this presentation make sense to them, but it stimulated additional discussion about the successful and less-than-successful cases and how this knowledge could influence further practice.

Timing Is Critical

Another critical factor in presenting evaluations is timing. In some cases, the evaluation needs to be critically timed to match a decision or an initiative or a funding cycle. In others, the information is part of ongoing practice and may be presented at any point throughout the year. Obviously, the agency personnel involved in the project will be able to provide insightful feedback on how the relevant information fits with agency timing related to decision making. In one evaluation project, the findings provided some useful information about the timing and importance of aftercare contacts. The agency wanted this information disseminated prior to an initiative to revamp aftercare to serve as both the intelligence behind the innovation and a tool to promote momentum. So, the evaluation findings needed to be completed and circulated on a stringent timeline.

In other cases, evaluation can be presented as ongoing information that can be used to inform routine events, such as case planning or supervision. Data that might come from clinical assessments of families can be presented routinely as part of an assessment process. In one agency, summarized reports of family contacts by specific workers were vital parts of the supervision. The clinical supervisor and the individual family workers would examine these data to discern if all families were given the needed supports; if not, possible explanations for the discrepancies could be explored.

Using an Agreeable Format

Later in this chapter, we will consider report structures and writing style; but it is critical to think about the presentation of the material in a manner that is easy for the users to consume. In a recent class of administration students, a chart of family contact data was presented on a sheet of paper with about nine rows and six columns of numbers. The students, fresh from a budgeting class, immediately begin circling individual numbers and doing their own additional calculations. While this is rare for most audiences, it illustrates the importance of matching the presentation format to the audience. In another case, some key outcome data was a vital part of an agency-wide annual staff presentation. The data was presented in a story format: "If you were to follow 100 of our youth for 5 years, x% would be in prison, x% would be living at home. . . ." This seemed more palatable than a table of numbers.

Another valuable tool is the presentation of numerical data in a graphic format. Graphic formats, when prepared correctly, can illuminate evaluation findings (Alvero, Bucklin, & Austin, 2001; Patton, 1997; Poertner & Rapp, 2007; Salkind, 2007). Whether presenting the results to small groups of practitioners or agency boards of directors, graphic presentations can have great impact. The findings tend to be easier for many audiences to grasp, and the discussion seems to move more quickly to the implications of the findings. Little time is spent on explaining the presentation of the data.

Checking Vitals

Framing the evaluation to meet the needs of users is critical. This may differ depending on the place of the end user in the organization; direct service practitioners will be interested in material that is more relevant to their practice, while executives would more likely be focused on an agency-wide point of view.

Clinicians are comfortable with language that relates to treatment, whereas a manager would more likely identify with language that summarized information across a program.

Likewise, a clinician would be interested in information organized around single clients, whereas an executive would most likely prefer agency-wide summaries.

The timing of evaluation data is critical, ranging from data that may be used in an ongoing fashion to findings that must meet a very tight timeframe.

Efforts made to package the data in a manner that suits the audience using graphs or vignettes can have significant returns.

SHARING THE RESULTS

While the traditional strategy for spreading the word about the wonderful things learned in an evaluation project is typically a report, there are many other alternatives to consider. We suggest allowing your plan for to use to guide your decisions about any specific dissemination plans. Patton (2002) understands that reports often may be required, but that impact actually occurs outside the report in more personal interactions. Traditional reports also can be used to spread the word to important constituents who may not necessarily be central to service improvement (Patton, 2002). This chapter will spell out a variety of these options, including written reports. In the process of listing the options, some attention will go to writing style and supplementary techniques for supporting dissemination.

Writing Style

Some resources will address the task of writing a technical evaluation report (Booth, Colomb, & Williams, 2008; Pyrczak & Bruce, 2007), but this task does not receive adequate attention given its prominence in the evaluation enterprise. Often evaluation reports are written as if they are being submitted to a refereed publication where the value will be based on the methodological rigor, which requires complete and full disclosure of all details of the evaluation. Again, we are revisiting the tricky balance required to construct a reliable evaluation report. The report needs to be written in a fashion that is accessible to the readers but also addresses the tension to fully disclose the details of the method. This transparency about the method also provides some credibility by making the procedures for collecting, analyzing, and interpreting the data very clear. The written description of the method and respective findings is sometimes difficult to boil down to easily digestible nuggets when a complex evaluation design or sophisticated statistical technique is employed.

Writing is a central component of the many ways to spread the word about evaluation findings. As stated, writing an evaluation report for an agency is very different than writing a report for a federal grant or an article for a refereed journal. Agency practitioners are more interested in the practice implications of your findings and most likely less interested in the technical aspects of your research method. Furthermore, while many of your potential users have had, and most likely did well, in research classes, it is not their natural orientation to adopt the frameworks of an evaluation researcher, so the written material needs to be clear and straightforward. In research classes, students have been asked to think about the audience as a relative who does not work in the field. This material needs to be stated in a way that can be easily grasped by a person who is not in the field. Grob (2004) calls this the "Mom Test" (p. 605).

One of the mantras of this book is to involve agency staff in all facets of the evaluation process. This is particularly relevant to the development of written materials to disseminate the findings. Agency staff should be involved in reviewing written materials and providing feedback about clarity and readability. For example, in one project, a complex statistical modeling technique was used to analyze data from multiple statewide data systems. The users of the data made helpful suggestions in the preparation of the report and actually convinced the authors to write a section of the report with a technical focus and another section that emphasized the practice implications of the research. The end result was two sub-reports within the single report. While our report would have contained this information, it would have been organized in a more traditional academic linear fashion (intro, literature review, methods, findings, etc.) that would have forced readers, especially the practitioner types, to wade through the material. This tactic proved to be useful in this case, as it forced many practitioners to read the report; many confessed that without this structure, they would not have made the effort. Prior to this feedback, technical details around method had been relegated to separate sections, typically appendices. Both of these strategies allow full disclosure of method while giving less technical readers the chance to focus on the practice implications of the evaluation. Not all reporting situations allow this amount of flexibility, but during report preparation, it can be fruitful to investigate possibilities for organizing and presenting written reports. When possible, the report can be tailored to agency practitioner needs. Grob (2004) spells out six different formats that can serve as a menu of options to match the specific reporting needs (p. 610).

Checking Vitals

Regardless of the technique, the presentation needs to utilize a writing style that will be acceptable to the needs of the user.

Users are a great source of information about the style of writing that best meets the needs of the consumers of the evaluation.

PREPARING THE REPORT

End users of information can be great resources in the overall report production process. Reports are often produced in stages, a format that provides opportunity for feedback and discussion of findings before a final report is disseminated. Evaluators develop and give users a draft of the evaluation report for feedback. The reviews of the draft report usually generate valuable discussion about the findings and possible use, as well as the actual written product. Language that may seem neutral to the report writer may be inflammatory to users. For example, in a report that provided statewide findings about consumer satisfaction for private foster care providers, the evaluators were informed that focusing on a single agency was inflammatory. While the authors chose a specific agency to illustrate the various types of information provided by the study, the agencies did not agree. The agency being highlighted perceived itself as being singled out in a less constructive manner, while some of the other agencies felt the highlighted agency was receiving preferential treatment. After receiving this information in a draft, the report was revised to provide a more equalized treatment. Three examples were created where the agencies' scores were similar or the differences were more balanced. The point of the report was to illustrate the various types of consumer satisfaction data and not make judgments about respective agency performance.

In some cases, evaluation findings will not be flattering. It is important to be clear that the suggestions for reporting should not compromise the honesty of the evaluation findings. If agency staff have been involved throughout the evaluation, the findings should not be too surprising. Furthermore, agency staff ideas can have a distinct presence in the interpretation of the findings and recommendations.

In the evaluation of a large multi-agency collaboration of services to encourage the payment of child support, the findings did not show extensive evidence of increased payments. After an initial draft was completed, the agencies asked the evaluators to more fully describe the service recipients' history, including the length of nonpayment and the degree of economic hardship. In addition, a small group of consumers receiving the full complement of the multi-service regimen began making payments. This was an encouraging finding, and the agency coalition forwarded a recommendation about enhancing the services across the organizations, an admittedly difficult implementation struggle. Both of these additions were compatible with a credible evaluation report and represented a more complete report from the perspective of the agency collaboration.

Report Structure

Figure 13.2 presents a possible report structure. A couple of the features of this potential layout warrant some explanation. Although an evaluation project may have been all consuming to those who have devoted a year or more to its completion, many users and other constituents will have little time to devote to reading any type of report. Therefore, an executive summary becomes an important element. This section of the report should be 2 or 3 pages long and include a short background, the findings, the recommendations, and enough method detail to make the evaluation look credible (Grob, 2004; Patton, 2002). The executive summary is written for the constituents who do not have the time to invest in reading your report. When you write executive summaries, remember that readers with questions or curiosity about more details can always refer to the more elaborate report. In some cases, constituents simply need a brief overview. Their role may be one of supporting or endorsing changes that require various types of organizational support. In many agency settings, they do not have the time or energy to know intimate details of the project, which is totally acceptable.

Another unique feature of this proposed structure is the use of appendices. Many aspects of the evaluation need to be included in a report to establish the

Figure 13.2	Possible Report Structure

Executive summary	2- or 3-page short review of highlights.
Literature review	Summarized report of relevant literature.
Method	Evaluation design, sample, data collection, and data analysis.
Findings	Results of study.
Recommendations	Discussion of implications, with specific ideas for program improvement strategies supported by evaluation findings.
Appendices	Critical information that may not be vital to the description of the above, method details, data analysis details, in depth aspects of the analysis, consent forms, etc.

credibility of the findings and to make the evaluation process transparent; however, to include these matters in the evaluation text can be overwhelming and create a disincentive for interested readers. The appendices provide an option for, in effect, storing these documents for easy access for the inquisitive reader. Appendices are often used for consent forms that service consumers complete prior to personal interviews or written surveys. Many times an analysis may require multiple steps to reach the final set, and the various steps can be included and explained in detail in the appendices. While Figure 13.2 proposes a possible structure, the users should have considerable input into the structure and the level of detail of the evaluation reports.

Checking Vitals

Report preparation should engage the users in reviewing a draft version for feedback and suggestions.

A standard report structure should include an executive summary, a literature review, methods, findings, and recommendations.

The executive summary should be a concise 2- or 3-page version of the report with an emphasis on findings and recommendations.

Appendices can be used to store important details in the study that would be less than interesting to most readers.

Alternative Feedback Mechanisms

We would agree with Patton (2002) that the most impactful methods of communicating are typically more interpersonal than a final report. Historically, every evaluation project culminates in a report; therefore, we strongly encourage agency evaluators to consider a variety of different methods, instead of or in addition to this traditional alternative. As mentioned previously, there are many different purposes for sharing evaluation findings and many users with differing intentions. In this section, we will present some additional mechanisms beyond the written report.

Briefings—presentations customized to specific purposes—can be useful. Hendricks (1982) describes this method as an important vehicle in the repertoire of evaluators. These types of presentations are designed with a specific audience in mind. In one case, a program team was given data about their clients with specific changes in mind. This briefing included a program manager, the treatment team, an outside consultant, and the evaluator. The issue of aftercare was the topic. The program manager gave some background on the challenges of implementation. The types of family contacts for the previous 6 months were presented by location (in the agency, in the family home, and in the community). The team then discussed the implications of the findings and possible solutions.

In another case, agency-wide briefings were held throughout this children's service agency's multi-state locations. The agency was facing severe budget shortfalls and was entertaining new service delivery approaches. The briefings focused on the recidivism rates for the clients, the state of the fiscal crisis, and open discussions of new possible models. The intent of these briefings was to include the entire agency staff in the agency's need for a new direction; the evaluation data and fiscal data painted a fairly clear picture of the need to consider changes.

Report cards are sometimes used to report multiple areas of performance on an ongoing basis. This mechanism can be used to monitor overall performance across a number of different areas. The data could be focused on a single agency or make comparisons across multiple agencies. It can also be framed from an agency point of view, as in Figure 13.3, or can be put together from the perspective of consumers to reflect their point of view. A consumer report card could report options related to health care or education (Gormley, 2002).

Figure 13.3	Report Card for Community Shelter

Area of performance	Measure #1	Measure #2	Measure #3
Coverage	# of ongoing clients	# of new intakes	# of outreach contacts
Service use	# of occupied beds	# of case management clients	% of resident families with children attending school
Outcomes	# of new applications for housing subsidies	# of clients in secure housing	% of clients completing job interviews

Checking Vitals

Alternative methods to reporting can be powerful strategies for sharing the evaluation information.

Short briefings and/or short presentations for specific audiences can be created and modified for specific groups.

Report cards can be used to share ongoing evaluation data on a regular basis for a select number of crucial measures.

SUPPORTING THE DISSEMINATION PROCESS

The previous discussion has focused on a variety of ways to disseminate the findings from an evaluation. Some of these have been general, overall reporting mechanisms, whereas others have been very specific. This section will list some strategies that have been used effectively to support the dissemination process, with the intention of getting the findings utilized to support constructive decision making.

An Active Role for Data Users

There are a number of different ideas for supporting the dissemination process. In almost all cases, it is fruitful to involve the agency personnel. This can be a powerful way to support the use of the evaluation. If a specific staff person has been active in the evaluation in any capacity—from its design to collecting the data to using the results to improve practice—his or her role can bring credibility to the presentation of the evaluation findings. In the development of a school social work model, the assistant superintendent for specialized services became a strong supporter of the new model, especially the value of school social workers in the planning and development of follow-up service plans. Whether the presentation is a large production to an entire agency or to a single treatment team, teaming with agency personnel involved in the evaluation can bring credibility to the process and product.

Data Review Meetings

These staff gatherings focus on examining specific information related to service delivery. One of the briefing examples mentioned earlier described an evaluation presentation to a treatment team to examine the types of interaction with client families. The briefings became an ongoing meeting to discuss family contact data. In Kansas, reports come from the state mental health department describing service activity and client outcomes every quarter. Some mental health centers schedule off-site meetings to discuss this data with specific treatment teams. The focus of the "data parties" is to compare and contrast those doing well and those who are struggling in certain areas. These gatherings provide recognition to those showing success and support to those with areas of practice that need attention.

A similar activity occurs in a private foster care provider in Kansas. The agency has a well-developed data system that reports on contractual outcomes. Routinely, the middle managers and program managers review data and discuss strategies for service improvement in targeted areas. Meetings of this type are viewed as a supportive mechanism to the review and possible usage of data for program assessment and improvement.

Decision-Making Model Reviews

Oftentimes, decision-making models are used to help agency staff consider possible uses of the data (see Chapter 8, Program Description: Evaluation Designs Using Available Information). Part of the design of the evaluation is to develop potential strategies for using the evaluation data to make decisions. In some cases, there may be a structured decision model. In others, the agreement may be to examine service patterns related to certain client groups. These mechanisms can facilitate the value of the evaluation, but the agreement, what-ever it might be, needs to be documented during the evaluation design and then reinforced during the data collection, as well as after the findings have been deter-mined. While decisions made during the simulation of a decision process may not be followed exactly, these models make a great template for considering action.

CUSTOMIZING THE DISSEMINATION FOR THE INTENDED ACTION

Throughout the book, the common theme has been to invest resources in the users of the evaluation in all facets of the evaluation process. That same ideal has been reinforced in this section. One last element may be helpful to the concept of customizing dissemination. When trying to define the best method of presenting findings, it can be beneficial to consider the purpose of the dissemination effort. Figure 13.4 describes a number of distinct purposes that could be possible goals of an evaluation presentation. For any single evaluation, there can be different purposes of the activity. In addition, multiple strategies can be employed for a single evaluation. The ideas forwarded in Figure 13.4 are intended to stimulate different ways of thinking about informing users of the evaluation.

Figure 13.4   Purpose of Dissemination Efforts

Type	Explanation	Action Intended
Contribute to knowledge base	Share valuable practice findings discovered in an evaluation that may be useful to a specific audience	Increase the expertise of the practice community
Raise awareness	Educate key agency, community, or consumer constituents about service needs or challenges	Build goodwill for the agency
Gain support	Engage organizational, community, or consumer actors in support of specific program improvements	Provide needed resources to participate in program change
Influence change	Persuade key actors to engage in program improvement strategy	Participate in program change

If, for instance, the evaluation results were targeted at making specific changes in the delivery of services, then the direct service staff might receive the evaluation in more and greater detail than the executive level of the organization. The level of detail needed by each group may be different. The way they digest information and the intended action of each group may also be different. In this case, the direct service staff are being asked to change their daily practices, while the executive personnel are asked for more supportive actions that are less drastic in their daily routines.

Checking Vitals

Dissemination efforts can be enhanced by including specific users in the presentation of the information.

Data review meetings can be held to discuss the use of specific data with the possible consumers of the information.

The decision-making models and processes that were developed in the design of the evaluation should be reviewed and implemented.

There are a variety of different actions that could be influenced by distributing evaluation information, and those specific possible actions should be considered when determining possible dissemination tactics.

This chapter has suggested that evaluators should carefully plan any evaluation dissemination efforts and should consult the key agency, community, and consumer players involved in the evaluation process. The deliberations should consider a range of options for "getting the word out" about the evaluation. When crafting this plan, evaluators should consider the intent of the dissemination efforts with diverse uses as possibly distinctly different tactics that can be utilized for different groups of consumers. As Patton (2002) suggests, written reports rarely stimulate the use of evaluation results by consumers. The intent of this chapter has been to suggest a variety of different options for disseminating evaluation findings and to encourage readers to think about a variety of ways to match the possible tactic with the intent. As with all chapters in this book, the focus is on supporting the users of the evaluation in the application of the information for the provision of better services.

REVIEW AND REFLECT

Big Ideas

• Disseminating the evaluation is a vital aspect of the evaluation that should be thoughtful, and its planning should be inclusive of the eventual users.

• While traditional reports are the typical method for distributing evaluation information, other alternatives may be more influential.

• Plans for sharing the evaluation findings should consider a variety of alternatives based on the intended action desired from users and the input of the agency personnel.

Discussion Questions

• What is one method for framing evaluation findings? Give an example. (The example should include a hypothetical finding and how it should be framed.)

• What are some ways that potential users can be involved in the planning for dissemination?

• What are some strategies for improving the readability of a written evaluation report?

• What is the difference between alternative dissemination strategies and the activities that are seen to support those strategies?

• Which of the purposes for dissemination do you think are the most common, and why are they the most common?

Activities

• Which of the different methods for dissemination are the most common, and which do you think have the greatest potential?

• Pick one of the purposes of dissemination and develop a plan for sharing the evaluation findings to address your choice.

• Describe your views on the sharing of evaluation data. What do you think are the biggest struggles in getting evaluation information to the end users? Which of the various reporting ideas in this chapter do you find the most compelling? Which of the various reporting ideas do you find the least compelling? Please describe your rationale in each case.

Resources

• *Evaluation toolkit: Reporting.* (n.d.). Retrieved from http://wkkf.org/Default .aspx?tabid=90&CID=281&ItemID=2810021&NID=2820021&LanguageID=0

• *Evaluation toolkit: Tips on writing effective reports.* (n.d.). Retrieved from http://wkkf.org/Default.aspx?tabid=90&CID=281&ItemID=2810045&NID= 2820045&LanguageID=0

• *Chapter 7: Reporting the results of mixed method evaluations.* (n.d.). Retrieved from http://www.nsf.gov/pubs/1997/nsf97153/chap_7.htm

Addendum

Families as Evaluators

One of the important themes of this book is the involvement of information consumers in all aspects of the evaluation process. Admittedly, that discussion has focused on practitioners and other professionals, with some vague references to families. Familial involvement in evaluation is an important development. Additionally, it is well-suited to the ethical and practice principles forwarded in this book. In this section, we will highlight this unique aspect of evaluation practice that is overlooked in many discussions.

A well-developed tradition in mental health services arenas is the role of families as advocates for their own services, as well as for the services needs of others in similar circumstances (Faulkner, Scully, & Shore, 1998; Grosser & Vine, 1991; Hatfield, 1981). As families have become formidable advocates, they have increased their role in the evaluation of services. This has been a natural development on two fronts. As advocates, their voices need to be included in the evaluation process to make the findings more meaningful. Also, as advocates, their enhanced role in the evaluation process keeps them informed, and an informed advocate is a better advocate (Greene, 1997; Slaton, 2004).

"Family voice" is a term to reflect the insights that are unique to families with a child receiving services (Slaton, 2004, p. 1). While families may be excluded from any meaningful role in the evaluation process for a number of reasons, such as lack of formal training, loss of objectivity, perceived lack of interest in evaluation, and so forth, Slaton contends that evaluation teams that include families are more likely to generate evaluations that address the most pressing questions in a comprehensive fashion.

Many of the chapters in this book address agency-based evaluation challenges that can be addressed by the real involvement of family members in the evaluation process. Chapter 4 (Ethical Challenges for Evaluators in an Agency Setting: Making Good Choices) provides extensive advice on the respectful treatment of service consumers who are used as participants in the collection of various evaluation data. Families can translate the sound ethical practices presented by human subjects into procedures that should be palatable to families and provide warnings when the same may be viewed as offensive. Chapter 6 (Cultural Competency and Program Evaluation) offers helpful suggestions on the sensitive treatment of families who share cultural and ethnic backgrounds that are different from the evaluation team. Family members on the evaluation team from similar circumstances can truly have an impact on the potential difficulties of data collection by alerting the evaluators early in the process to possible barriers.

Despite the best intentions, a well-meaning evaluation team can perpetuate a variety of struggles that occur in the service world. Language differences that are not apparent can be bridged by a family member's review. The purpose of the evaluation can be expanded by a family member who understands the type of data that will most likely help the community. Slaton (2004) says it best: "Team members cannot cover each other's backs, if they have no idea what the other team members are facing" (p. 5).

A diverse evaluation team complete with meaningful family representation can expand the understanding of the challenges that the evaluation will face and help to develop effective resolutions.

Chapter 7 (Program Definition: Using Program Logic Models to Develop a Common Vision) emphasizes the importance of examining program information needs within the context of a solid program understanding. Additionally, the process for developing this understanding calls for an inclusive set of viewpoints. The perspective offered by family members not only is unique but also adds to the comprehensive nature of the program model. Chapter 8 (Program Description: Evaluation Designs Using Available Information) encourages the evaluation team to review multiple sources of available data to address program information needs. A family member with the point of view of a service recipient can offer a valuable critique of the existing information sources and what it might represent from that point of view. While existing data may rely on a service plan or a family contact record, a consumer voice about the significance of this information could be valuable. For example, if a service plan is going to be a valuable tool for assessing service delivery, then families typically need to be included in these plans.

The last chapter, Chapter 13 (Dissemination: Spreading the News), addresses the distribution of the evaluation information. This task could greatly benefit from the advice and input of family members with a feeling for the service community. Advice could be used to get the evaluation information to the service consumers, a task that is lacking in most evaluations. The family evaluation member could also review the information that is being portrayed to ensure that it is not "sugar-coated" to make a constituent happy. Furthermore, as advocates, the family members would have valuable insights into the type of assessment that is suggested in that chapter; in other words, who needs to hear what information?; when?; and how should it be delivered? The other chapters in this book are focused on the application of specific research methods in an agency setting. A family member on the evaluation team can work with the team to match the needs of the method with data collection practices that are acceptable to service consumers who will most likely be providing the data. Additionally, consumers need to be convinced that evaluation projects are not a waste of time; their lack of interest can be devastating, if they refuse to participate. Family members can assist the evaluators with "selling" the credibility of the evaluation to their own and other families, especially if they have an ownership in the project that has been cultivated by their meaningful involvement (Osher & Adams, 2000; Slaton & McCormack, 1999).

This section of this book highlights the myriad of benefits provided by having an active family member on the evaluation team. The benefits of having an active family member in the evaluation process provide an excellent complementary addition to the rest of our text. Special thanks go to Barbara Huff, former executive director of the Federation of Families for Children's Mental Health, for her wisdom and for inspiring us to add our insights to this additional segment. She provided access to valuable training materials on evaluation (Osher & Adams, 2000; Slaton & McCormack, 1999).

References

Alter, C., & Egan, M. (1997). Logic modeling: A tool for teaching critical thinking in social work practice. *Journal of Social Work Education, 33*(1), 85–102.

Alter, C., & Murty, S. (1997). Logic modeling: A tool for teaching practice evaluation. *Journal of Social Work Education, 33*(1), 103–117.

Alvero, A. M., Bucklin, B. R., & Austin, J. (2001). An objective review of the effectiveness and essential characteristics of performance feedback in organizational settings (1985–1998). *Journal of Organizational Behavior Management, 21*(1), 3–29.

American Evaluation Association. (2004). *Guiding principles for evaluators.* Retrieved June 15, 2006, from www.eval.org/Publications/GuidingPrinciples.asp

Barber, J. P., Gallop, R., Crits-Christopher, P., Frank, A., Thase, M. E., Weiss, R. D., et al. (2006). The role of therapist adherence, therapist competence, and alliance in predicting outcome of individual drug counseling: Results from the National Institute Drug Abuse Collaborative Cocaine Treatment Study. *Psychotherapy Research, 16*(2), 229–240.

Bear, M., & Sauer, M. (1990). Client satisfaction with handyman/chore services in a pilot-shared cost-service coordination program. *Journal of Gerontological Social Work, 31*(3/4), 133–147.

Bell, J. B. (2004). Managing evaluation projects. In J. S. Wholey, H. Hatry, & K. E. Newcomer (Eds.), *Handbook of practical program evaluation* (2nd ed., pp. 571–603). San Francisco: Jossey-Bass.

Berg, B. L. (2004). *Qualitative research methods for the social sciences* (5th ed.). Boston: Pearson.

Berg, M. (1992). Learning disabilities in children with borderline personality disorder. *Bulletin of the Menninger Clinic, 56*(3), 379–392.

Bernard, H. R. (2002). *Research methods in anthropology* (3rd ed.). Walnut Creek, CA: Alta Mira Press.

Bloom, M., Fischer, J., & Orme, J. G. (2003). *Evaluating practice: Guidelines for the accountable professional.* Boston: Allyn & Bacon.

Booth, W., Colomb, G., & Williams, J. (2008). *The craft of research* (3rd ed.). Chicago: University of Chicago Press.

Brandell, J. (1989). Monitoring change in psychotherapy through the use of brief transcripts. *Journal of Independent Social Work, 4*(2), 113–134.

Brislin, R. (1993). *Understanding culture's influence on behavior*. Fort Worth, TX: Harcourt Brace.

Campbell, D. T., & Stanley, J. C. (1966). *Experimental and quasi-experimental designs for research*. Chicago: Rand McNally.

Caudle, S. L. (2004). Qualitative data analysis. In J. S. Wholey, H. P. Hatry, & K. E. Newcomer (Eds.), *Handbook of practical program evaluation* (pp. 417–438). San Francisco: Jossey-Bass.

Cheon, J., & Kapp, S. (2007). *Examining the relationship between demographics, service histories, consumer satisfaction, and outcome using causal modeling.* Children's Mental Health Research Team, University of Kansas.

Children's Services Practice Notes. (1999, February). *Culturally competent practice: What is it and why does it matter?* Retrieved August 7, 2009, from www.practicenotes.org/v014_n01/culturally_competent_practice

Clausen, J. A. (1998). Life reviews and life stories. In J. Z. Giele & G. H. Elder, Jr. (Eds.), *Methods of life course research: Qualitative and quantitative approaches* (pp. 189–212). Thousand Oaks, CA: Sage.

Cross, T. (1997, Summer). *Five steps to becoming culturally competent.* National Resource Center for Youth Services (newsletter). Tulsa: University of Oklahoma.

Cocks, A. (2008). Researching the lives of disabled children: The process of participant in seeking inclusivity. *Qualitative Social Work, 7*(2), 163–180.

Colorado Trust. (2002). *Guidelines and best practices for culturally competent evaluations.* Retrieved August 7, 2009, from www.colorado.gov/cs/satellit

Community Research Associates. (1989). *Evaluating juvenile justice programs.* Washington, DC: Office of Juvenile Justice and Delinquency Prevention. Retrieved July 31, 2009, from http://www.ojjdp.ncjrs.org

Cook, J. R., & Kilmer, R. P. (2004). Evaluating systems of care: Missing links in children's mental health research. *Journal of Community Psychology, 32*(6), 655–674.

Cook, T. D., & Campbell, D. T. (1979). *Quasi-experimentation: Design and analysis issues for field settings.* Boston: Houghton Mifflin.

Cooke, R. A., & Lafferty, C. (2007). *Organizational Culture Inventory (OCI).* Retrieved from Human Synergistics Web site: http://www.humansyn.com/products/oci.aspx

Cousins, J. B., & Leawood, K. A. (1986). Current empirical research on evaluation utilization. *Review of Educational Research, 56*(3), 331–364.

Denzin, N. (1989). *Interpretative biography.* Thousand Oaks, CA: Sage.

Denzin, N., & Lincoln, Y. (Eds.). (1994). *Handbook of qualitative research.* Thousand Oaks, CA: Sage.

Diener, E., Suh, E., Lucas, R. E., & Smith, H. L. (1999). Subjective well-being: Three decades of progress. *Psychological Bulletin, 125*, 276–302.

Dilley, J., & Boysun, M. (2003). *Culturally competent and efficient surveillance strategies.* Retrieved August 7, 2009, from http://ncth.confex.com/ncth/2003

Drisko, J. (1997). Strengthening qualitative studies and reports: Standards to enhance academic integrity. *Journal of Contemporary Human Services, 79*(1), 62–74.

Dybicz, P. (2004). An inquiry into practice wisdom. *Families in Society, 85*(2), 197–203.

Emerson, R., Fretz, R., & Shaw, L. (1995). *Writing ethnographic field notes.* Chicago: University of Chicago Press.

Epstein, I. (2001). Using available clinical information in practice-based research: Mining for silver while dreaming of gold. In I. Epstein & S. Blumenfield (Eds.), *Clinical data-mining in practice-based research: Social work in hospital settings* (pp. 15–32). Binghamton, NY: Haworth Press.

Epstein, I., & Blumenfield, S. (2001). *Clinical data-mining in practice-based research: Social work in hospital settings.* Binghamton, NY: Haworth Press.

Epstein, I., Zilberfein, F., & Snyder, S. (1997). Using available information in practice-based outcomes research: A case study of psycho-social risk factors and liver transplant outcomes. In E. J. Mullen & J. L. Mangabosco (Eds.), *Outcome measurement in human services* (pp. 224–233). New York: NASW Press.

Faulkner, L. R., Scully, J. H., Jr., & Shore, J. H. (1998). A strategic approach to the psychiatric workforce dilemma. *Psychiatric Services, 49,* 493–497.

Fischer, R., & Valley, C. (2000). Monitoring the benefits of family counseling: Using satisfaction surveys to assess client perspective. *Smith College Studies in Social Work, 70*(2), 271–286.

Franklin, C., & Ballan, M. (2001). Reliability and validity in qualitative research. In B. Thyer (Ed.), *The handbook of social work research methods* (pp. 273–292). Thousand Oaks, CA: Sage.

Geertz, C. (1971). Deep play: Notes on the Balinese cock fight. In C. Geertz (Ed.), *The interpretation of cultures* (pp. 412–453). New York: Basic Books.

Gilman, R., & Huebner, E. S. (2004). The importance of client satisfaction in residential treatment outcome measurement: A response. *Residential Treatment for Children and Youth, 21*(4), 7–17.

Glisson, C., & Green, P. (2006). The effects of organizational culture and climate on the access to mental health care in child welfare and juvenile justice systems. *Administration and Policy in Mental Health and Mental Health Services Research, 33*(4), 433–448.

Goode, T. (2004). *Promoting cultural diversity and cultural competency.* Retrieved from Georgetown University Center for Child and Human Development: http://www11.georgetown.edu/research/gucchd/nccc/documents/ChecklistBehavioralHealth.pdf

Gormley, W. T. (2002). Using organizational report cards. In J. Wholey, H. Hatry, & K. Newcomer (Eds.), *Handbook of practical program evaluation* (pp. 628–648). San Francisco, CA: Jossey-Bass.

Graue, M. E., & Walsh, D. J. (1998). *Studying children in context.* London: Sage.

Greene, J. C. (1997). Evaluation as advocacy. *Evaluation Practice, 18,* 25–35.

Greig, A., & Taylor, J. (1999). *Doing research with children.* London: Sage.

Grinnell, R. (1997). *Social work research and evaluation: Quantitative and qualitative approaches.* Itasca, IL: Peacock Press.

Grob, G. (2004). Writing for impact. In J. Wholey, H. Hatry, & K. Newcomer (Eds.), *Handbook of practical program evaluation* (pp. 604–627). San Francisco: Jossey-Bass.

Grosser, R. C., & Vine, P. (1991). Families as advocates for the mentally ill: A survey of characteristics and service needs. *American Journal of Orthopsychiatry, 61*(2), 282–290.

Hanks, R. S., & Carr, N. T. (2008). Lifelines of women in jail as self-constructed visual probes for life history research. *Marriage & Family Review, 42*(4), 105–116.

Hartnett, H., & Kapp, S. (2003). Establishment of quality programming. In K. Yeager & A. Roberts (Eds.), *Evidence-based practice manual: Research and outcome measures in health and human services* (pp. 939–948). London: Oxford Press.

Hatfield, A. B. (1981). Families as advocates for the mentally ill: A growing movement. *Hospital Community Psychiatry, 32,* 641–642.

Hatry, H. (2004). Using agency records. In J. Wholey, H. Hatry, & K. Newcomer (Eds.), *Handbook of practical program evaluation* (pp. 396–412). San Francisco: Jossey-Bass.

Haynes, D., Sullivan, K., Davis, T., & Yoo, S. (2000, June). *Evaluating the Texas Integrated Funding Initiative.* Presentation at Systems of Care Conference, Austin, TX.

Hendricks, M. (1982). Oral policy briefings. In N. L. Smith (Ed.), *Communication strategies in evaluation* (pp. 249–258). Thousand Oaks, CA: Sage.

Hennessy, E. (1999). Children as service evaluators. *Child Psychology & Psychiatry, 4,* 153–161.

Hodges, S. P., & Hernandez, M. (1999). How organizational culture influences outcome information utilization. *Evaluation and Program Planning, 22*(2), 183–197.

Holt, J., & Lawler, J. (2005). Children in need teams: Service delivery and organizational climate. *Social Work and Social Service, 12*(2), 29–47.

Horst, P., Nay, J. N., Scanlon, J. W., & Wholey, J. S. (1974). Program management and the federal evaluator. *Public Administration Review, 34*(4), 300–308.

Howard, J. A. (2001). *On being adopted: Narratives of young adopted women.* Unpublished doctoral dissertation, University of Chicago.

Huer, M. B., & Saenz, T. I. (2003, May). Challenges and strategies for conducting survey and focus group research with culturally diverse groups. *American Journal of Speech-Language Pathology, 12,* 2–13.

Huer, M. B., Saenz, T. I., & Doan, J. H. (2001). Understanding the Vietnamese American community: Implications for training educational personnel providing services to children with disabilities. *Communication Disorders Quarterly, 23,* 27–39.

Humphreys, L. (1970). *Tearoom trade: Impersonal sex in public places.* Chicago: Aldine.

Hyde, J. (2005). From home to street: Understanding young people's transitions in homelessness. *Adolescence, 28*(2), 171–183.

Ingram, B. L., & Chung, R. S. (1997). Client satisfaction data and quality improvement planning in managed health care organizations. *Health Care Management Review, 22*(3), 40–52.

Inouye, T., Yu, H. C., & Adefuin, J. (2005). *Commissioning multicultural evaluation: A foundation resource guide.* Oakland, CA: Social Policy Research Associates.

Isajiw, W. (2000). Approaches to ethnic conflict resolution: Paradigms and principles. *International Journal of Intercultural Relations, 24,* 105–124.

Johnston, T. (2002). *No more victims, Inc.: Evaluation of a school-based program.* Austin, TX: Hogg Foundation for Mental Health.

Kapp, S. A. (1997). *Examining life in the juvenile justice system: A qualitative approach employing life history interviews and reflexivity.* Unpublished doctoral dissertation, Michigan State University, East Lansing, MI.

Kapp, S. A. (2000). Defining, promoting, and improving a model of school social work: The development of a tool for collaboration. *School Social Work Journal, 24*(2), 20–41.

Kapp, S., & Grasso, A. (1993). BOMIS: A management information system for children and youth service providers. In A. Grasso & I. Epstein (Eds.), *Information systems in child, youth and family agencies: Planning, implementation, and service enhancement* (pp. 33–48). New York: Haworth Press.

Kapp, S. A., & Propp, J. (2002). Client satisfaction methods: Input from parents with children in foster care. *Child and Adolescent Social Work Journal, 19*(3), 227–245.

Kapp, S. A., Robbins, M. L., & Choi, J. J. (2008). *A partnership model study between juvenile justice and community mental health: Finding-FY 2008.* Lawrence, KS: The University of Kansas, School of Social Welfare.

Kapp, S., Schwartz, I., & Epstein, I. (1994). Adult imprisonment of males released from residential care: A longitudinal study. *Residential Treatment for Children and Youth, 12*(2), 19–36.

Kapp, S. A., & Vela, H. R. (2004). The parent satisfaction with foster care services scale. *Child Welfare, 83,* 263–287.

Kirkpatrick, D. L. (1998). *Another look at evaluating training programs.* Alexandria, VA: American Society for Training & Development.

Klein, W. C., & Bloom, M. (1995). Practice wisdom. *Social Work, 40*(6), 799–807.

Kopczynski, M. E., & Pritchard, K. (2004). The use of evaluation in nonprofit organizations. In J. S. Wholey, H. Hatry, & K. E. Newcomer (Eds.), *Handbook of practical program evaluation* (2nd ed., pp. 649–669). San Francisco: Jossey-Bass.

Krueger, R. A., & Casey, M. A. (2000). *Focus groups* (3rd ed.). Thousand Oaks, CA: Sage.

Kuperschmidt, J. B., & Coie, J. D. (1990). Preadolescent peer status, aggression, and school adjustment as predictors of externalizing problems in adolescence. *Child Development, 61*(5), 1350–1362.

Lewinson, P., Redner, J., & Seeley, J. (1991). The relationship between life satisfaction and psychosocial variables: New perspectives. In F. Strack, M. Argyle, & N. Schwarz (Eds.), *Subjective well-being: An interdisciplinary perspective* (pp. 192–212). New York: Plenum Press.

Locke, L. D., & McCollum, E. E. (1999). Client views of live supervision and satisfaction with therapy. *Journal of Marital and Family Therapy, 27*(1), 129–133.

Lofland, J. (1971). *Analyzing social settings.* Belmont, CA: Wadsworth Publishing.

Lord, B., & Pockett, R. (1998). Perceptions of social work intervention with bereaved clients: Some implications for hospital social work practice. *Social Work in Healthcare, 27,* 51–66.

Lowery, C. (2001). Ethnographic research methods. In B. Thyer (Ed.), *The handbook of social work research methods* (pp. 321–332). Thousand Oaks, CA: Sage.

Magill, R. S. (1993). Focus groups, program evaluation, and the poor. *Journal of Sociology and Social Welfare, 20*(1) 103–114.

Maluccio, A. (1979). *Learning from clients.* New York: The Free Press.

Manteuffel, B., & Stephens, R. L. (2002). Overview of the national evaluation of the Comprehensive Community Mental Health Services for Children and Their Families Program and the summary of current findings. *Children's Services, 5*(1), 3–20.

Marty, D., & Barkett, A. (2002). *Data analysis workbench*. Office of Adult Mental Health, University of Kansas School of Social Welfare, Lawrence, KS.

Masumoto, D. (1994). *Cultural influences on research methods and statistics*. Pacific Grove, CA: Brooks/Cole Publishing.

Mayer, B. (1989). Mediation in child protection cases: The impact of third-party intervention on parental compliance attitudes. *Mediation Quarterly, 24*, 89–106.

McClintock, E. (2004). Integrating program evaluation and organizational development. In A. R. Roberts & K. R. Yeager (Eds.), *Evidence-based research practice manual: Research and outcome measures in health and human services* (pp. 598–605). New York: Oxford University Press.

McLaughlin, J. A., & Jordan, G. B. (2004). Using logic models. In J. S. Wholey, H. P. Hatry, & K. E. Newcomer (Eds.), *Handbook of practical program evaluation* (pp. 7–31). San Francisco: Wiley & Sons.

McMurtry, S. L., & Hudson, W. W. (2000). The client satisfaction inventory: Results of an initial validation study. *Research on Social Work Practice, 10*(5), 644–663.

McNeese, C. A. (2004). The 7 secrets of a successful veteran evaluator. In A. R. Roberts & K. R. Yeager (Eds.), *Evidence-based practice manual: Research and outcomes measures in health and human services* (pp. 592–597). New York: Oxford University Press.

Measelle, J. R., Weinstein, R. S., & Martinez, M. (1998). Parent satisfaction with case managed systems of care for children and youth with severe emotional disturbance. *Journal of Child and Family Studies, 7*(4), 451–467.

Miles, M. B., & Huberman, A. M. (1994). *Qualitative data analysis*. Thousand Oaks, CA: Sage.

Mirabito, D. M. (2001). Mining treatment termination data in an adolescent mental health service: A quantitative study. In I. Epstein & S. Blumenfield (Eds.), *Clinical data-mining in practice-based research: Social work in hospital settings* (pp. 71–90). Binghamton, NY: Haworth Press.

Moore, T., & Press, A. (2002). *Results oriented management in child welfare*. Retrieved August 1, 2009, from University of Kansas School of Social Welfare Web site: http://www.rom.ku.edu

Moore, T., Rapp, C. A., & Roberts, B. (2000). Improving child welfare performance through supervisory use of client outcome data. *Child Welfare, 74*(5), 475–497.

Morgan, D. L., & Scannell, A. U. (1997). *The focus group guidebook*. Thousand Oaks, CA: Sage.

Morris, M. W., Leung, K., Ames, D., & Lickel, B. (1999). Views from inside and outside: Integrating emic and etic insights about culture and justice judgment. *The Academy of Management Review, 24*(4), 781–796.

National Association of Social Workers. (1999). *Code of ethics of the National Association of Social Workers*. Washington, DC: Author. Retrieved July 1, 2008, from http://www.socialworkers.org/pubs/code/code.asp

Nay, J. N., Scanlon, J. W., Graham, L., & Waller, J. D. (1977). *The National Institute information machine: A case study of the National Evaluation Program*. Washington, DC: Urban Institute.

Olson, D. H., Russell, C. S., & Sprenkle, D. H. (1983). Circumplex model of marital and family systems: VI. Theoretical update. *Family Process, 22*(1), 69–83.

Osher, T., & Adams, J. (2000). *The world of evaluation: How to make it yours* (Course II). St. Louis, MO: Federation of Families for Children's Mental Health.

O'Sullivan, E., & Rassel, G. R. (1989). *Research methods for public administrators.* New York: Longman Press.

Oswalt, W. (2002). *This land was theirs: A study of Native Americans* (7th ed.). Boston: McGraw Hill.

Parette, H. P., Brotherson, M. J., & Huer, M. B. (2000). Giving families a voice in augmentative and alternative communication decision making. *Education and Training in Mental Retardation and Developmental Disabilities, 35,* 177–190.

Patton, M. Q. (1997). *Utilization-focused evaluation* (3rd ed.). Thousand Oaks, CA: Sage.

Patton, M. Q. (2002). *Qualitative research and evaluation methods* (3rd ed.). Thousand Oaks, CA: Sage.

Pennell, J., & Anderson, G. (2005). *Widening the circle: The practice and evaluation of family group conferencing with children, youths, and their families.* Washington, DC: NASW Press.

Poertner, J., & Rapp, C. (2007). *Textbook of social administration: The consumer-centered approach.* Binghamton, NY: Haworth Press.

Poister, T. H. (2004). Performance monitoring. In J. Wholey, H. Hatry, & K. Newcomer (Eds.), *Handbook of practical program evaluation* (pp. 98–126). San Francisco: Jossey-Bass.

Posavac, E., & Carey, R. G. (2007). *Program evaluation: Methods and case studies* (7th ed.). Upper Saddle River, NJ: Prentice Hall.

Practice Notes. (1999, February). Culturally Competent Practice: What is it and why does it matter? *Jordan Institute for Families,* North Carolina, vol. 4, no. 1.

Primm, A., Gomez, M., Tzolova-Iontchev, I., Perry, W., Thi Vu, H., & Crum, R. (2000). Severely mentally ill patients with and without substance use disorders: Characteristics associated with treatment attrition. *Community Mental Health Journal, 36*(3), 235–246.

Public Health–Seattle & King County. (n.d.). *Gay, lesbian, bisexual and transgender health.* Retrieved August 7, 2009, from www.kingcounty.gov/healthservices/health/personal/glbt.aspx

Pyrczak, F., & Bruce, R. (2007). *Writing empirical research reports.* Los Angeles: Pyrczak Publishing.

Reamer, F. (2001). Ethical issues. In B. Thyer (Ed.), *The handbook of social work research methods.* Thousand Oaks, CA: Sage.

Rehr, H. (2001). Foreword. In I. Epstein & S. Blumenfield (Eds.), *Clinical data-mining in practice-based research: Social work in hospital settings* (pp. xv–xxiii). Binghamton, NY: Haworth Press.

Rodgers-Farmer, A. Y., & Potocky-Tripodi, M. (2001). Gender, ethnicity, and race matters. In B. Thyer (Ed.), *The handbook of social work research methods* (pp. 445–454). Thousand Oaks, CA: Sage.

Rossi, P. H., Lipsey, M., & Freeman, H. E. (2004). *Evaluation: A systematic approach* (7th ed.). Thousand Oaks, CA: Sage.

Rostoscky, R. R., Riggle, E. D. B., Dudley, M. G., & Wright, M. L. C. (2006). Commitment in same-sex relationships: A qualitative analysis of couples' conversations. *Journal of Homosexuality, 51*(3), 199–223.

Rounds, K. A. (1988). Aids in rural areas: Challenges to providing care. *Social Work, 33*(3), 257–261.

Royse, D. (1992). *Program evaluation: An introduction.* Chicago: Nelson-Hall.

Royse, D., Thyer, B., Padgett, D., & Logan, T. K. (2005). *Program evaluation: An introduction* (4th ed.). Belmont, CA: Brooks/Cole Publishing.

Rubin, A., & Babbie, E. (1993). *Research methods for social work* (2nd ed.). Pacific Grove, CA: Brooks/Cole Publishing.

Rubin, A., & Babbie, E. (2005). *Research methods for social work* (5th ed.). Belmont, CA: Wadsworth Publishing.

Rutman, L. (1980). *Planning useful evaluations: Evaluability assessment.* Thousand Oaks, CA: Sage.

Salkind, N. (2007). *Statistics for people who (think they) hate statistics* (2nd ed.). Thousand Oaks, CA: Sage.

Savas, S. A. (1996). How do we propose to help children and families? In P. Pecora, W. R. Seelig, F. A. Zirps, & S. Davis (Eds.), *Quality improvement and evaluation in child and family services: Managing into the next century* (pp. 37–52). Washington, DC: Child Welfare League of America.

Savas, S. A., Epstein, I., & Grasso, I. (1993). Client characteristics, family contacts and treatment outcomes. In A. Grasso & I. Epstein (Eds.), *Information systems in child, youth and family agencies: Planning, implementation, and service enhancement* (pp. 33–48). New York: Haworth Press.

Scambler, G. (2007). Sex work stigma: Opportunist migrants in London. *Sociology, 41*(5), 1079–1096.

Schön, D. (1983). *The reflective practitioner: How professionals think in action.* New York: Basic Books.

Schumacher, J., Bye, L. L., Chen, M. S., McCarthy, W. J., Tang, H., & Cowling, D. (2003). *Collecting culturally competent data.* Retrieved from http://ncth.confex.com/ncth/2003

Schwartz, I., Kapp, S., & Overstreet, E. (1994). Juvenile justice and child welfare: Longitudinal research in the state of Michigan. In E. Weitekamp & H. J. Kerner (Eds.), *Cross-national longitudinal research on human development and criminal behavior* (pp. 111–115). Dordrecht, The Netherlands: Kluwer Academic.

Senge, P. (1994). *The fifth discipline: The art and practice of the learning organization.* New York: Doubleday.

Slaton, E. (2004). *Family engagement in evaluation: Lessons learned.* Retrieved May 30, 2009, from Federation of Families for Children's Mental Health Web site: www.ffcmh.org

Slaton, E., & McCormack, M. (1999). *The world of evaluation: How to make it yours.* St. Louis: Federation of Families for Children's Mental Health.

Sluyter, G. V. (1998). *Improving organizational performance: A practical guide for the human services field.* Thousand Oaks, CA: Sage.

Stewart, D. W., & Shamdasani, P. M. (1990). *Focus groups: Theory and practice.* Thousand Oaks, CA: Sage.

Stroul, B., et al. (1980). *Final report of the exploratory evaluation of the National Institute of Mental Health Community Support Program* (Appendix B). Silver Spring, MD: Macro Systems.

Sturg, D., Ottoman, R., Kaye, J., Saltzberg, S., Walker, J., & Mendez, H. (2003). Client satisfaction and staff empathy at pediatric HIV/AIDS programs. *Journal of Social Service Research, 29*(4), 1–22.

Takkinen, S., & Suutama, T. (2004). Life-lines of Finnish people aged 83–87. *International Journal of Aging and Human Development, 59,* 339–362.

Taut, S. M., & Alkin, M. C. (2003). Program staff perceptions of barriers to evaluation implementation. *American Journal of Evaluation, 24*(2), 213–226.

Thyer, B. (Ed.). (2001a). *The handbook of social work research methods.* Thousand Oaks, CA: Sage.

Thyer, B. (2001b). Single-system designs. In B. Thyer (Ed.), *The handbook of social work research methods* (pp. 239–255). Thousand Oaks, CA: Sage.

Tracy, E., Whittaker, J., Pugh, A., Kapp, S., & Overstreet, E. (1994). Network characteristics of primary caregivers in high risk families: An exploratory study. *Families in Society, 75*(8), 481–489.

Uehara, E. S., Farris, M., Graham, T., Morelli, P., Phillips, R., Smith, L., & Bates, R. E. (1997). A collaborative-comparative approach to learning qualitative data analysis. *Journal of Teaching in Social Work, 14*(1/2), 45–67.

Ward, L. (1997). *Seen and heard: Involving disabled children and young people in research and development projects.* York, UK: Joseph Rowntree Foundation.

Wholey, J. S. (1983). *Evaluation and effective public management.* New York: Little Brown & Co.

Wholey, J. S. (1994). Assessing the feasibility and likely usefulness of evaluation. In J. S. Wholey, H. P. Hatry, & K. E. Newcomer (Eds.), *Handbook of practical program evaluation.* San Francisco: Jossey-Bass.

Yeager, K., & Roberts, A. (Eds.). (2003). *Evidence-based practice manual: Research and outcome measures in health and human services.* London: Oxford Press.

Index

Statistical regression, 216–217
Structure versus fluidity, 28–30
Study, concluding, 78–81
Success
  coding youth comments about,
    259 (table)
  four takes on, 262 (table)
Summative evaluation, 29.
    See also Evaluation process;
    Program evaluation
Survey instrument, 271–273
Systematically gathered data, advantages
  of, 167

Tearoom Trade, 66
Treatment documentation, 167
  advantages of, 168

data, using to study client
    termination, 171–172
service delivery and, 172
Treatments
  diffusion of, 217
  imitation of, 217
Triangulation, 262–263
Tuskegee Syphilis Study, 65
Tutoring program, 29 (example)

University-based evaluators, 89–96,
  102–104

VSQ-9 (Patient Satisfaction Survey), 308–309

Working Alliance Inventory (WAI),
  319–320

About the Authors

Stephen A. Kapp, MSW, PhD, is an Associate Professor at the University of Kansas School of Social Welfare. Dr. Kapp has focused his career on agency-based program evaluation of children and family programs. He has more than 20 years of experience working both externally and internally on agency evaluations. His teaching and writing efforts have focused on evaluation, with an emphasis on the use of information by agency staff and giving service recipients a voice in the evaluation process. Currently, he is directing multiple research grants that examine the service experience of youth and their families in the Kansas Mental Health System. He received his PhD from the School of Social Work at Michigan State University and his MSW from the University of Michigan.

Gary R. Anderson, MSW, PhD, is the Director of the School of Social Work, College of Social Science, at Michigan State University. He came to Michigan State University from Hunter College (New York City). At Hunter, he was a Professor and the founding Director of the National Resource Center for Permanency Planning. Dr. Anderson has written a number of books and articles on policy and practice related to children and families. His most recent book, with Joan Pennell, *Widening the Circle: The Practice and Evaluation of Family Group Conferencing With Children, Youths, and Their Families*, was published by the NASW Press. He is the former editor of the journal *Child Welfare*. He has directed over 25 funded projects addressing aspects of child welfare, and is currently leading projects on child welfare worker recruitment and retention, and conducting research related to post-adoption services and training. He received his PhD from the School of Social Service Administration at the University of Chicago, and his MSW from the University of Michigan.

Supporting researchers for more than 40 years

Research methods have always been at the core of SAGE's publishing program. Founder Sara Miller McCune published SAGE's first methods book, *Public Policy Evaluation*, in 1970. Soon after, she launched the *Quantitative Applications in the Social Sciences* series—affectionately known as the "little green books."

Always at the forefront of developing and supporting new approaches in methods, SAGE published early groundbreaking texts and journals in the fields of qualitative methods and evaluation.

Today, more than 40 years and two million little green books later, SAGE continues to push the boundaries with a growing list of more than 1,200 research methods books, journals, and reference works across the social, behavioral, and health sciences. Its imprints—Pine Forge Press, home of innovative textbooks in sociology, and Corwin, publisher of PreK–12 resources for teachers and administrators—broaden SAGE's range of offerings in methods. SAGE further extended its impact in 2008 when it acquired CQ Press and its best-selling and highly respected political science research methods list.

From qualitative, quantitative, and mixed methods to evaluation, SAGE is the essential resource for academics and practitioners looking for the latest methods by leading scholars.

For more information, visit **www.sagepub.com**.